O9-BHK-002

THE HAIR STYLIST HANDBOOK

Achieve professional-quality hair results with this full-color, comprehensive book from award-winning hair and makeup pros, Gretchen Davis and Yvette Rivas. In *The Hair Stylist Handbook: Techniques for Film and Television*, you'll learn how to create that sought-after "complete look" by learning the newest hair techniques that are in demand on film and television sets. Learn how to break into the industry, what products to use to achieve specific effects, how to maintain a look throughout the day, what quick techniques to use to achieve certain textures, and much more. With input from hairstylist Yvette Rivas, this step-by-step guide makes complex techniques clear, allowing you to achieve the most coveted results. Here, you will find:

- An extensive chapter on men's grooming techniques and hair products
- Specific techniques for dramatic and long-lasting hair color
- Lists of the best hair tools and instructions on how to use them to achieve different looks
- Information about how production schedules, cast, and crew are all affected and influenced by the hair and makeup team
- Details on how to run a successful and organized hair and makeup trailer on set

Whether you are a professional in the field, or a student looking to break into the industry, this book will provide you with secrets and information that you cannot find anywhere else.

Gretchen Davis is a highly sought-after makeup artist and writer for the entertainment industry, where she has worked for high-profile clients in film, television, and digital media as a personal hair and makeup stylist or department head. In 2012 Gretchen was nominated for an Emmy, highlighting her work on *Hemingway and Gellhorn*. Some of her clients have included Cate Blanchet—who in her Oscar's acceptance speech thanked Gretchen personally—Gerard Butler, Jonathan Groff, Russell Tovey, and Rob Lowe. Gretchen also keyed projects like feature films *Milk* and *Steve Jobs*, and NBC's *Trauma*. She has been featured in *SF* magazine, where critics praised her work on the film *Blue Jasmine*. She has also been featured on various blogs and in print articles.

Yvette Rivas is a freelance hair stylist with a long history in the entertainment industry. Her experience includes contributing to the design of dolls in the likeness of the Spice Girls, Britney Spears, Kate Winslet, and Pamela Anderson. Yvette has been a department head for films, television shows, web series, and national commercials. She is also a Primetime Emmy-nominated hair stylist for HBO's *Hemmingway and Gellhorn*, and was recognized at the Oscars for her work on *Blue Jasmine*.

THE HAIR STYLIST HANDBOOK

TECHNIQUES FOR FILM AND TELEVISION

Gretchen Davis

With contributions by Yvette Rivas

NEW YORK AND LONDON

First published 2016
by Focal Press
711 Third Avenue, New York, NY 10017

and by Focal Press
2 Park Square, Milton Park, Abingdon, Oxon OX14 4RN

Focal Press is an imprint of the Taylor & Francis Group, an informa business

© 2016 Focal Press

The right of Gretchen Davis to be identified as author of this work has been asserted by her in accordance with sections 77 and 78 of the Copyright, Designs and Patents Act 1988.

All rights reserved. No part of this book may be reprinted or reproduced or utilized in any form or by any electronic, mechanical, or other means, now known or hereafter invented, including photocopying and recording, or in any information storage or retrieval system, without permission in writing from the publishers.

Trademark notice: Product or corporate names may be trademarks or registered trademarks, and are used only for identification and explanation without intent to infringe.

Library of Congress Cataloging in Publication Data
A catalog record for this book has been requested

ISBN: 978-1-138-81514-8 (pbk)
ISBN: 978-1-138-67597-1 (hbk)
ISBN: 978-1-315-74692-0 (ebk)

Illustrations by Robert Revels, revelsart@gmail.com
Typeset in Avenir and Chaparral by
Servis Filmsetting Ltd, Stockport, Cheshire

Printed and bound in India by Replika Press Pvt. Ltd.

"On TV people look at your hair and then they look at your skin, and then they look at your clothes, and by the time they're listening to what you're saying you're off the screen."

Doug Coupland

Contents

Acknowledgments ix

Introduction 1

1 CHAPTER ONE – *Anatomy* 3

2 CHAPTER TWO – *Color* 27

3 CHAPTER THREE – *Tools* 65

4 CHAPTER 4 – *Men's Grooming* 97

5 CHAPTER FIVE – *Design* 119

6 CHAPTER SIX – *Education* 207

Glossary 228

Index 235

Acknowledgments

Thank you to Yvette Rivas, the most incredible hair stylist, for all your wisdom and your talent for explaining techniques that will pave the way for beginning hair stylists looking for that career in film. You are a major contributor to this book, and it's been inspirational to watch you work. Without you this handbook would never have been written.

Thank you to all the gifted stylists who work day in and day out, and who educate us all to be better at what we do. Special thanks to the stylists who make clients, actors, and models beautiful through the art of hair styling.

Thank you, Bumble and Bumble, and expert stylist Tiffani Patchett. We could not do without these products in the hair and makeup trailer.

Davines, a must-have product line to correct and beautify our actors—thank you for your continued support and knowledge.

Thank you, Patrick Evan, at Patrick Evan Salon, for your insight into color, and Vanessa Mills, who makes color, and color corrections, a little easier for us film folk.

Don Jusko, your RCW color wheel is a valuable tool in my kit. Thank you for those last-minute questions you so patiently explain.

Thank you, Teri Eaton, of SenSpa, San Francisco. No one can take care of our clients better. Health inside and out is key.

Thank you, Kenny Myers, for answering all my emails and texts to explain effects and products even though you are incredibly busy! The actors are grateful! (Chuckle.)

Thank you to all the support team at Temptu over the years. Airbrushing has never been so fun!

Thank you, Lennotch Taplet, for your fantastic clipper cuts and product knowledge. I'm considering a buzz cut at your shop TopNotch Barber.

Aileen Nunez, International Manager of Education and Style for Andis, your insight was very educational! I can't live without my Andis Phat!

Jill Glaser, thank you for putting your time and skill into your school Makeup First, an educational achievement. We need great minds like yours and Dave Bova's to pave the way for young talent. It's a selfless job and not anyone can do it. Thank you both for your insight and words.

Thank you, Jennifer Stanfield, a very talented makeup artist and hair stylist. Hope you are out this way again!

Thank you, Kentaro Yano, you have always been a huge support for me! I'll never be able to thank you enough for all those last-minute designs you so expertly bring to life.

Jenny Boot, what can I say but WOW! Your work is truly inspirational!

Lars Carlson, thank you once again for your expertise in all things!

Thank you, Kathleen Courtney, for your insight into what it is like to work and work with a UPM.

Thank you, Judith Blinick, for your knowledge in accounting, a very important part of our job.

Janice McCafferty, CEO and founder of Janice McCafferty Communications Inc., thank you for your contributions!

Thank you, Susan Stone, for all the hard work on my last project and your expertise on wig blocking at San Francisco Opera.

Thank you to the leaders in our field, who keep hair stylists and makeup artists working creatively: Wella, Logics, Redken, Clairol, Matrix, Oribe, Davines, Bumble and Bumble, Kenra, DevaCurl, Carols Daughter, Sheer Technology, PPI, Matthew Mungle, Kamisori, Lord & Cliff, FHI Heat, Oster, Wahl, Iwata, Fellow Barber, Topshop, Sonia Kuska, Dermalogica, Murad, Proactiv, and so many, many more.

Introduction

One of the things friends and even strangers ask us is: How do I get into the business? Many, if not most, think of hair stylists in terms of what they see on television: a celebrity artist or stylist making a beautiful actress more beautiful for the red carpet, or someone on "makeover" shows prettying up a normal-looking woman. New upcoming hair stylists know we work in film and television with famous actors and fantasize about us arriving in a limo at the trailer to work our magic on some "A" list actor or actress. Nothing could be further from the truth.

The reality is when working on a television show or film, the alarm clock usually goes off at 4 am, sometimes sooner, and sometimes, if we're fortunate, as late as 5:45 am. It's a bleary-eyed drive to crew parking, all the while fielding phone calls about this or that mini crisis. We're in the trailer about an hour later, and after a 12- to 15-hour day hopefully we are done. Just another long day shared by our colleagues and other crew members, who are highly skilled vagabonds in the film and television industry.

But why do the hundreds of other stylists and artists toil—and yes, that's the correct word, toil—in this business?

That's what this book is all about: showing new artists what to expect on a film. What hair techniques are already known to work by others in the industry, and lastly what products are used to pull off the incredible characters expected in film and television or a web series.

To keep getting jobs in this business you need a skill set that's highly sought after and highly respected. These skills also include thinking on your feet, common sense, and quickness. For the most part, the scripts don't call for someone who can "fluff and puff" or "comb and blow dry" the characters.

The actors are your canvas and in this book we will help you discover some of the skills and products you'll need to succeed. And when you do, make sure you also buy a good alarm clock.

Gretchen Davis and Yvette Rivas

CHAPTER ONE
Anatomy

Movie and video hair stylists are creative forces to be reckoned with. Creative thinking outside the box goes a long way for this exclusive group of men and women. With individualistic artistic talent, hair stylists mold, shape, cut, and manipulate hair to create images that may linger for ever in your memory. In film, hair stylists are asked to do just about anything and everything. Those requests from actors, writers, directors, and producers span the spectrum from beauty to special effects through all media. As a multi-media hair stylist, you'll encounter many situations that require knowledge of facial anatomy, as well as the structure of the hair follicle. For example, you might encounter diseases, inflammation, burned or broken follicles while working with an actor. You could be asked to create or fit a wig, extensions, or visually reshape the head using these items. Sadly, problems often arise for hair stylists who are just beginning their career, and that's why it's important that professional hair stylists know how to solve unexpected problems quickly. Experienced hair stylists know how to correctly decide what styles, hairpieces, or products work best under different circumstances.

> "The impulse behind our interest is the urge both to locate an invisible 'self' beneath the skin and to 'read' what the surface appearance tells us."
>
> Sandra Kemp, *Future Face*, p. 35.

Starting with the skeletal system, hair stylists should focus on understanding what is holding and shaping the head. The head in its most basic form includes your sensory organs: the nose, ears, skin, and eyes. The skull protects the brain. For hair stylists, the occipital and parietal bones and the crown have the most impact in determining cutting, styling, or applying hair-like extensions. Head shapes determine what styles work best for the individual.

The skull is often used by makeup artists for anatomically correct measurements for beauty or effects makeup.

The skull is in two parts.

The neurocranium protects the brain, and forms the base of the skull. Eight bones form the cranium: the occipital, sphenoid, frontal, ethmoid, two parietal and two temporal bones.

The viscerocranium is the facial skeleton. The facial skeleton consists of nasal and oral cavities, mandible, vomer, maxilla, palatine, nasal, zygomatic, lacrimal, conchae, and inferior nasal bones.

Medical science tells us the epidermis helps the skin protect us from diseases and other biological threats and retains water. Also, layers of fat in the skin help to retain energy while holding in heat. The skin is the largest organ of the body. Hair is made up of proteins and

Figure 1.1 Skull anterior

amino acids. Hair grows down into the dermis, originating from the epidermis. As cells form, older hair is pushed outward. As hair grows it goes through keratinization, a process by which epithelial cells lose their moisture and are replaced by horny tissue. Proteins in hair are bonded by amino acids known as polypeptides, and polypeptides in different states allow us to manipulate hair by blow drying, using irons, or tinting, for example.

A professional hair stylist should know what happens to hair when cut, plucked, or chemically removed. Will the hair grow back quickly? Has the hair been damaged? Will cutting hair make it grow faster? There are several factors involved in how hair grows back, or grows back texturally different. Hair can also grow back much slower or not at all.

Hair growth happens in four phases. Anagen is the phase in which hair grows. Depending on heredity, environment, or chemical abuse, hair can grow at a fast pace, or stop growing at a certain length. This phase can last two to eight years. Catagen is a transition between active growth and rest. Telegen is the phrase at which hairs are dead, and shedding can occur daily. This phase lasts between two to four weeks. Lastly, exogen is a phase in which several hairs in one follicle are shed.

HUMAN HAIR GROWTH

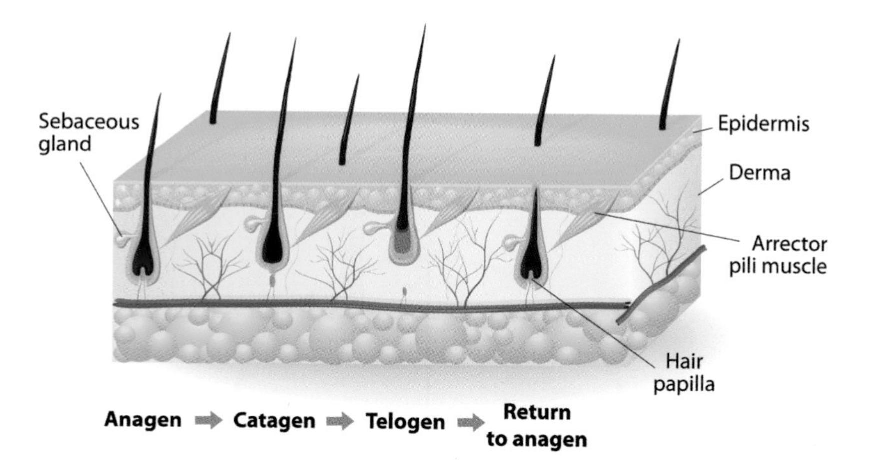

Figure 1.2 The skin and hair growth

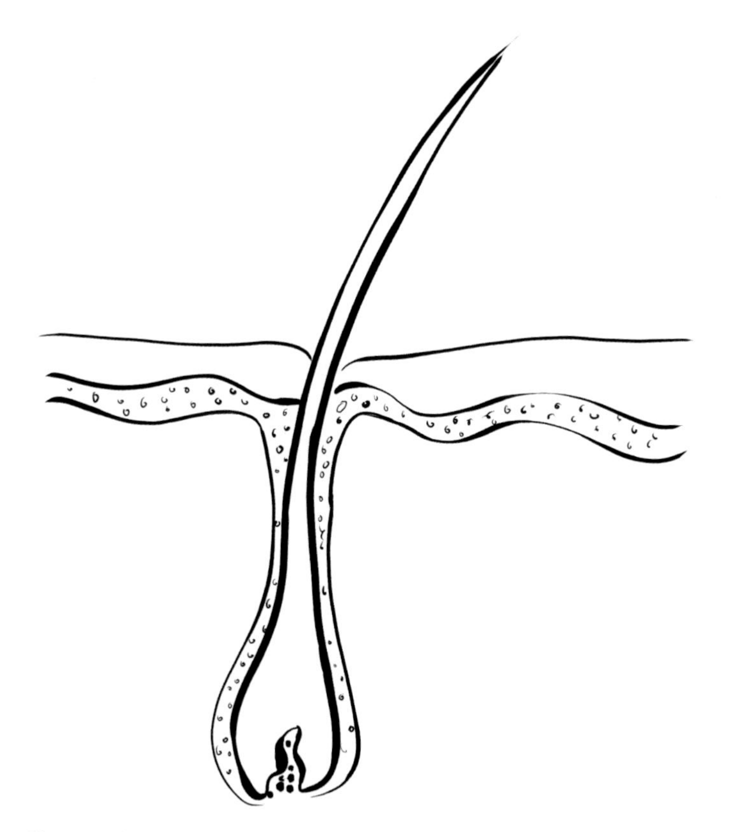

Figure 1.3 Hair structure

Hair is often admired for its color. But hair fibers have no color. Cells produce pigments called melanin, the same chemical that colors our skin. Cells (melanocytes) are found in the dermis (skin), but also in the bulb of hair follicles, so that pigments are distributed to growing hair.

How is this done? Simply put, keratinocytes produce hair fiber that contains melanosomes, that in turn form color.

Head Shapes

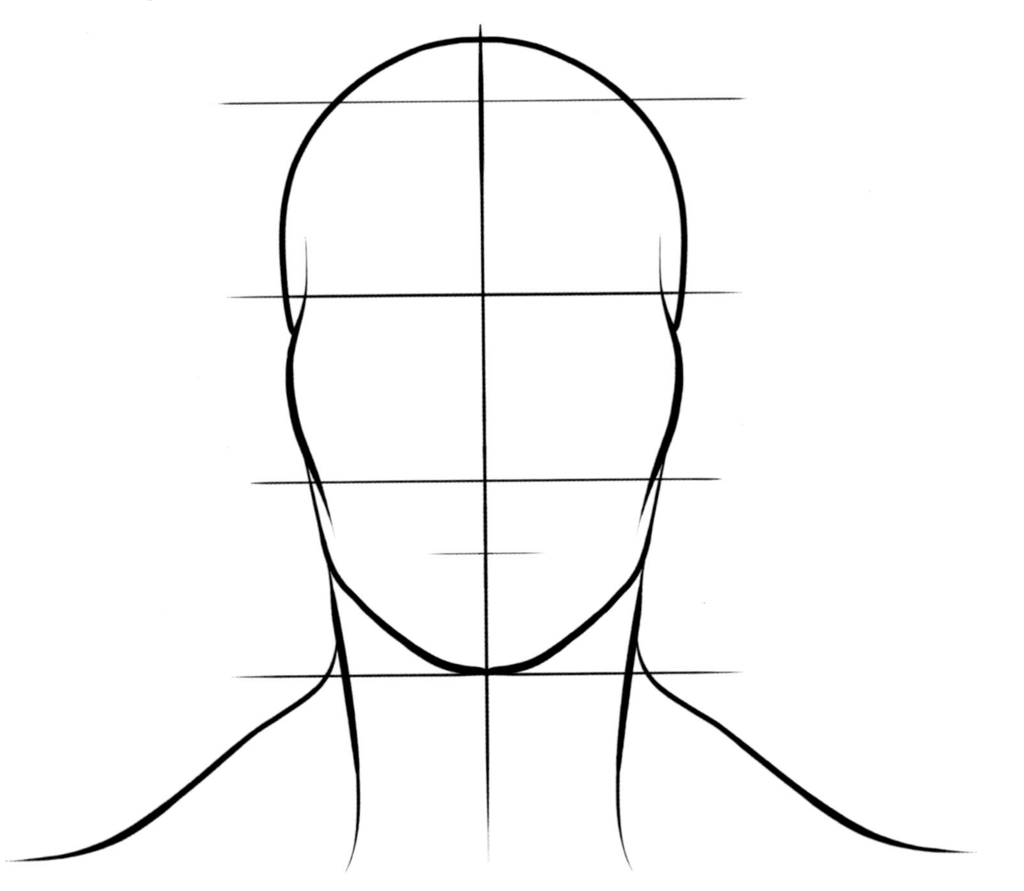

Figure 1.4 Proportions of the head

> "There is certainly no absolute standard of beauty. That precisely is what makes its pursuit so interesting."
> John Kenneth Galbraith

Men's and women's face shapes are generally the same. Men tend to sway towards a more macho appearance, and their hair styles and facial hair will often reflect this.

> "It's not uncommon for people to have a combination of face and head shapes. Most importantly it was observed that the proportion of the features were nearly identical on everyone regardless of sex or nationality."
>
> William L. Maughan, *Drawing the Head*, p. 60

Skeletal, head, and neck shapes will influence the way you cut, style, or color hair, although for film and television you'll probably be styling most often for a specific character. For example, the crown or top of the head is seen in a variety of shapes. A flat top (crown) would need more volume on top. How the head curves downward forming a parietal ridge determines head shapes such as round or square. Jennifer Stanfield, makeup artist for films like *San Andreas* and *The Hobbit* trilogy says, "When creating looks for period pieces, head and face shapes can differ. Fuller appearances are achieved through shading, highlighting, hair color, extensions, and wigs." Your personal evaluation and experience will be a deciding factor in the final outcome.

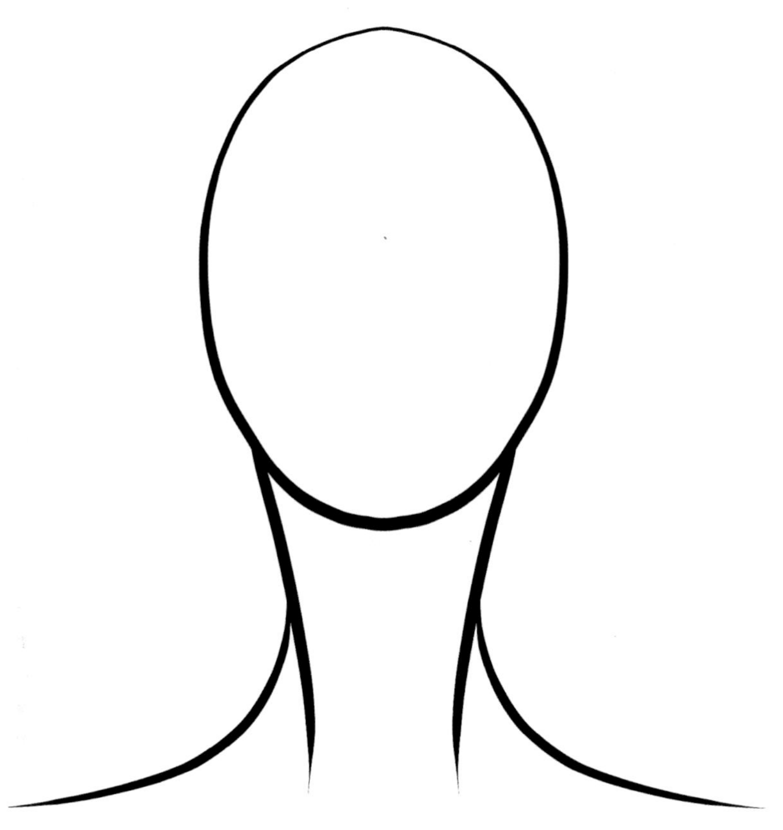

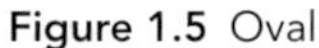

Figure 1.5 Oval

Oval

Oval shapes are considered the ideal head shape. Most wigs and hair styles will work well with this shape, as will facial hair such as moustaches, goatees, and one-day beard growth.

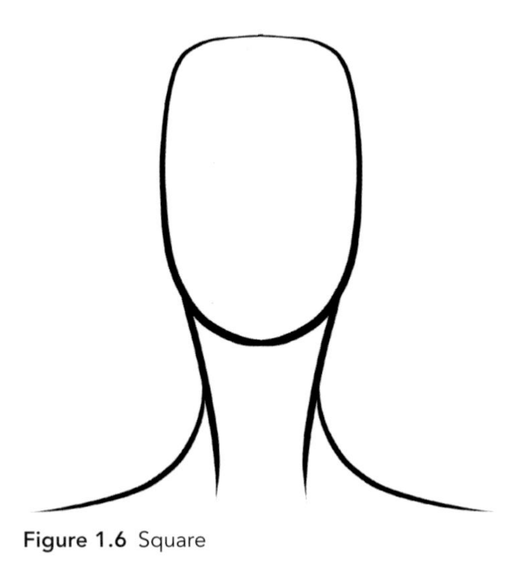

Figure 1.6 Square

Square

Men love this shape, so hair styles, cuts, and wigs should emphasize a strong jawline. Beards shaped with hard lines at the edges will deemphasize the jawline. Haircuts and facial hair can be short but shaped to balance forehead and jaw.

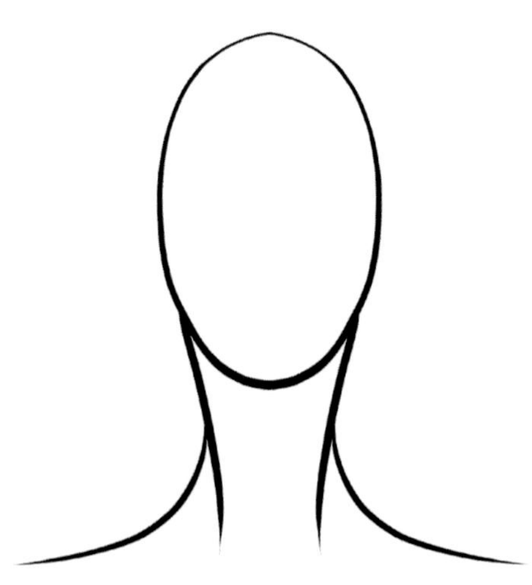

Figure 1.7 Oblong

Oblong

This head shape looks best with wigs or haircuts evenly styled. For women, texture around the face and bangs look good. Men can be styled shorter on the sides but not shaved. Blend sides shorter, versus the top, which can be slightly longer. For beards, men should be trimmed and groomed. Beard or facial hair should give the appearance of a shorter face shape.

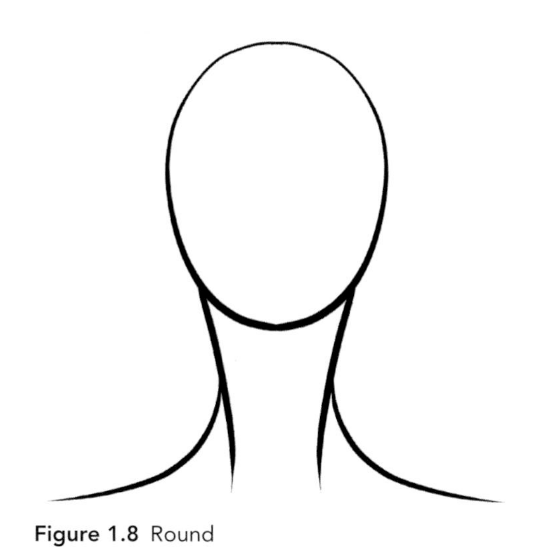

Figure 1.8 Round

Round

Round shapes should have volume on top, with longer, soft, textured hair on the sides of the face for women. On men, beards and moustaches should be shaped to slim the face. Round shapes can also take crisp outlines from facial hair. Necks should be kept hair free.

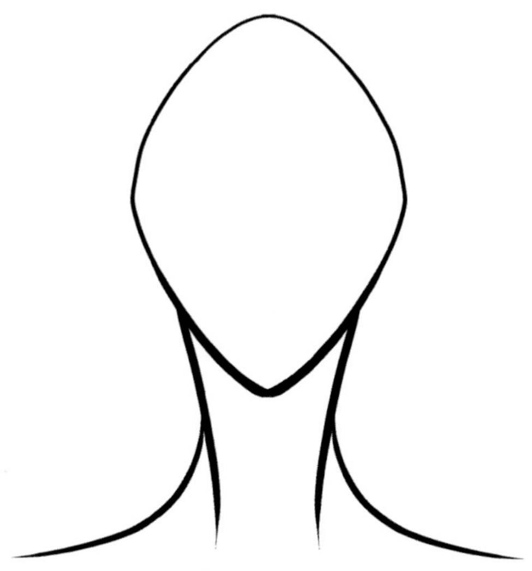

Figure 1.9 Diamond

Diamond

The head shape is narrower in the forehead and chin. Wigs and hair should be styled longer and wavy with fullness at the chin. Facial hair should be trimmed to square off this shape, although it can be elongated with sideburns.

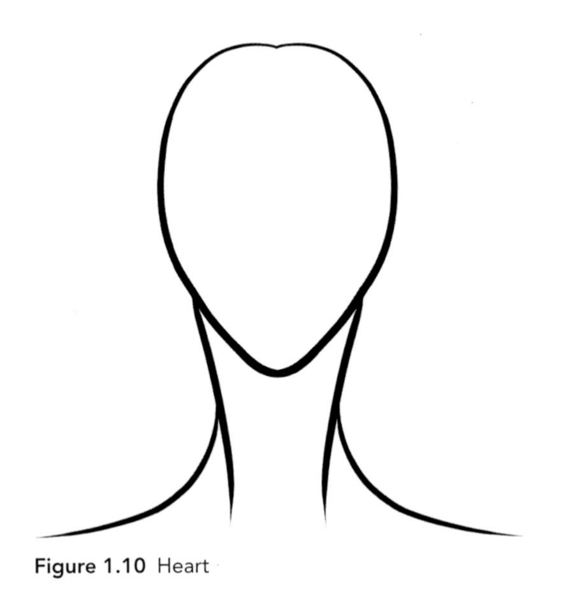

Figure 1.10 Heart

Heart

Longer styles with texturing are flattering to this shape. Hair should be swept over the forehead slightly. Men often sport facial hair shaped to give a stronger jawline.

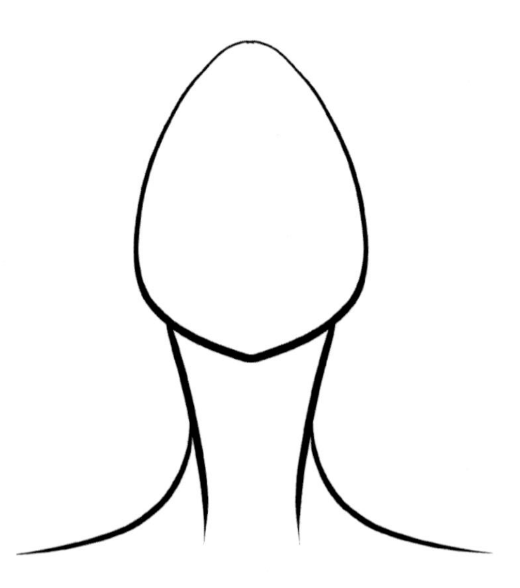

Figure 1.11 Pear

Pear

Foreheads are smaller compared to the jawline. Wigs and hair styles should have volume on top and over the forehead.

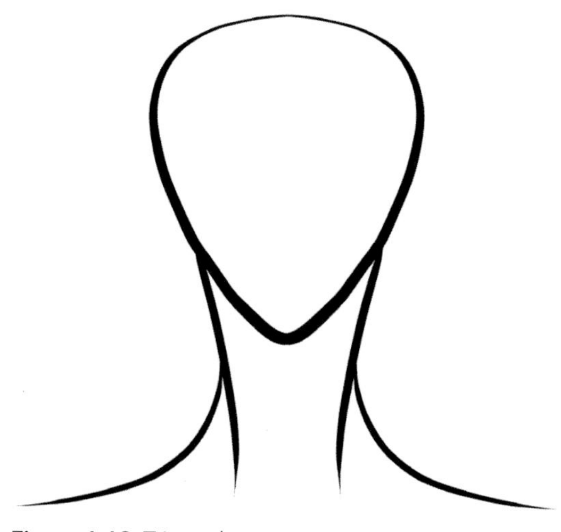

Figure 1.12 Triangular

Triangular

This shape is wider on the forehead and jawline, and smaller on the chin. Short styles look good. Beards help to strengthen the jawline, taking away from the narrow chin. Facial hair can be grown longer in length.

Hair Textures

Figure 1.13 Different hair textures

It's really hard to "type" hair textures. Most people can exhibit several textures of hair on their heads. Hair can be coarse, tight, fine, curly, natural, nappy, or cotton candy, just to name a few different textures. Flat irons, weaves, and extensions all come into play in how a person's hair looks and feels.

Yvette explains: "If you don't have confidence in your ability to work with all hair textures, you'll be afraid to tackle the challenges facing you in the hair and makeup trailer."

"To eliminate this instant negative between you and the person in your chair, start a conversation that's honest and upfront. For example, ask, 'What products do you like to use?' 'Are there products you need to use I should know about?' 'Your hair looks great. Give me some knowledge about your hair.' Soon your client will feel a lot more comfortable, knowing you will take good care of the hair."

In general, texture is broken down into different categories. There are hair stylists who use charts describing textured hair. Those systems are useful in deciphering all the ranges of textured hair, yet words used to describe hair typing can be interpreted in a number of ways, making the topic a little confusing. Because of ongoing debates about hair typing and hair textures, I feel approaching each actor as an individual works out best, especially when working in film, which requires split-second decisions. Feeling the hair, asking questions, and observing the individual are the some of the tools you'll need to become a competent hair stylist. Over time you will begin to recognize all the variety of hair textures and what products to use. Below are some examples of those tools. We include a demonstration of working with the tightest to the loosest of curls, followed by straight, fine, coarse, and male hair textures.

Yvette: "First rule: Do not comb, or brush through curly hair. Second rule: When styling anybody's hair with heat, be sure to use a heat-protective product first. People assume that tighter curls or hair that is coarse can tolerate high heats. This is not so. Hair can break and burn when temperatures are set too high. Third: Maintain good hair by using product systems for your hair texture. Example: Dry hair works well with No Poo (no-suds shampoos)."

Quick Change: Five-minute product and styling decisions for textured hair

If needed, rewet hair using Evian water spray. Only mist enough to get your desired effect. For dry, damaged hair, apply and leave in the conditioner. Then, using your fingers, massage the conditioner around the coils. Follow with a moisture creme to help put water back into the hair.

Figure 1.14 Style curls by misting with Evian. Apply leave-in conditioner

Figure 1.15 Apply a leave in conditioner and let dry naturally. Finish with Bumble and Bumble Spray Shine

Figure 1.16 Bumble and Bumble Spray Shine or leave-in conditioner. Finish with a Bumble and Bumble Spray Shine for luster.

Mist sections of hair with the Evian spray. Next, warm a pomade in the palms of your hands. Then, bring the product down the hair shaft from root to ends for each section. Hit the hair with a dryer equipped with a diffuser. Follow with an anti-frizz product and small curling iron. Wrap the hair in sections around the curling iron.

Figure 1.17 Mist, pomade, dry with diffuser, and curl, wrapping the hair around the iron

Suggestion: Do not spray a product like Bumble and Bumble Spray Shine directly onto the hair. Apply a small amount in your hands, then using your palms and fingers work the product through the hair.

Fine curls respond well to mousse products. Apply the mousse throughout the hair using your fingers. Air dry. This can be done the night before shooting the next morning.

Figure 1.18 Fine curls

Figure 1.19 Twist your curls with a moisture product

Use a moisture cream, twisting the product with your fingers into individual curls. Dry the hair naturally or with a dryer with a diffuser.

Figure 1.20 Spray mist and gels

Rewet with a water spray mist. Apply a gel from root to ends in sections. Hit with a dryer attached with a diffuser.

Figure 1.21 Protect with Kenra Hot Spray

Use a hair-protecting product like Kenra Hot Spray before using curling irons or flat irons. Follow with a heavier gel to style.

If you don't use the right product for straight coarse hair, you'll never keep the curl. It's simplest to use a heat-protective product that also holds curl. Kenra Hot Spray is a must in your kit. Apply spray to the hair and follow with a curling iron.

Figure 1.22 Heat Protective Products Holds Curl

Figure 1.23 Needs volume

Thinning, fine, straight hair needs volume. Start by applying a thickener spray such as Bumble and Bumble Prep. Follow with blow drying with a round or paddle brush, then style.

Jennifer Stanfield: Another quick solution is to put in big rollers. Send the actress to makeup. After makeup is done, have the actress sit back in your chair. Remove the rollers and style.

Suggestion for dreads: Use a conditioning product for dreads to alleviate dryness. Be aware that new dreads can easily fall apart and unravel. Asking questions is important to find the most effective product for your client.

Recommended products: DevaCurl Products Shampoo System, Carol's Daughter, BB Spray Shine, Davines, Kenra Hot Spray, Frédéric Fekkai Curl Cream, BB Prep Thickening Spray, and Crew.

Figure 1.24 Kenra Hot Spray; **Figure 1.25** Bumble and Bumble Invisible Oil; **Figure 1.26** Bumble and Bumble Thickening Hairspray ; **Figure 1.27** Davines Curl-Building Serum; **Figure 1.28** Davines Authentic Moisturizing Balm; **Figure 1.29** Davines Moisturizing Mousse

Weather conditions

Weather outside or the conditions found on different sets can greatly affect the way your hair styles maintain their hold. Using the right products makes a world of difference. For example, it could be cool and dry outside, but inside the set hot and humid. Head stylist with Bumble and Bumble, Tiffani Patchett, suggests how to work with a variety of weather conditions.

Dry, Hot Weather

If you live or work in areas where the conditions found are dry and hot, your hair could suffer the consequences. The sun and wind can cause hair to be dull, frizzy, and lifeless.

Tiffani Patchett: "For dry hair use a weekly hair mask. Choose a mask that best fits your specific hair needs. Use one with reparative properties for color-processed hair, such as

1.30 1.31 1.32 1.33 1.34

Figure 1.30 Bumble and Bumble Invisible Oil Shampoo; **Figure 1.31** Bumble and Bumble Invisible Oil Conditioner; **Figure 1.32** Bumble and Bumble Brilliantine; **Figure 1.33** Bumble and Bumble Mending Masque; **Figure 1.34** Bumble and Bumble Quenching Masque

Bumble and Bumble Mending Mask, or extra moisture for heat-styled hair. Quenching masks work great for thirsty hair. Also, if working in dry conditions, a leave-in mask like Quenching Complex gives the hair that much-needed moisture. If the hair is dull, focus on shampoos and conditioners that contain oil. Finish your hair with an oil product. I recommend Bumble and Bumble Hairdresser's Invisible Oil Shampoo and Conditioner, and Hairdresser's Invisible Oil for all hair types to add extra shine. Use Brilliantine for thick or coarse textures."

Humidity

People with hair that is already damaged or dry experience frizz in climates with humidity. This seems odd, but dry hair absorbs the moisture in the air.

Tiffani Patchett: "Set yourself up with the right styling products. Humidity can wreak havoc. Come to set armed with an oil-absorbing powder like Bumble and Bumble Pret-a-Powder just in case the actor starts to sweat. Also bring a smoothing serum and hairspray. On days like these it's smart to have a hair dryer handy for any resetting of the hair or to keep hairlines/ backs of necks dry."

Heat

The sun breaks down the outer layer of hair. When this happens the hair loses moisture.

Tiffani Patchett: "Use the same products as in dry hot weather. If you are shooting outdoors I recommend Color Minded Family by Bumble and Bumble, which has UV protection."

Figure 1.35 Bumble and Bumble Heat/UV Protective Primer Invisible Oil

Figure 1.36 Bumble and Bumble Quenching Complex

Rain

Rain can contain natural elements that might cause the hair to expand. It will frizz again! If you get caught out in the rain, be sure to shampoo your hair when you get in. Rain can carry chemicals from environmental contamination.

Tiffani suggests: "Before styling hair, analyze the texture in order to choose the right product. For finer hair use a structure product for hold, like Bumble and Bumble Thickening

Hairspray, before blow drying. Then layer a light anti-frizz serum such as Hairdresser's Invisible Oil. If your actor has coarser or curly textured hair choose a taming product like Bumble and Bumble Defrizz. Once outside, protection is key: umbrellas and a can of light-hold hairspray to gently lay down any stray hairs."

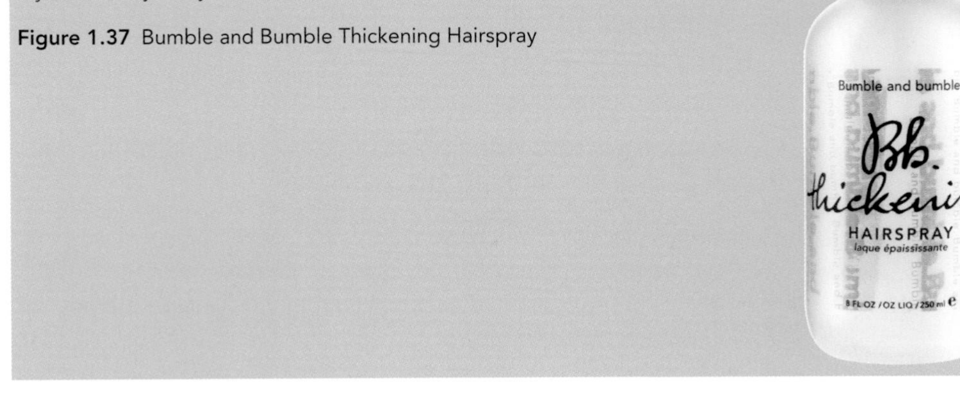

Figure 1.37 Bumble and Bumble Thickening Hairspray

Cold, Dry Weather

In cold environments the scalp can be itchy and flaky. Indoor heat and a lack of humidity results in a dry, lackluster mane.

Tiffani Patchett: "The same rules apply in cold, dry weather as in dry, hot weather."

Most Common Hair Damages Incurred on Set

Burns from Curling Irons/Flat Irons

How to correct: First keep flat irons and curling irons on a lower heat. Coarse hair can take a bit more heat, but be careful. Don't risk it if you are inexperienced working with different hair textures. Lower heat might take longer, but the hair will not burn. Always use a heat-protective product.

Chemical Damage from Tinting

How to correct: Start with trimming as much of the split ends as you can. Use a deep-conditioning hair mask a few times a week and a daily conditioner for damaged hair caused by coloring. Do not wash hair every day.

Overbrushing Hair

How to correct: Overbrushing causes split ends. Start with changing brushes to a good set that won't tangle the hair. Trim off any split ends.

Prosthetic Glues

How to correct: What a disaster this can be. Using the wrong glues and the wrong removers is one of the most painful things to experience. The makeup artist and hair stylist should never use an actor as a test subject.

Mark Garbarino: "Adhesives for hair that are easily removed are Telesis Silicone Adhesive, or SilPak Inc. MA-200, which is half the cost and has the same properties. I also use isopropyl myristate for removing most adhesives from hair or skin. 244 Fluid is a makeup thinner that also works fantastically for non-oily removal of Pax paints, Pros-Aide, tattoos, and cabo transfers to skin or hair."

See Chapter 5 for more information on adhesives plus removers.

Blood

How to correct: Blood is another area that can be done all wrong. Especially in the hair. Hair stylists and makeup artists need to work closely together to achieve the desired look while keeping in mind what the products are doing to the hair.

Suggestion: Treat blood products the same for use in hair or on skin. Choose what bloods work for the effects at hand, keeping in mind color, old or new, texture, staining, and so on. Start cleaning up blood in hair with a warm, damp towel, working the product out of the hair. Follow with a product like shave cream to lift the stain that blood products can leave behind. Finish with a shampoo-of-choice rinse.

See Chapter 5 for more information on blood.

Diseases and Disorders that Affect the Hair and Scalp

Diseases can have a devastating effect on their sufferers, and many of the symptoms reveal themselves in the sufferer's hair. Diseases often cause individuals to experience discomfort as well as humiliation, especially when symptoms occur on the face and scalp.

"Sufferers attempt many remedies. They may groom themselves excessively, such as brushing their hair for hours."
Daniel McNeill, *The Face*, p. 288.

The following will give you a guideline on what symptoms occur and how you can spot them. Always have a list of dermatologists you trust on hand. If you don't know any, contact the nearest medical school or teaching hospital and speak to someone in the Dermatology department for a recommendation. Sending an actor for professional treatment and advice is a huge plus. Many makeup artists have cosmetician licenses and are up on the latest treatments and can perform spa services and handle medical treatments, but if what you are using isn't getting immediate results, then consulting a dermatologist is the best solution. If an actor has been diagnosed with any of the conditions below, he or she probably already has been prescribed treatment products by his or her physician. Below are some other suggested products to help your actor stay camera ready.

Dandruff

Dandruff is a condition whereby dead skin cells flake off from the scalp. It's usually not a serious condition. Although dandruff is associated with a dry scalp, flaking can be thick and oily. Use conditioners and shampoos with deep-moisturizing scalp masks. Also, warm, wet towels used in combination with moisture products can help relieve itching and redness.

Psoriasis

This is a common condition that causes the skin to itch, resulting in redness and irritation. Look for red skin with white patches. Medicated, antifungal shampoos are often used. At work, use gentle alcohol-free products.

Seborrheic Dermatitis

This skin condition forms yellowish-white scales on an oily surface and is found on the scalp or ears. Shampoos containing mint, tar, and antifungal ingredients are a good choice. Oils such as olive, peppermint, and tea tree make good hair masks. You can also apply a mild corticosteroid cream.

Alopecia Areata

This condition causes round patches of hair loss on the scalp and body. The hair follicles are not damaged, so it's possible for hair to grow back on its own. To treat this condition a doctor is necessary. You can, however, give the illusion of hair by painting in by hand with Skin Illustrator or other tattoo palettes. Also consider using lace hair or facial hairpieces.

Trichotillomania

A psychological disorder when a person needs to pull out their hair. Although there is no known cure for this disorder, therapy and diet changes in combination with medicines are successful. Try using shampoos, conditioners, and hair products that contain soothing properties. Have a relaxing, even tempo when working in the trailer. Refrain from suggesting any oral herbal remedies. Herbal supplements taken with prescribed medicine can have negative results.

Hypothyroidism

This condition prevents the thyroid gland from producing enough thyroid hormones, and causes dry and brittle hair. Use shampoos and conditioners that repair damaged hair, in combination with thick moisture masks and conditioners. Refrain from suggesting foods or vitamin supplements such as high fiber, soy, calcium, or iron supplements, for example. Foods can negatively affect thyroid medications.

Anorexia Nervosa

An eating disorder. People are underweight and hair can become dry and brittle. Use products to help repair damage to the hair, and use low-heat or no-heat tools for styling. If the hair is thinning, use hair fillers or hair extensions. Use caution when applying hair extensions, however: Not properly applied, the hair could pull, causing further damage.

Figure 1.38 SenSpa scalp treatment

Spa Treatments

Spa treatments are more than a luxury service. Many of the hair and skin conditions talked about can approve significantly with spa services. When there is no time to treat conditions in the hair and makeup trailer, send your client to a reputable spa that performs the services you have requested. Work closely with technicians, massage therapists, cosmeticians, and dieticians, for example. You can request services on the menus, so custom blend products and services that will fit the actor's needs—for example, scalp treatments and back facials are often-overlooked treatments performed in a spa.

"Our scalp needs the same nourishment and attention as other parts of the body," says Teri Eaton, Outreach Manager at SenSpa in San Francisco. "Before starting a treatment, voice your wants and concerns to the service provider. What products are you using now? What products will the provider be using? Do you have any flaking or itching on the scalp? Do you have any sores in the scalp, contagious disorders, or are you in chemotherapy? Any of these issues can affect the hair and scalp. Disclosure between you and the provider enables him or her to better fit you with the correct treatment services. Treatments for hair and scalps improve follicular strength, microcirculation of the scalp, protecting hair from harsh shampoos, and damage done by chemical agents. All of these things destroy the outer cuticle of the hair. SenSpa, for example, has services that address these concerns with its Drenched and Quenched hair and scalp treatments. The services, besides soothing and relaxing, treat those hair and scalp concerns. Our scalp treatments use jojoba oil with vitamin E to nourish the scalp and promote hair growth."

To perform a similar scalp treatment, massage the hair with a warm, dry towel and a vitamin-blend product to protect the hair follicles and encourage hair growth at the root.

Credits

www.americancrew.com
www.bumbleandbumble.com
www.carolsdaughter.com
www.davines.com
www.devacurl.com
www.everydayhealth.com
www.fekkai.com
www.kenra.com
www.senspa.com
www.imdb.com/name/nm08221451 (Jennifer Stanfield)
www.youbeauty.com

References

Atlas of Human Anatomy, Frank H. Netter (Saunders)
Clinical Atlas of Human Anatomy, Peter H. Abrahams, Johannes M. Boon, Jonathan D. Spratt (Mosby)
Drawing the Head, William L. Maughan (Watson-Guptill Publications Inc.)
Future Face, Sandra Kemp (Profile Books)
The Face, Daniel McNeill (Penguin Books Ltd)

CHAPTER TWO
Color

Figure 2.1 Don Juskos Color Wheel

Hair coloring is an age-old art. Plants, henna, and indigo, for example, were often used for tinting hair in ages past. The sun was another alternative, and still is now, for creating highlights. When synthetic dyes were discovered, women began frequenting beauty parlors or salons for their color, and today there are so many choices for color that hair stylists need to know the science behind it. Not only will a hair stylist need to know hair dyes: He or she will have to make decisions about color with temporary tint products.

Understanding the color wheel is the first step. When working, you'll discover that using the color wheel and colored hair swatches for reference will help you make the right hair color choices. Color wheels, like Pantone charts, will also determine what colors can be used for many different things, including makeup colors, hair colors, and fashion.

You can break down color combinations by determining what your client's natural color is when he or she first sits down in your chair. To do this, you must first find the client's level of color, using the color wheel. Then, proceed to the opposite side of the wheel. Remember, hair color has many levels of darkness ranging from 1 to 12, with 1 being the lightest and 12 being the darkest.

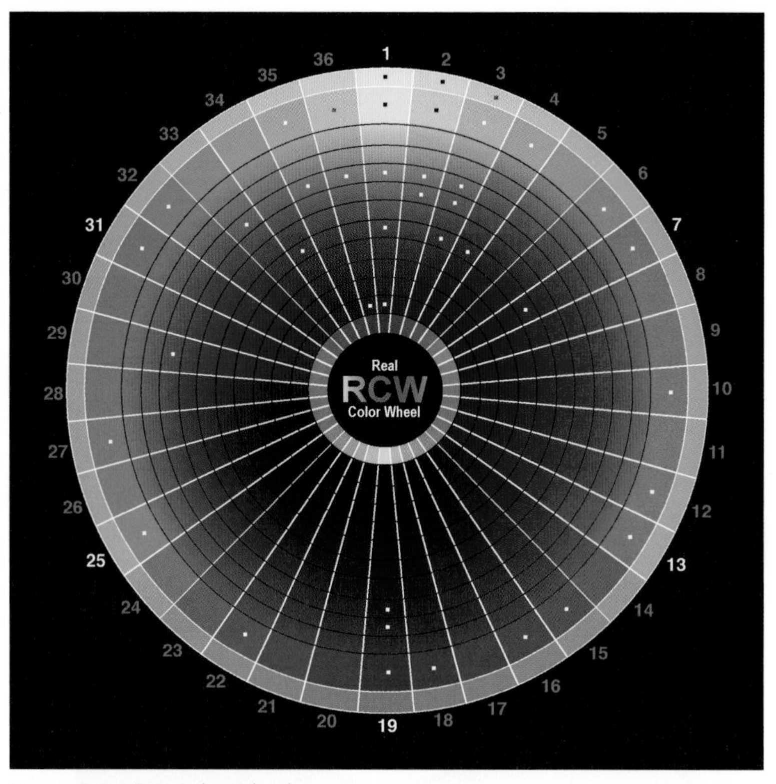

Figure 2.2 RCW Color Wheel

Figure 2.3 Wheel of hair on ring

Suggestion: Press the color wheel against the client's skin to quickly determine what color decisions would be best for him or her. This is especially important when time and space is of the essence in a busy hair and makeup trailer.

Hair color and skin tones can either complement or compete with each other. If you remember that fact, you'll have an easier time deciding how to bring out an actor's beauty, enhance his or her personality, or match his or her look with the time period of the film. For example, when you choose unflattering colors that are opposite to the actor's skin tone, you'll automatically create a visual disturbance, a little trick used for effect by makeup and hair professionals.

Today's world is a menagerie of color undertones. Carefully study your client before beginning to work on his or her look. Check out their eye color, skin tone, and natural hair color. Think of all those ingredients together and individually. Keep in mind people can fib about what their natural hair color is. Be patient and vigilant. Ask them about their hair and makeup history, especially what products they've used in the past and what they're using now. The products they use every day provide an important clue to their skin tone.

Figure 2.4 Dark hair, warm skin tones

Figure 2.5 Sonia Kashuk makeup palette, suitable for dark hair and warm skin tones

Black/dark brown hair and warm skin tones suit earth tones: orange, reds, and golds. Colors with a gold base are complementary to this skin tone. Remember to avoid the darkest shades.

Figure 2.6 Warm skin tones with yellow

Figure 2.7 Sonia Kashuk makeup palette, suitable for warm skin tones with yellow

Warm yellow-based skin tones work best with golden browns, coppers, and red tones.

Figure 2.8 Warm skin tones with red

Figure 2.9 Topshop eyeshadow and lipstick. Suitable for warm skin tones with red.

Gold works best if you have a warm skin tone with red undertones, but remember to avoid red colors.

Figure 2.10 Blonde hair with cool skin tones

Figure 2.11 Sonia Kashuk makeup palette , suitable for blonde hair with cool skin tones

For blonde, light brown, golden, white blonde, blue/black hair, think cool skin tones such as pinks, greens, blues, and blue/reds. Ash blonde or reds are the colors of choice for cool skin tones. To represent health and vibrancy, try warm colors on pale skins.

Figure 2.12 Dark hair with burgundy

Figure 2.13 Sonia Kashuk makeup palette, suitable for dark hair with cool skin tones

With dark/black hair, use cool undertones with blue/reds, burgundy, or garnet.

Figure 2.14 Don Jusko color swatches

Hair Dyes, Tints, and Bleaches

Figure 2.15 Davines Toner Burnt Umber

Figure 2.16 Davines Toner Orange

Figure 2.17 Davines Toner Red

Figure 2.18 Davines Toner Violet

Figure 2.19 Davines Toner Yellow

Figure 2.20 Davines Toner Ultramarine

Dyes are used to reduce or add color to the hair, and that's why hair dyes, tints, toners, and bleaches are common products in every hair and makeup trailer. Sometimes the challenge is too great for what's on hand and the actor is dispatched to a color expert for specific care, but using outside help may cause a conflict with production over budget issues, legal issues, and time restraints for an outside colorist. Sometimes, instead of sending the actor to the colorist, the colorist is sent to the trailer, hopefully a couple of days before shooting or prep days. Both options rely upon the appropriate financial approval from production. The important thing is to be honest with yourself and your skills. If you're unsure whether or not you can handle the job, don't attempt it, but talk to production about getting extra help, including possibly employing someone else on your crew.

Temporary Hair Colors

These are the easiest choice, but they need to be reapplied often. Temporary colors do not contain bleach, so they won't lighten the hair.

Semi-Permanent Hair Colors

These last longer than temporary colors, but not as long as permanent ones.

Permanent

Permanent hair dye lifts the original color from the hair and adds new color. Permanent dye contains oxidizers such as hydrogen peroxide. It lasts the longest and has to be touched up with new hair growth.

Streaking Products

These are temporary or permanent products that are used to highlight sections of the hair.

Vegetable-Based Products

These temporary dyes are sourced from plants, flowers, or fruit.

Henna

Henna, a plant product, is used for tattoos and hair coloring.

Bleaching

This is used to reduce color.

Tints

A tint is a temporary color that covers the existing shade of the hair without lifting it. You can add silicone for shine too. Shampooing will fade or wash out the tint within a few weeks. Tints do not cover gray effectively.

Patrick Evan, Color Expert

The Patrick Evan Salon is an exclusive establishment employing expert stylists for a number of services. Precision cuts, extensions, color, and highlights are just the tip of the iceberg. Patrick lends us here his vast knowledge on color and working with new clients, and his advice on products.

Patrick Evan: "Properly prepare your client by consulting with him or her about what hair color to use. It's best to speak with new clients a few days before the actual appointment. This gives enough time to properly prepare for the service. Ask the client to bring in sample pictures of the color he or she would like to see for their hair.

"Have your client use a clarifying shampoo the day before the appointment. The shampoo will remove built-up waxes and other products, insuring your coloring will last a long time.

"There are many factors that go into deciding what colors to mix for a client. You have to ask the questions: What color have they chosen? Is there gray hair? What tones has the client chosen? What is the condition of the hair? What does the client want to see, and is that really different than the pictures he's shown you, or appeals he or she has made? You can see by these questions that communication is important before you select the products for the session. As far as my choices, I usually use Logistics Colorcremes and Wella Koleston products, which are perfect for permanent tints."

Patrick goes on: "Never mix colors from different brands. Specific brands mix their products with complementary ingredients in exact amounts. Mixing brands destroys that balance and can and has produced unpredictable results.

"Always perform a patch test on new clients to determine allergy sensitivity. Dab a small amount of the desired color behind the client's ear or on the client's elbow. Let it dry and wait 24 to 48 hours to see if there's any kind of reaction. Ask the client if they have any skin allergies or other conditions that might be affected by coloring. If there's redness, itchiness, or other irritation, *don't* use the product. Discuss with your client alternatives such as colored hair extensions."

More about Color Charts

Patrick continues: "Using color charts can be tricky because every color line has its own slightly different shade of the same color. Don't mix color charts. Stick to the same color line when at the beginning of the session. You can also use natural color swatches, because the colors do not change, but remember the swatches are made using naturally 100 percent white hair and, thus, the color you desire may not match the swatch when it's applied on your client. Use the swatches as a reference but not as the final decision on what the desired color will look like."

Mixing Colors for a Beginner Client

"The best advice is to keep it simple and not go overboard on change. Use a color that is close to what your client already has: For example, don't go from blonde to brunette. So the first step is to figure out exactly your client's level of color using a natural swatch if available. Next, you need to find the desired level of tone: for example, red, gold, or ash. Try for something close to his or her existing color but one level lighter or darker to start."

Coloring Mistakes

Patrick advises, "The most common mistake is not knowing exactly what color or tone you're starting from. If you don't know, you can't mix the right color. For example, you have a client with dark brown hair who wants to be a golden blonde. If you pick a golden blonde off the chart, your client will probably end up with orange hair. A colorist must learn how to recognize and compensate for how much red is naturally in the hair, and that means using just enough color to counteract the red. Unfortunately many stylists fail to take this step, and you see, as I have in my career, a lot of orange hair. Again, understand what happens to natural hair color during the lifting process so you can achieve the shade both you and your client desire."

Coloring Different Hair Textures

"Different hair textures take differently to coloring. Fine hair will process more quickly, and if not diligently monitored will be damaged. Also, by absorbing color more quickly, the desired color may be darker or lighter than hoped for. A shorter process time and weaker solution may be required. Conversely, coarser hair has a stronger structure and is resistant to color. A longer processing time and a stronger solution may be needed," Patrick concludes.

Taking Patrick's knowledge and applying it to a hair and makeup trailer, be prepared to do the following.

How to Apply Basic Color

Set-Up in the Trailer

Before starting you'll need tinting bowls, tinting brushes, hand towels, set-up towels, protective gloves, a drape, several tail combs, a timer, and cotton neck protectors.

Figure 2.21 Supplies for coloring

Prepping Your Client

First, sit your client in a comfortable position. Protect his or her neck with cotton and use a drape over the cotton. Next, have a bottle of water or other beverage of choice for your client to sip during the session. Also, any reading material is a plus and his or her choice of music can sometimes help keep someone calm and still. Once everything is set, section the hair on the head into four parts (front to back, sectioned in half, then ear to ear) before applying color.

Figure 2.22 Mixing bowls

Applying Color

First, put on your protective gloves, then mix the desired color in a mixing bowl.

Figure 2.23 Applying color

Take a small section of hair at the top of the four parts and apply the mixed color, working your way down the hair. Each segment is worked on individually, so for each segment start at the part and apply color, then fold the foil and continue working downward until that section is done.

Go to another section and repeat until the desired color is complete.

Make sure you keep track of the time the color is on the hair. As mentioned before in this chapter, be aware of how different hair textures, dry hair, and damaged hair affect how long it will take for the color to set. Use a timer to remind you when to check the color and when the process is finished. When the hair reaches the desired color, quickly rinse and shampoo, but remember shampooing after a coloring is optional. You don't want to risk washing out or fading the color. Using a tinted shampoo and conditioners will enhance or correct but not fade the color.

Figure 2.24 Davines Tinted Shampoo Chocolate

Figure 2.25 Davines Tinted Shampoo Red

Figure 2.26 Davines Tinted Shampoo Tobacco

Figure 2.27 Davines Tinted Shampoo Silver

Figure 2.28 Davines Tinted Shampoo Copper

Figure 2.29 Davines Tinted Shampoo Golden

Figure 2.30 Davines Tinted Conditioner Chocolate

Figure 2.31 Davines Tinted Conditioner Red

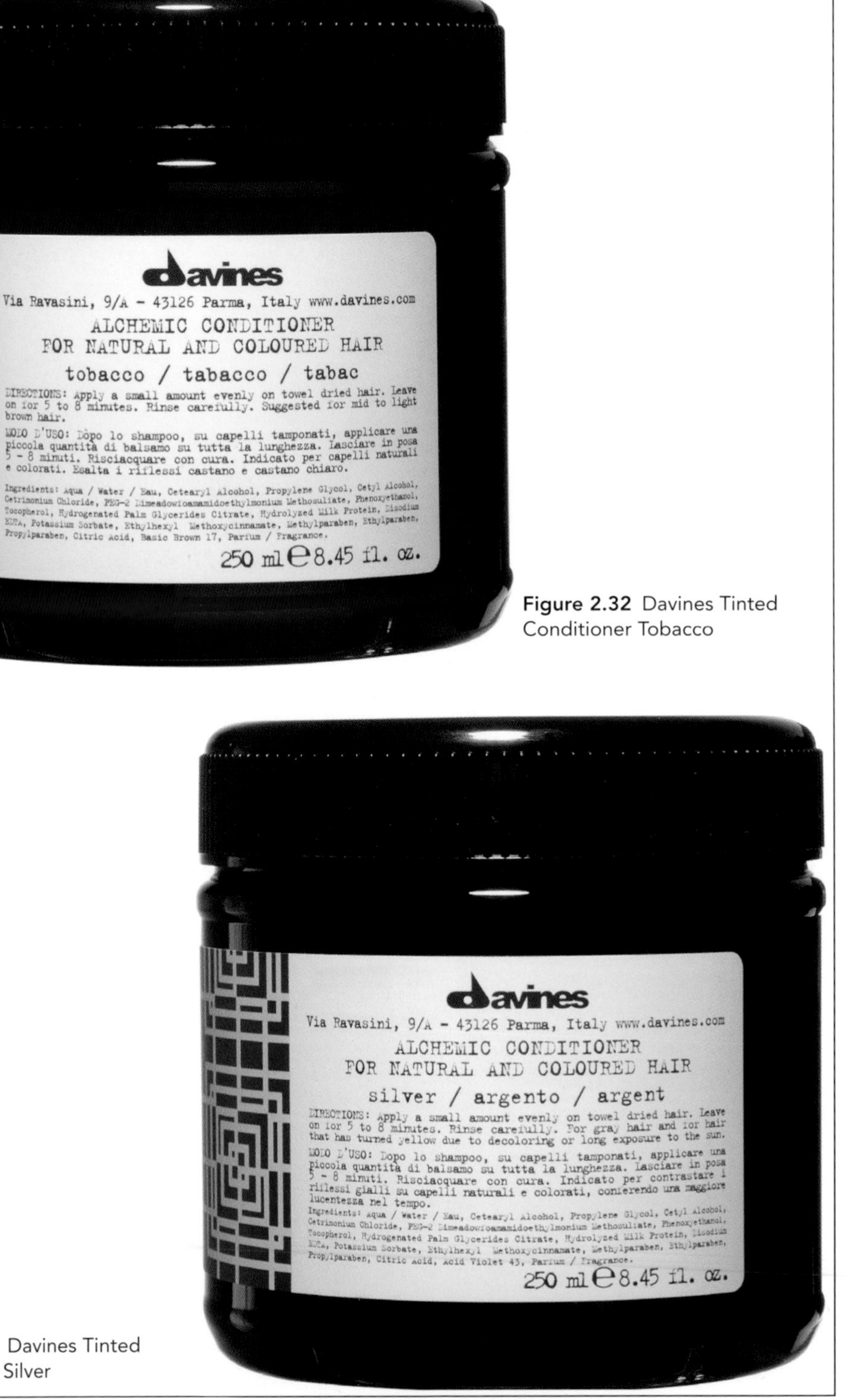

Figure 2.32 Davines Tinted Conditioner Tobacco

Figure 2.33 Davines Tinted Conditioner Silver

Figure 2.34 Davines Tinted Conditioner Copper

Figure 2.35 Davines Tinted Conditioner Golden

Suggestions: First, proper ventilation is important, especially when you're working in a hair and makeup trailer. Make sure all the windows and doors are open and fans running on high. Just as important, make sure other actors are not in the trailer while the work is being done. Second, keep a bottle of dishwashing liquid nearby. It can be used in an emergency to remove color stains on the skin.

Hair Lightening Using Bleach

It's not common, but there are times where bleaching whole heads of hair in the hair and makeup trailer is necessary. Bleach removes color from your hair by using the process of oxidation and there can be major mishaps with the process.

Figure 2.36 Vanessa Mills

Vanessa Mills is a colorist at Patrick Evan Salon. Her 15-year career has been based entirely in San Francisco. Vanessa started out as an assistant to one of the highest-profile colorists, training exclusively in the art of color. Her extensive training includes Wella, Logics, Redken, and Clairol. Her background also includes stints in New York and LA with Matrix. Vanessa loves the many aspects of color and the chemistry behind it. Creating long-lasting reds, rich warm brunettes and multi-dimensional blondes is a passion. Vanessa's creativity flows when correcting color, with all the science it entails.

Vanessa's shares her professional expertise on the bleaching process here, giving advice and tips to help you to keep the process safe and effective.

Vanessa: "Before you start to change your color from brown to blonde, consider a few factors. Has the hair been previously colored? How many levels of light do you want to go? What is the condition of the hair?

"Using color (tint) is an effective and gentle way to lighten hair, but not many people can use this method. If your client has had a previous color, you will need to use a lightener (bleach) instead.

"Also, if the client wants a color that is three to four shades lighter than her own, then bleaching is recommended. If you attempt to use color with these two factors you will end up with orange hair. Hair color is limited to how light it can go. Bleach is not limited. But bleach can have harsh qualities. If not done correctly, there can be serious side effects, such as hair breakage and scalp burns, which should be immediately attended to."

Double process is a full bleach, a procedure that includes bleaching and then toning to the desired color.

Vanessa: "When lightening, the hair goes through different stages of lift. Red to orange and yellow to pale yellow. When lightening brown hair to a sunny blonde, the process will have to reach yellow to pale yellow, then tone accordingly afterwards.

"First begin by applying a high developer like 30–40 volume mixed with bleach. Apply the mixture to the mid-shaft of the hair, at least half an inch from the scalp. Next, apply scalp lightener on the roots, close to the scalp. Lastly, apply the bleach mixture of 30 volume to the ends of the hair. Process until the desired level of lightness is achieved and then tone with your desired shade.

"Gentle process is a little safer because you can control the outcome. Apply a full head of highlights using back-to-back foils. Afterwards, use a base adjunct (a product that lightens base levels by one to two levels). If you are going three to four levels lighter, use a tint.

"Hi Lift works well to lighten hair. Most lines that carry Hi Lift colors are a level 12 mixed with double the amount of 40-volume developer."

Note: To be a candidate for Hi Lift colors you must not have had a previous color or the desire to go lighter than four shades from where you start.

Color tinting stops working at the 45-minute mark. The process is completely done at this point. If your color is not the desired tone, most likely the formulation was wrong. Add toner or high lights to fix it.

How to Apply a Color Tint

Set-Up

Bleach powder, peroxide, color toner (if needed), color tints, color bowl, color brush, gloves, cape, timer.

Bleaching Steps

Start with clean, washed hair free of conditioners and hair products such as hairsprays.

Mix the desired amount of peroxide plus bleach for the hair color that is to be lightened—for example, a percentage strength ratio of 30–9. It's best to follow the manufacturer's directions, then adjust those combinations to your client's needs.

Protect your hands by wearing gloves. Try to avoid latex gloves because there's a powdery residue on latex and your client may be allergic to latex.

Apply from the ends of the root evenly through the hair, or only as far as the hair needing to be lightened. The ends of the hair generally will take color differently than the roots, especially if the hair has previous color.

The bleach can lift any time between 15 to 40 minutes. You can check your progress by wiping a small amount off a few strands of hair. If the level of lift is satisfactory, it's time to rinse and condition. At this point you may need to use a corrective toner to remove unwanted brassiness, or to retint to the desired colors. Follow the manufacturer's instructions as a guide.

Monitoring the health of your client's hair afterwards is very important. Actors will need regular conditioning a few times a week. The length of the project will determine how many times color will have to be applied again.

Figure 2.37 Davines Bleach Powder

Figure 2.38 Davines Paste

Maintaining Blonde

Vanessa: "Hair that has been colored blonde is not difficult to maintain, if the lightening process has been done correctly. Blonde hair has a tendency to appear dull, and blonde hair absorbs light rather than reflects it. Maintain blonde hair's shine by using a glaze once a month. This keeps the hair cuticle sealed.

"You want to control the brassiness. To do this, you can use purple-tinted shampoos and conditioners once a week. Using it more often can turn hair gray.

"Daily conditioning is needed for lightened hair (not tinted). That, along with a weekly deep-conditioning mask, will keep hair healthy and shiny.

Suggested Products

Hair masks: Oribe Signature Moisture Mask, Oribe Gold Lust Transformative Mask, Kerastase Masque Chroma Riche.

Hair glazes: Redken Shades EQ, Logics Color Insider, and Wella Color Touch.

Tinted shampoo and conditioners: Oribe Conditioning for Beautiful Color, Davines.

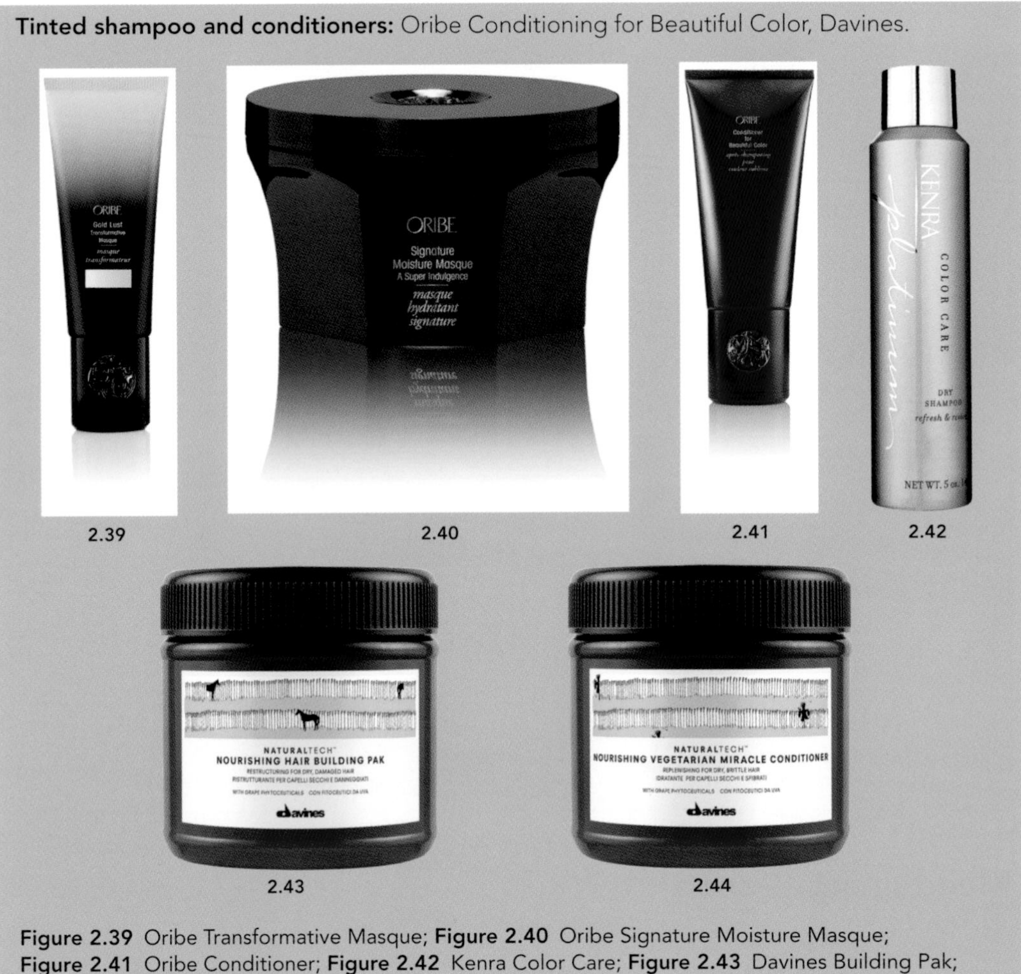

Figure 2.39 Oribe Transformative Masque; **Figure 2.40** Oribe Signature Moisture Masque; **Figure 2.41** Oribe Conditioner; **Figure 2.42** Kenra Color Care; **Figure 2.43** Davines Building Pak; **Figure 2.44** Davines Nourishing Vegetarian Conditioner

Color Correcting

Color correcting is a great way to help hair that is drab with little or no color. By lightening or darkening an existing color, you might also need to correct, but make sure to use discretion, because correcting color can be complicated and hard to achieve in certain situations, such as color correcting on actors in the hair and makeup trailer.

Use warmer red-based colors to darken blondes and to grab the hair without turning the color green or gray. Use cool-toned shampoos or conditioners to tone down any brassiness between color applications.

If you want to darken blonde hair, you should add warmer or red-based colors first. Without this step your newly applied darker color could grab the hair, turning the color green or gray.

If you have been going blonde, your color will most likely have cool tones, or will have done in the past. Using your color wheel, you can see that red is opposite to green, which makes the brown hair dye neutral.

If your hair color is too orange, try a blue-based shampoo, and if it's too red, use a green shampoo to tone down the color.

Brow and Lash Tinting

The most common service in a hair and makeup trailer is brow and lash tinting, and there are some very good products with which to do this. Many mascaras can cause irritation, therefore tinting makes sense. Brows can be darkened or lightened according to the character being portrayed, or you might simply want to darken an actor's lashes so the eyes will stand out.

Like color for the hair, you'll need to check brow tints during the process to control the amount of lightness achieved.

When tinting eyelashes or brows use only reputable, known products. Follow any manufacturer's instructions. Make sure products are fresh, noting expiration dates. Heed warnings on the packaging.

Figure 2.45 Tinting: Step One. Cleanse the area to be tinted

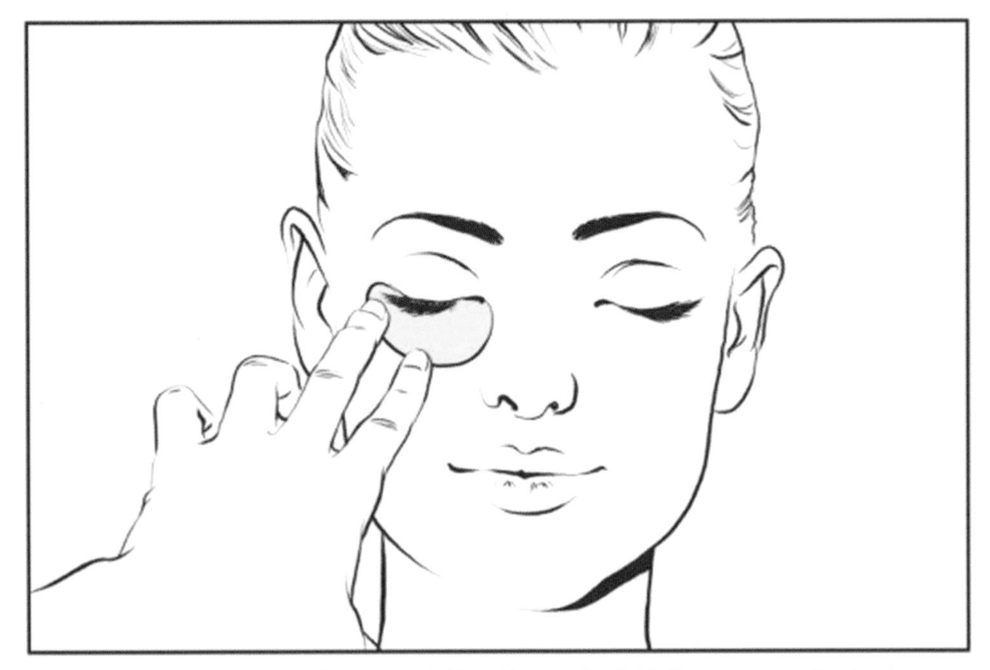

Figure 2.46 Step Two. Protect the eyes and skin with a small shield. If none come with the tint, cut a damp cotton pad in a moon shape. Use no shred cotton pads.

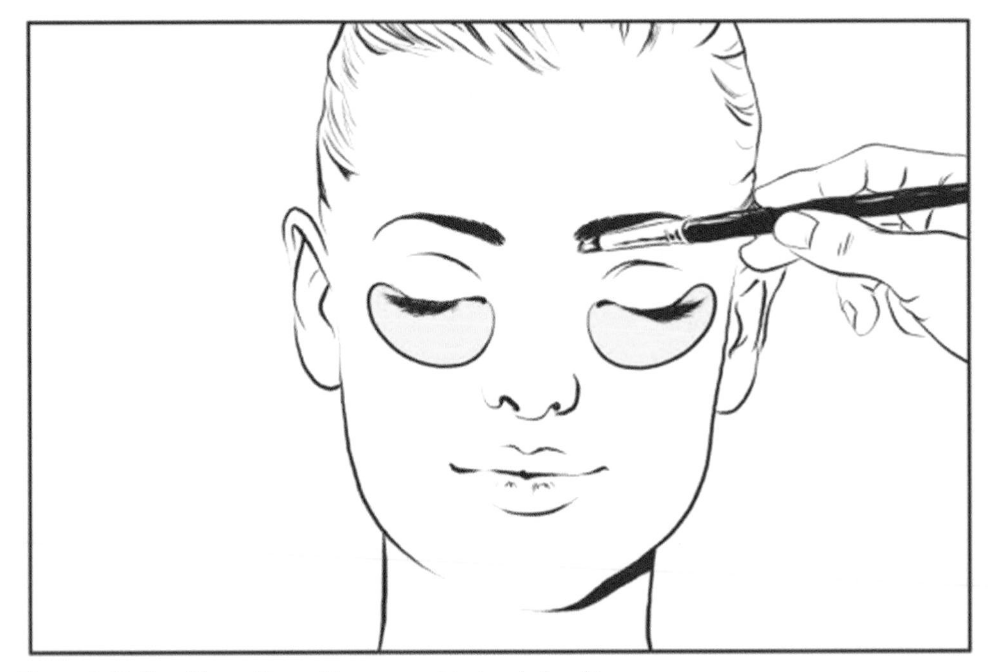

Figure 2.47 Step Three. Tint, taking care not to touch the skin.

After tinting eyelashes and brows, treat the area with gentle eye products to soothe and condition the area. Lashes are particularly vulnerable to falling out with constant rubbing, tinting, and wearing cosmetics. Cleanse the lashes with Gentle Lash Cleanser, following up with lipocils to stimulate regrowth of brows and lashes.

Figure 2.48 Talika Lash Conditioning Cleanser

Figure 2.49 Talika Lipocils

Caution: Dyes can irritate the skin and cause rashes on the scalp, hairline, ears, and neck. Facial swelling can also occur. Breathing in the dye fumes can cause respiratory problems, so be extra careful with all products.

Protect Yourself

Wear gloves and a cape. Make sure your client's face and eyes are protected. While working in the hair and makeup trailer keep all fans going and all doors open. Keep out crew and actors who don't need to be in the trailer. Test all dye products for allergic reactions and always follow judiciously manufacturer's directions. Wear gloves!

See www.fda.gov for up-to-date product safety advice.

Temporary Color Products

Figure 2.50 Colored hair extensions

Be prepared for any possibility. There are many products you can use for temporarily coloring hair. Quick and easy solutions can sometimes get you out of an unexpectedly tense situation. Remember, unless approved by the actor, director, and producers, you should never give an actor a permanent hair color. This includes stunt men and women. Films are not shot sequentially. Each day you're shooting different sections of the script, reflecting different continuity issues. Can temporary color be used for managing touch-ups between permanent colors, or fillers applied for a fuller hair look? Do brow colors need to alter or be reshaped? That's where temporary colors help you stay out of continuity trouble.

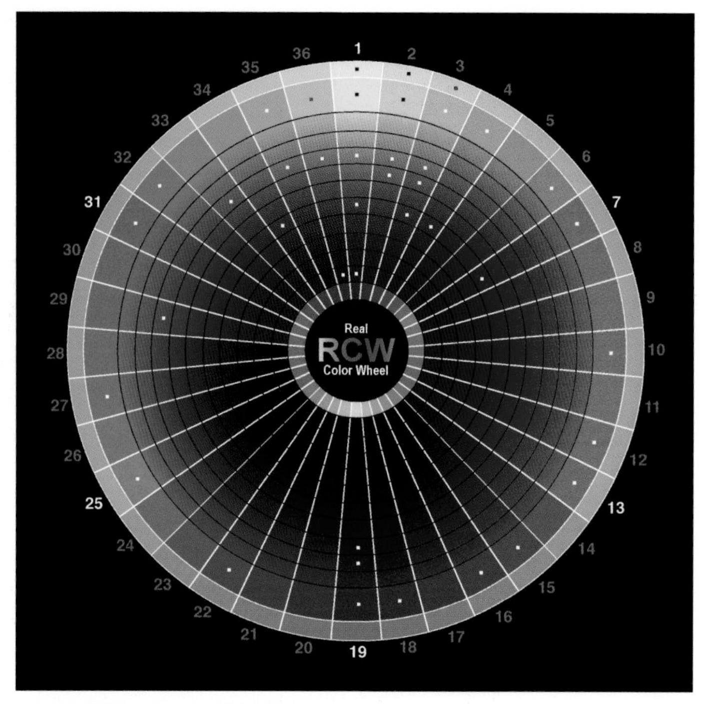

Figure 2.51 Don Jusko Color Wheel

Figure 2.52 RCW Color

Hair Chalks

Hair chalks come in a variety of colors and prices, so there are a lot of choices. It all depends upon your project. In film, chalks are sometimes used to create a whole different look. Chalks are also used in the hair and makeup trailer to create a bold contemporary look on actors without a trip to the salon. But remember that chalks can get on everyone and everything, so extra caution is needed to keep them away from hands, face, and wardrobe.

Applying Hair Chalks

Set-Up

You will need a spray water bottle, set-up towels, small face towels, hair dryer, flat iron, gloves, and chalk.

Steps:

1. First drape your client.
2. Spritz water onto sections of the hair you're going to color. Make sure it's damp and not soaked, because color adheres to the damp hair.
3. Working in a downward motion, apply the chalk while twisting and turning the hair that is being colored.
4. Use a flat iron on low heat to seal the color into the hair, followed by your choice of hairsprays.

Recommended Chalks for Different Hair Colors

Red hair: greens, purples.

Brown hair: pink, purple, green, yellow.

Blonde hair: pink, purple, blue.

Black hair: bright blue, red, pink, purple.

Tattoo Palettes

These products are used constantly for filling in hairlines for an illusion of thicker hair (a fan brush works great to do this) or for changing someone's color to reflect age or youth.

Figure 2.53 Illustrator Scalp

Figure 2.54 Dura Pro Temptu Hair

Tinted Gels, Foams, Mousse, Powders, Fibers, and Sprays

Foams and mousse are light products that help add volume to hair. Colored mousse is used to add temporary color.

Yvette Rivas tells us color foams can be a great way to temporarily change or alter hair color: "When using foams, let the client know the truth about the products being used. For example, the holding power of the products."

Goldwell

Pros: Goldwell works great on pre-colored bright red or similar-tinted hair. These colors tend to fade quickly. The colored foam keeps colors vibrant. This product does have a strong holding power! Apply on washed, towel-dried hair. Process the foam for 5 to 15, minutes then rinse.

Cons: It is super hard to remove from blonde or bleached hair. I have known an actress complain to production that the stylists turned her hair into a greenish tone—production dished out a lot of money to correct the color!

Suggested products: Goldwell, Alterna Night Highlights Temporary Color Mousse (Alterna comes with an attached brush applicator).

Sprays

These color products are aerosol sprayed.

Suggested products: Bumble and Bumble spray chalk, Bumble and Bumble Hair Powder, Streaks 'n' Tips (a great product to use on the fly).

Creams and Gels

Color gels are fantastic to use for a quick pop of bright or neon day-glo color. These products transfer onto clothes, so it's best not to use on long hair. Creams and gels work on all kinds of hair textures, and are easy to apply with fingers or a comb. Gels can leave a shine after drying.

Suggested products: Manic Panic Dye Hard, Color Spiking Gel, Kryolan Hair Gel, Washables.

Fibers

Most fibers contain synthetic or plant-based keratin protein that is dye matched to hair colors.

Figure 2.55 Million Hair

Figure 2.56 XFusion

Figure 2.57 Eclipse Hair Filler

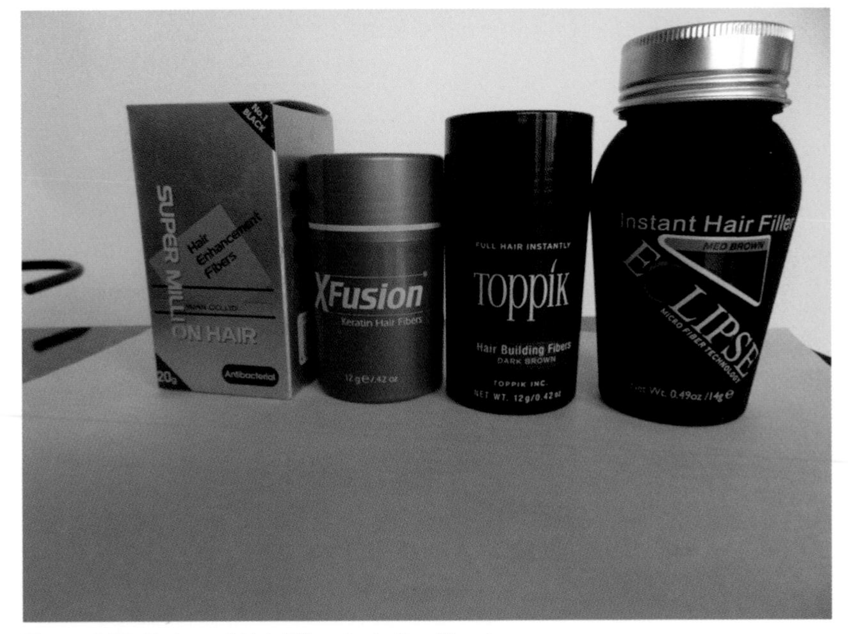

Figure 2.58 Variety of Hair Fillers including Toppix

Powder Tints

Most are talc based with added color. Applications will vary depending upon the other ingredients in the product.

Figure 2.59 Powder hair products

Crayons and Sticks

With crayons and sticks, the color is mixed with different compounds, such as waxes. Watch how you use temporary sticks: They can run if shooting in hot conditions, so be aware! Crayons and sticks work well for quick fixes. Everyone should have a set in their kit.

Suggested products: Roux 'Tween-Time Crayon, Daggett & Ramsdell Color Stick.

Airbrushes

Airbrushes are used to fill in hairlines, thinning hair on the scalp, and to fill in beards. Dura, for example, by Temptu, is an alcohol-based product that is effective in doing these things.

Figure 2.60 Temptu Air Brush System

Credits

www.colormevanessa@yahoo.com/Vanessa Mills
www.concoction.com
www.davines.com
www.eclipsehair.com
www.kenra.com
www.oribe.pro
www.oribe.com
www.patrickevan.com
www.realcolorwheel.com
www.skinillustrator.com
www.sleekhair.com
www.sleekhair.tumblr.com, Instagram.com/sleekhair
www.soniakashuk.com
www.target.com/Sonia Kashuk
www.supermillionhair.com
www.talika.com
www.temptu.com
www.toppik.com
www.topshop.com
www.xfusionhair.com

CHAPTER THREE
Tools

You need the right tools to create the best hairdo. As hair styles have changed over the decades, many hair stylists have come to rely heavily on their equipment. Hot irons, which made the Marcel wave so popular in the past, can be found today only in modern forms, and combs, brushes, dryers, rollers, and shears have all been updated to help hair stylists cut, backcomb, part, section, straighten, curl, and style hair. Working in modern media today, such as film, television, and web productions, you need the best equipment to achieve your "looks" quickly and efficiently, and a lot of productions require expertise with period hair styles, wigs, and extensions. You must know why you are buying that particular brush, for example, and for what purpose. Yvette Rivas, Department Head Hair Stylist, will suggest tools she uses right out of her kit throughout the chapter.

Brushes

Brushes are made with bristles. Stiff hair or feather, plastic or nylon, are all used to make various kinds of brushes.

There are many types of brushes available, but Yvette suggests, "Invest in a wood-handled small brush for slicking down baby hair. Also a medium wood-handled brush is great for teasing hair plus cleaning the heads of your clippers."

Types of Bristle

Boar Bristle

Boar bristles are hair from hog or wild boar. There are different textures and qualities of boar hair on the market. Boar hair is used in brushes for a variety of reasons, although the bristles are hard, which has stylists divided on what hair textures are good for boar brushes. Boar hairs also brush smooth, and distribute the natural oils in hair.

Nylon Brush Hair

This is nylon that has been spun into microfilaments to create synthetic brushes. There are many different sizes, shapes, and usages for nylon brushes. They tend to be less expensive and can be found mixed in with boar hair or other animal bristles.

Badger

Various types of badger hair are used for shaving brushes, although the English badger is now a protected species.

Silvertip Badger

The most expensive of all badger-hair brushes, silvertip badger claims to hold lather well when mixed with water. Silver tips are naturally formed on the bristles.

Super Badger

Super badger has a black band around the middle of the brush. The brush is exceedingly soft.

Best Badger

Best badger is lighter brown or gray in color. It has a slightly rougher feel on the face.

Pure Badger

Pure badger is the most available of all the badger-hair brushes. Colors range from tan to black. The texture is rougher on the face.

Copper Coated

Copper-coated bristles are ball-tipped bristles that have been infused with copper. These brushes claim to kill bacteria and treat other scalp conditions by stimulating the scalp through brushing.

Types of Hair Brush

There are a variety of brushes on the market today. Choosing brushes is a personal decision. Yvette Rivas, who has brushes for every situation, has her favorites:

"Have a detangle brush. This brush undoes tangles and can be used on wet or dry hair. A must-have. Monroe brushes (there are many different kinds) work for parting or sectioning the hair. The Monroe brush with a ridge in the middle of the brush is used for backcombing. Spray the ridge with hairspray, then backcomb. This keeps the backcombing in place. Vent brushes are useful on set for quick touch-ups. It's important for the brush used on set to maintain a style without any fuss. Mason Pearson brushes are a must-have for their overall use, reliability, and craftsmanship."

3.1

3.2

Figures 3.1 and 3.2 Mason Pearson brushes

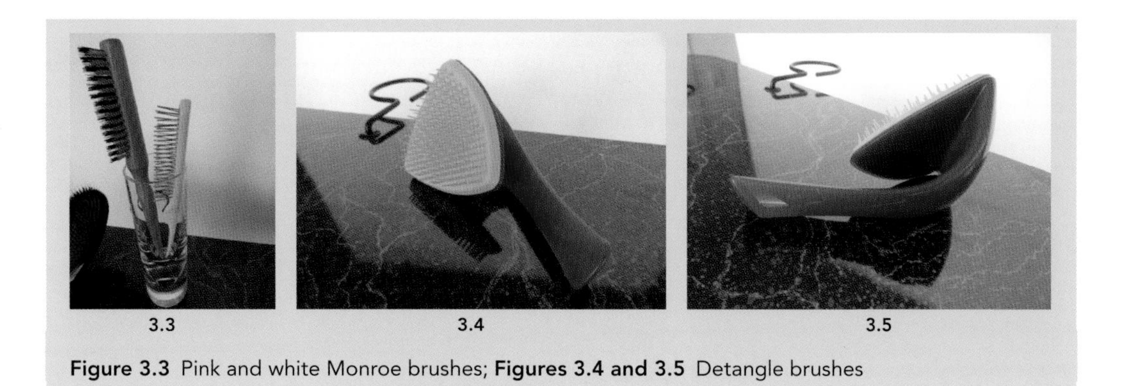

Figure 3.3 Pink and white Monroe brushes; **Figures 3.4 and 3.5** Detangle brushes

Round

Round brushes come in a variety of sizes. Round brushes can add volume and curl to straight hair, but also can be used to straighten curly hair while blow drying.

Teasing Brush

Teasing brushes can be used for backcombing, teasing, and adding volume.

Paddle

Paddle brushes work well to detangle long hair, smooth out hairdos and add volume to blow-outs.

Vent

Vent brushes add texture to hair. They also speed up blow drying and add volume.

Ceramic

Ceramic brushes retain heat and are used for different styling techniques.

Image Grooming Brushes

Grooming brushes are usually made with fine bristles and are used for men, women, and children. Grooming brushes promote good scalp stimulation, and shine to hair, while performing gently.

Pocket Size

Pocket-size or travel brushes are smaller in size. Pocket brushes come in all shapes and with all types of bristles.

Half Radial

Half radial brushes work by creating a good curve or bend in the hair, for example if you were to create hair that's turned under.

Ball Tipped

Ball-tipped brushes have little nylon balls attached to the bristles. This type of brush claims to promote a healthier scalp through massage induced by the bristles. It is also used for entangled hair.

Palm

Palm brushes can come in a variety of shapes and sizes, but they are usually a flat brush made with plastic or a stiff bristle, held in the palm of your hands. The brush is good for stimulating the scalp while brushing or shampooing.

Military Brushes

Military brushes tend to be oval, have no handles, and fit in the palm of the hand. They are usually made with a high-quality bristle that works well with short hair.

Facial Brushes/Shave Brushes

Shave brushes are used in the art of shaving. Tapered, flat, or rounded bristles are bound together and inserted into a wood, metal, ceramic, or glass handle. The bristles are usually made of badger. Shave brushes create lather when applied to shaving soaps mixed with water. The lathered brush is then applied to the beard for shaving.

Beard Brushes

Beard brushes not only brush the beard, but the stiffer bristles promote natural oils to lubricate the beard. They clean and detangle for a healthier, better-groomed beard.

Moustache Brushes

Moustache brushes are made with stiff bristles such as badger. The moustache brush cleans and shapes the moustache. Brushing a moustache keeps little hairs from sticking up in an unruly way.

Pro tip: If you have an actor with facial hair, keep a moustache brush or comb in your set bag for quick touch-ups. This will keep little hairs from sticking up and causing a not-so-great look on camera. If all else fails and you do not have a small stiff brush on hand, mix a small amount of resin-based glue with alcohol. Apply the mixture sparely with a flat cosmetic brush over the hairs that are sticking up.

Sponges

Coarse hair can achieve the style of different texture and knots with hair sponges.

To start the process, dampen the hair with water, then apply a grooming product to the hair. For example, creams, gels, leave-in conditioners or pomade work fine. We recommend Bees Wax, Pomade, or a pomade gel mix. Start circling the sponge on the hair in a circular motion on areas where you would like to have texture or a small dread. Always circle in the same direction. Circle on one side, opposite side, top, and back. Styles can also include a fade on the sides, with the textured dreads on top. The longer you circle the sponge to the hair, the more texture you will get.

Yvette Rivas recommends the following sponges: Nubian Twist, Tornado Coiler, Magic Twist.

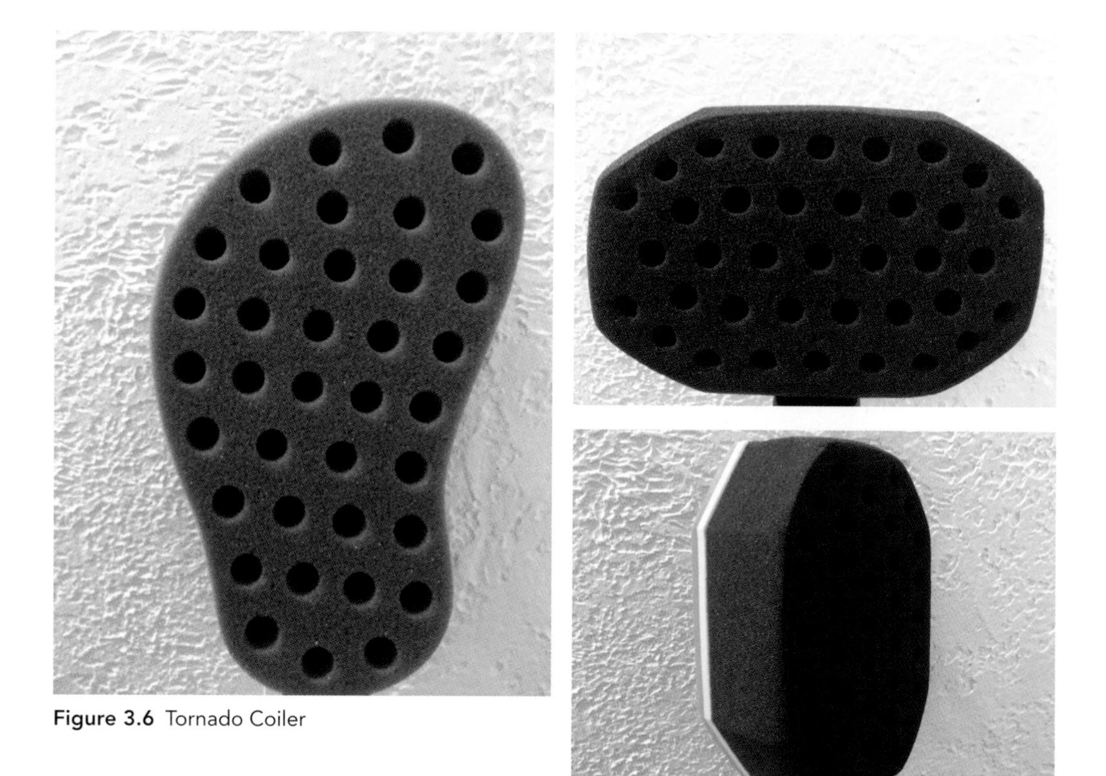

Figure 3.6 Tornado Coiler

Figures 3.7 and 3.8 Nubian Twist

Combs

Combs are an essential part of the stylist's toolkit.

Yvette explains, "My favorite combs are FHI black combs. Why? Well, FHI combs are heat resistant and used for cutting and styling. Silkomb combs are great all-purpose combs that also inhibit growth of bacteria. Silkomb has a comb that is angled in the middle. This comb's unique design allows stylists to trim hair close to the skin in hard-to-reach places. Another favorite is the Comare Mark II lift-and-style comb with stainless-steel fork. Comare is heat and chemical resistant. You can style, section, part, and backcomb. Combs with very fine teeth tapered on the ends work well on details, for example, the back of the neck. Lastly, who can go wrong with a basic styling men's grooming comb?"

Cutting

Cutting combs come in different sizes, colors, shapes, materials, and tooth variations. Cutting combs are used as a cutting guide with scissors.

Rattail

Rattail combs have a comb on one end, with a point on the other end, used as a sectioning hair tool or lifter.

Wide Toothed

Wide-toothed combs have extra space between the teeth of the comb. The extra-wide-toothed combs can be used for detangling wet or dry hair.

Barber

Barber combs are generally used on short hair with precise hair styles. Combs can also be used on many hair types and styles. Teeth on the comb vary in size from one end to the other. This gives the barber flexibility when creating styles. Rounded teeth on some combs have a gentler effect on the scalp.

Rake

Rake combs have larger teeth and come in many materials, and different sizes and shapes. The combs are used for thick, curly, textured, or tangled hair.

Styling and Lifting

A comb used for styling, lifting, and adding volume.

Detangling

This is like a rake comb, and detangles, separates, and combs curly hair. There are also brushes like Denman, or comb–brush combinations like KombBrush, that do the same thing.

Folding

A folding comb, also called a gentleman comb, is a compact comb that can be folded into a case. These combs are made from many different materials.

Spring

One side of this comb springs in, allowing hair to be pressed into the comb.

Grooming

These all-purpose combs are often inexpensive.

Teasing

The teasing comb comes with a pick.

Heat Resistant

These combs will hold up to heat.

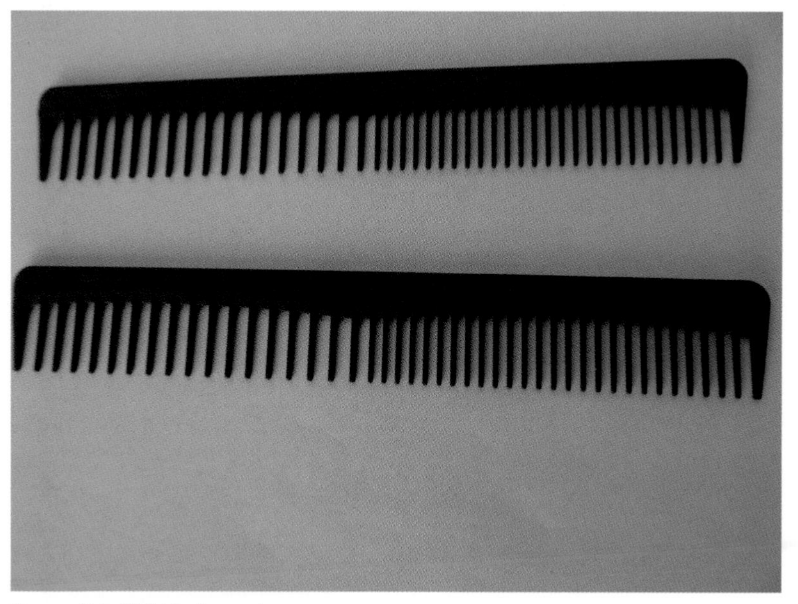

Figure 3.9 FHI black combs

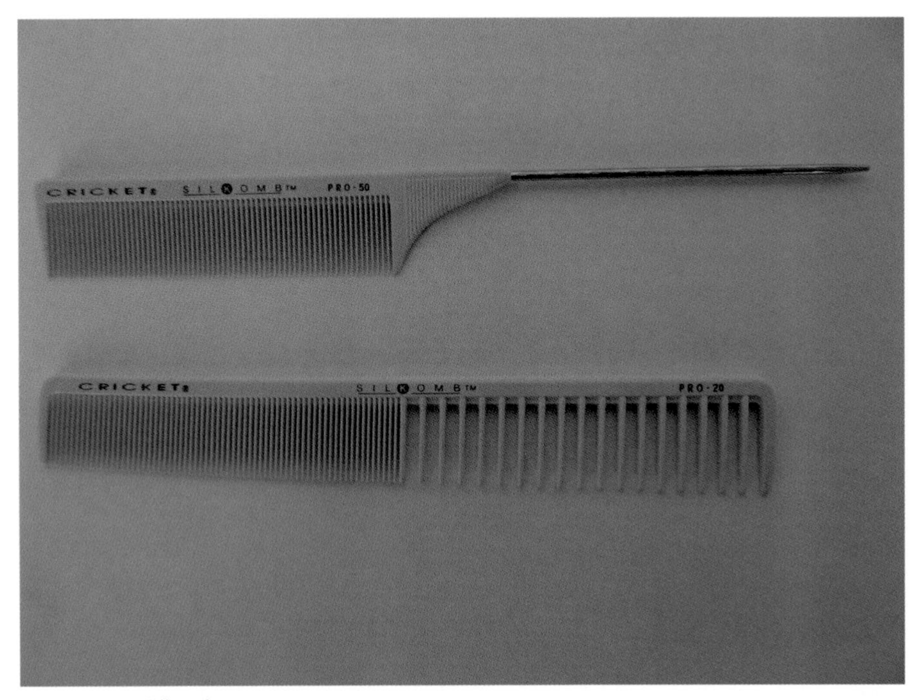

Figure 3.10 Silkomb

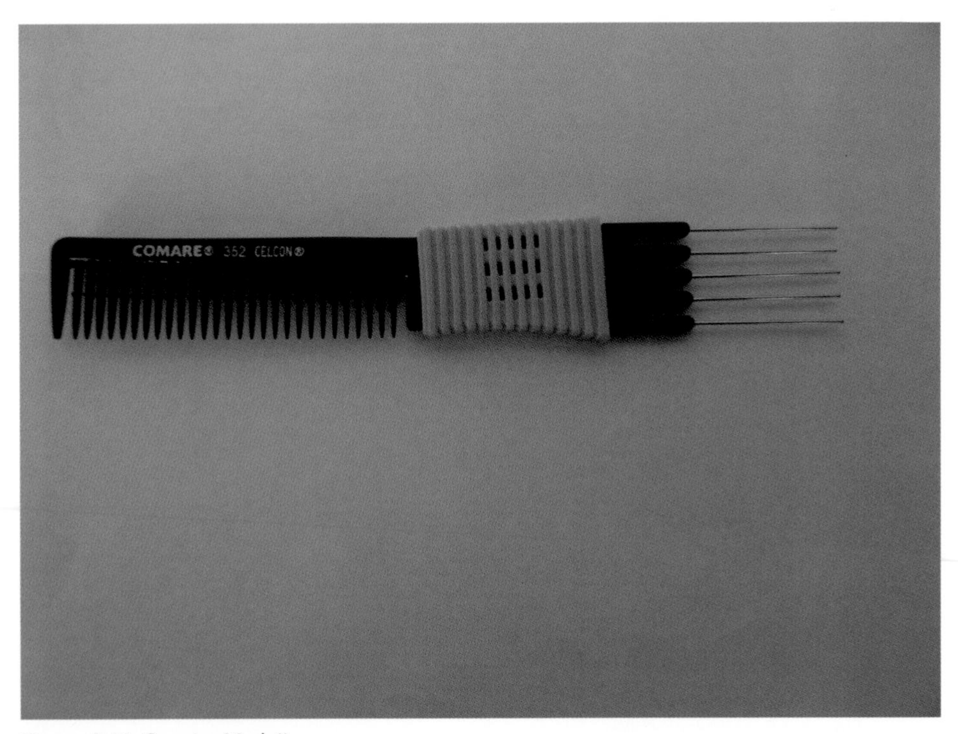

Figure 3.11 Comare Mark II

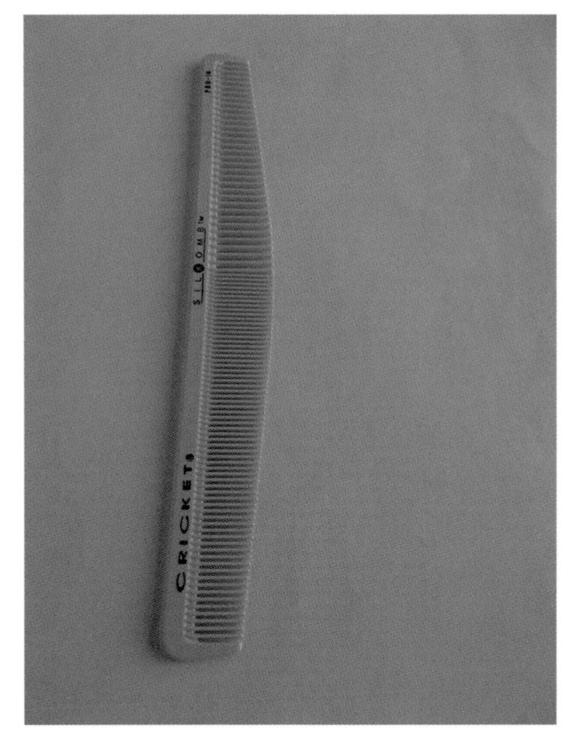

Figure 3.12 Cricket angle comb

Figure 3.13 Basic black grooming combs

Shears

Yvette never looks for the cheapest shears:

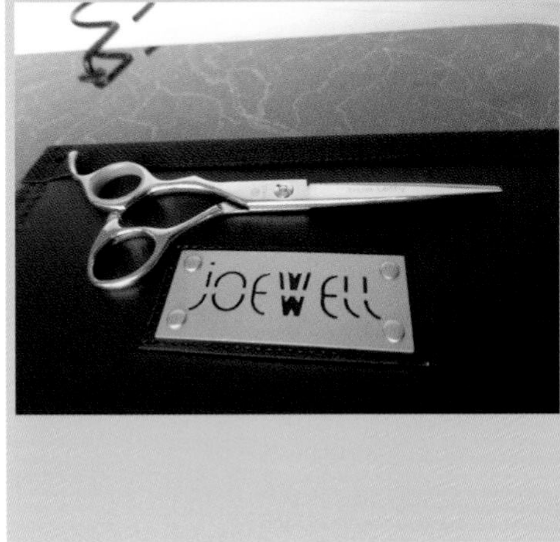

"Purchasing shears is a big investment. I still have and use my first pair. Things to consider are weight, how the scissors respond to opening and closing the blades, and whether you are left- or right-handed. Prices can vary widely. Once you do have your shears, keep them clean, and sharpened. Shears I use: Kamisori, from the Damascus collection, is made with Damascus steel. The shears are perfectly balanced and very sharp. Joewells are a reliable, well-made shear. Strong sharp blades with easy open-and-close movement. Joewell has good choices for lefties."

Figure 3.14 Joewell shears

Shears: A Lesson by Shear Technology

Handle configuration is one of the biggest choices you will make when purchasing shears. Opposing or straight-handled shears can put strains on your hand, wrist, arm and shoulders, neck, and back. Offset and crane handle configurations cause less strain. Bent-down thumb rings with space between the thumb and finger rings are also comfortable, especially with the use of finger inserts. These spacings should never be so large that your fingers and thumb go through past the knuckle.

Weight

When purchasing shears, take weight into consideration. You should have total control of your shears at all times.

Length

Choose a good fit for you. Measure the length of the blade against your middle finger and the overall length of the scissors against the extended palm of your hand. In general, longer lengths are used most often for scissors over comb and longer hair styles with texturizing.

Balance

Your shears should feel well balanced, not heavy or weighed down.

Level

In this type of shears, the handle is straighter or level.

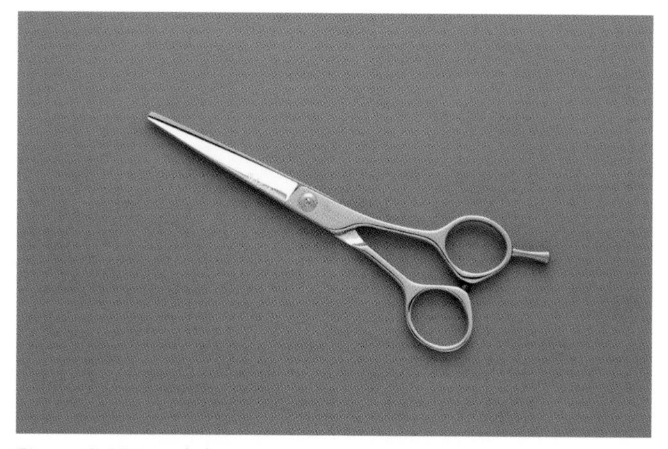

Figure 3.15 Level shears

Offset

One handle is longer than the other.

Crane

One side of the blade is longer than the other, but straighter.

Barbering

Barbering shears have longer blades, for using with a barber comb.

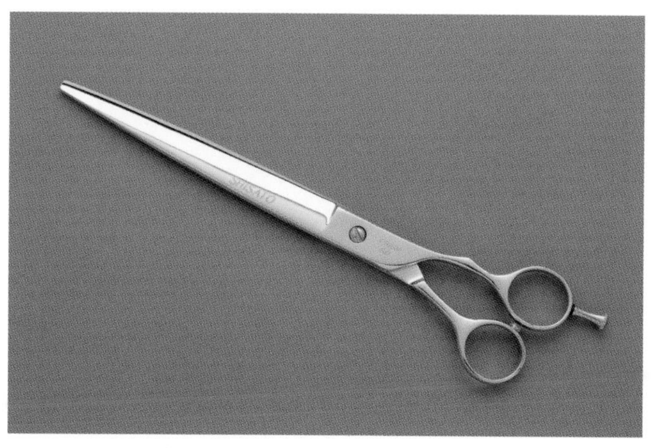

Figure 3.16 Barbering shears

Haircutting

This shorter shear is used with a cutting comb and the stylist's fingers lifting the hair to be cut.

Texturizing/Thinning

Texturizing shears are used to thin out hair and to put the final finishes on a haircut.

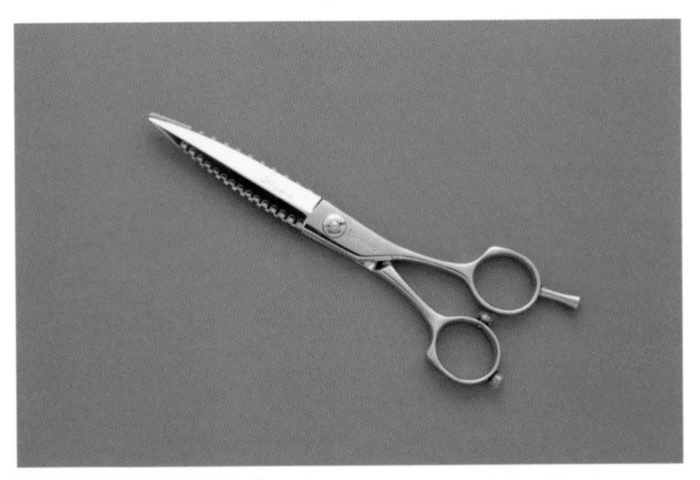

Figure 3.17 Texturizing shears

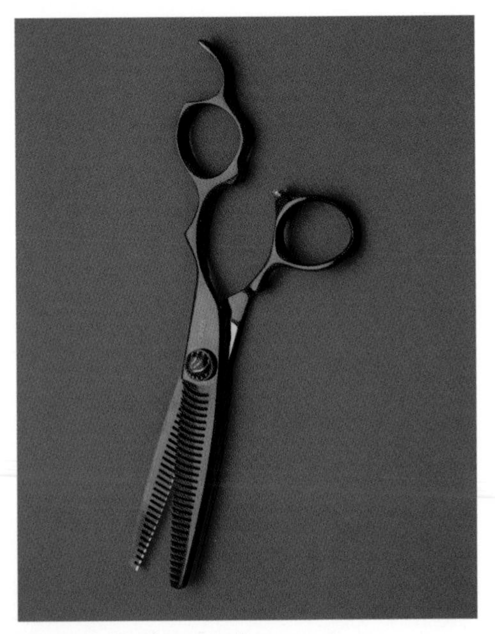

Figure 3.18 Thinning shears

Swivel

These shears allow the entire hand to rotate while cutting.

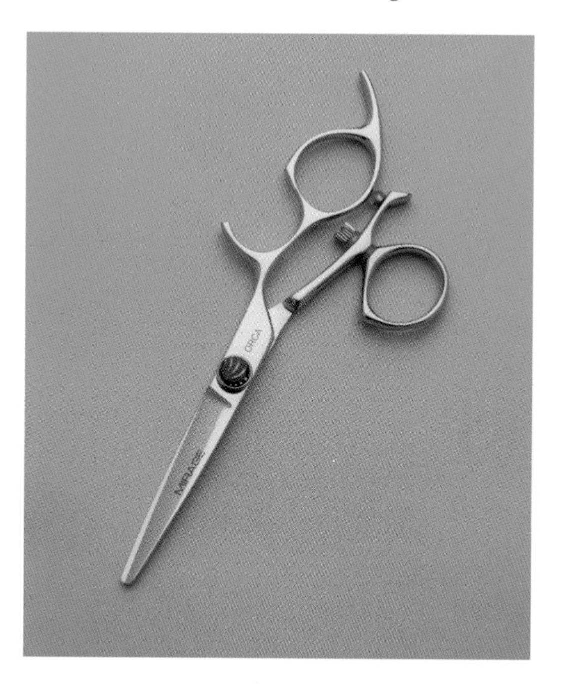

Figure 3.19 Swivel shears

Left-Handed

These shears are made specifically for left-handed stylists.

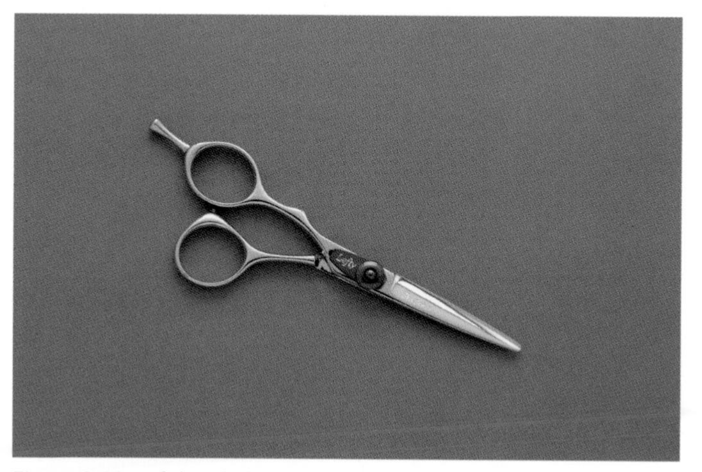

Figure 3.20 Left-handed shears

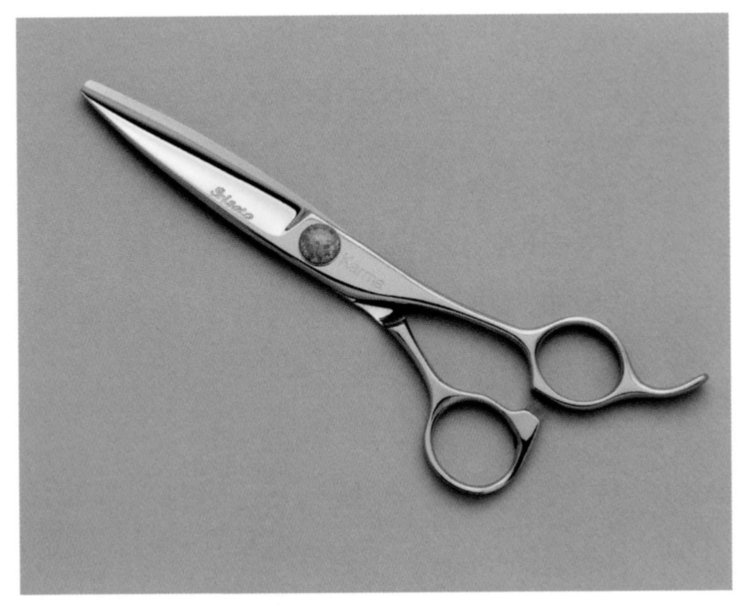

Figure 3.21 Slide cutting shears

Moustache Scissors

These are small, sharp, precision scissors made to trim and shape moustaches.

Maintenance

Shears that have been used with permed, colored, or hair containing any chlorine should be wiped down with alcohol then dried. Chemicals can dull the blades. Hair and dirt left on your scissors can cause rusting and pitting. Once a week, oil the scissors at their pivot point. When not cutting, store your scissors in a case or away from other people who might borrow your shears to cut paper or snip open tint bottles. Once a year have your shears cleaned, set, and balanced. Always use a qualified sharpener whom you know (for advice, contact Shear Technology at scissormall@astound.net).

Beard and Moustache Trimmers

These come in various sizes and head lengths.

Yvette advises: "Always have in a set bag portable trimmers that run without cords. Clippers are another must-have for hair stylists and makeup artists. Learning how to use clippers and trimmers ensures positive outcomes. If you are not a barber, don't try to be. But aim to be excellent in your skill and knowledge of using clippers and trimmers. Favorite clippers are Oster 76 Cordless, Oster Classic, and Andis T-Liners. Like all equipment, keep your clippers and trimmers working like new."

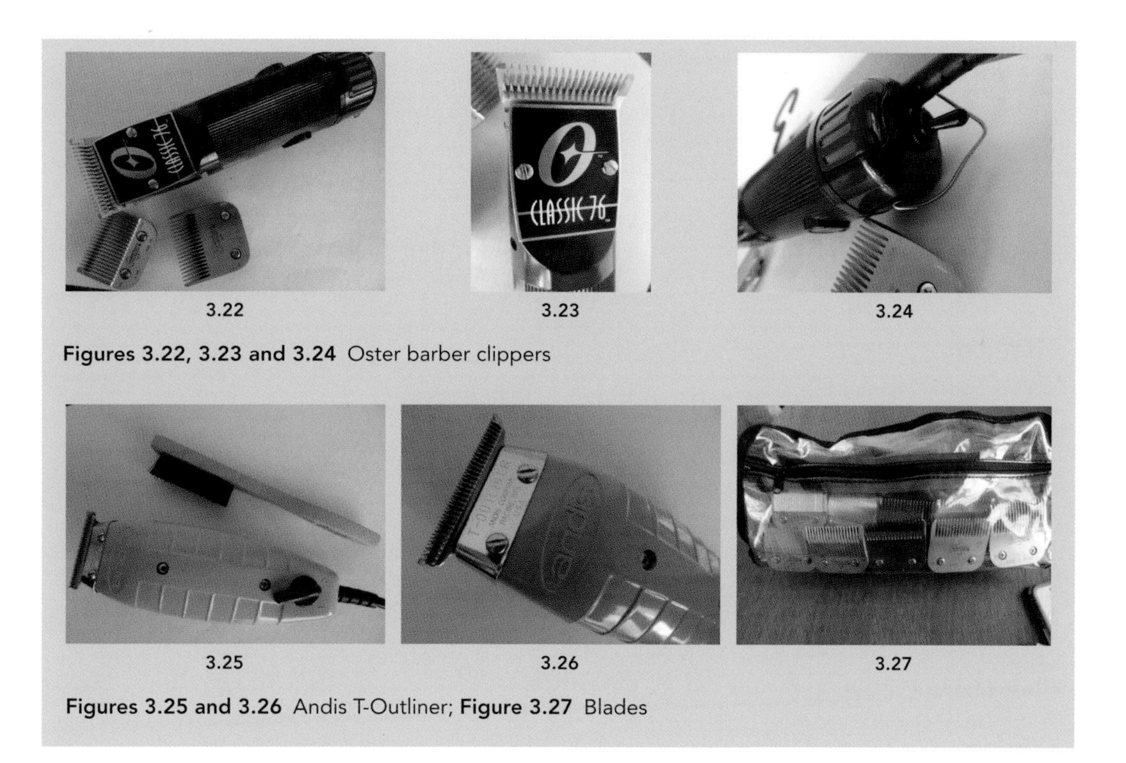

Figures 3.22, 3.23 and 3.24 Oster barber clippers

Figures 3.25 and 3.26 Andis T-Outliner; **Figure 3.27** Blades

Hair-Curling Irons

Curling irons add curl, volume, and texture to hair. They have to be used with care, however, as Yvette explains:

"One of the biggest mistakes using curling irons is keeping the heat on a high setting. This will burn the hair. It's better to keep the heat low and take several passes through the hair. Always use heat-protection products on the hair.

"There are a variety of curling irons. Use the curling iron appropriate to the work being done, hair texture, and shooting environment. For example, the Hot Tools Marcel Curling Iron has many usages. Hold the lever open, wrapping the hair around the barrel to curl. Or close the lever and wrap the hair around the whole barrel. When in a hurry you won't have to change out your irons for different textures and curls."

Besides the sizes and shapes or materials the iron is made of, it's the barrel of the iron that sets each apart, as this is where the heating elements are located. Here are a few examples of materials that curling irons are made of.

Teflon or Aluminum

An iron that is low tech in nature but works well for period looks.

Ceramic

Hair slides easily across the barrel of this type of curling iron.

Tourmaline

Using this material increases the heat level of the iron. Tourmaline curling irons are safe to use on wet or damp hair.

Titanium

These are really lightweight and usually inexpensive.

Types of Curling Irons

Here is a list of the different types of curling irons you'll find on the market today.

Spring

In this type, a spring works the barrels of the iron.

Clipless

These have no clamp on the iron.

Marcel

With Marcel irons, you apply your own pressure to the clamps.

Spiral

Spirals have shorter clamps, and a design molded into the barrel is used as a guide for the hair being curled.

Nano Titanium

A material often infused with another, such as ceramic, on a curling-irons barrel, allowing a more even distribution of heat.

Negative Ion Energy

An iron that produces negative ions that speed up the curling process, causing less static to the hair, therefore there is less chance of damage to the hair follicles.

FHI HEAT PLATFORM
1¼" TOURMALINE CERAMIC PROFESSIONAL CURLING IRON
www.fhiheat.com
FHI HEAT PLATFORM
1½" TOURMALINE CERAMIC PROFESSIONAL CURLING IRON
www.fhiheat.com

3.28

ON
OFF
FHI HEAT PLATFORM
ON
OFF
FHI HEAT PLATFORM

3.29

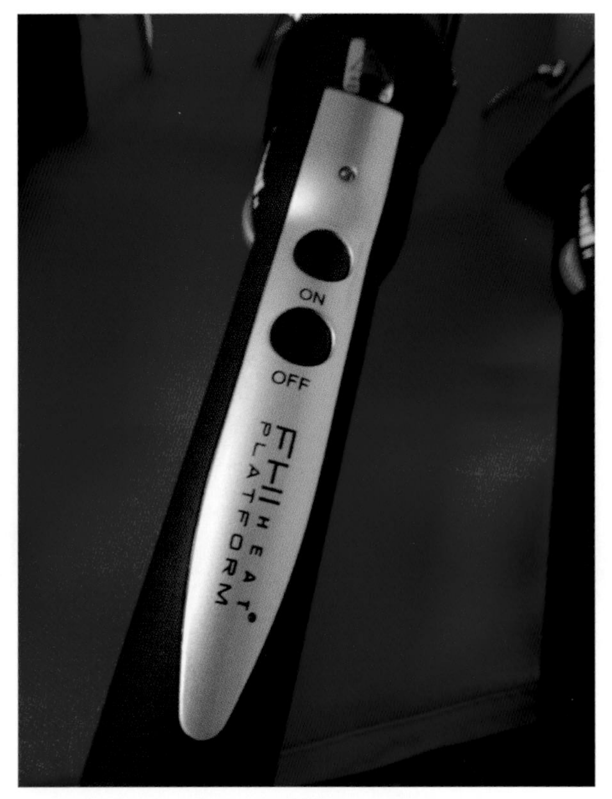

3.30

Figures 3.28, 3.29, 3.30 FHI Heat Platform series

Figure 3.31 Glamour Curling Iron

Figure 3.32 Hot Tools Marcel curling irons

3.33

3.34

Figures 3.33 and 3.34 Hot Tools Marcel Irons

Flat irons

Flat irons are similar to curling irons except that hair is usually ironed to take out or smooth out curly or wavy hair. Just like curling irons, flat irons are made from some of the same materials and heating elements. There are: tourmaline, ceramic, titanium, ionic, minis, and wet to dry.

Yvette says, "I use irons that are reliable, with multiple settings, that won't damage hair. Both curling irons and flat irons need to be cleaned and stored properly. If this is done, your equipment will last a very long time. Most of the flat irons I use have detachable heat mats. Just this simple difference comes in handy setting up in a trailer with limited room."

Figures 3.35 and 3.36 FHI Heat Platform series with detachable heat mat

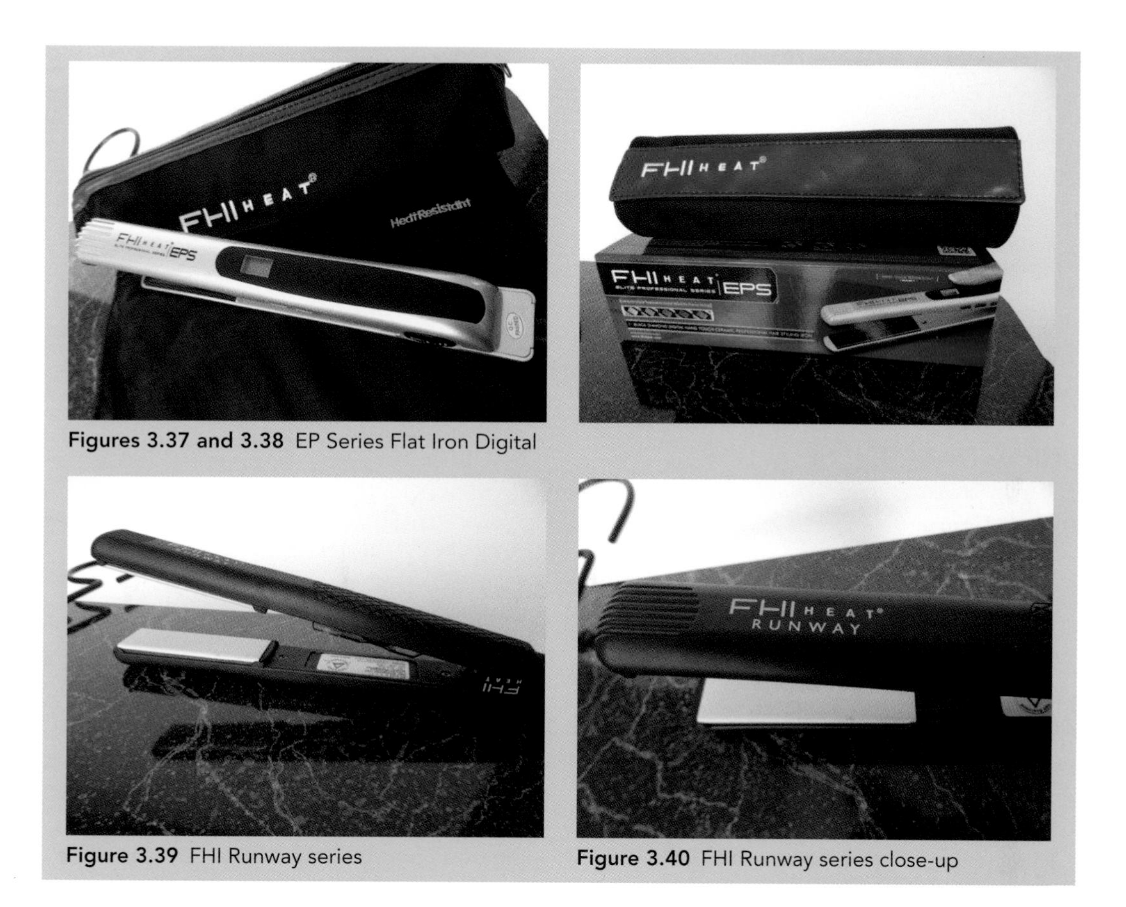

Figures 3.37 and 3.38 EP Series Flat Iron Digital

Figure 3.39 FHI Runway series

Figure 3.40 FHI Runway series close-up

Stove Irons

Stove irons are used in different kinds of work. The irons get hot quickly and can easily burn a surface you are working on. These irons can also burn human hair and lace pieces on ventilated wigs, in a matter of seconds. Whenever you start to use these, for the first few times practice on facial hair, or wigs that can be thrown away, or at least start with pieces in the back where it's not obvious for all to see. Always follow safety guidelines.

"Curling irons and flat irons can become very hot. Kevlar gloves can help protect your hands while working with high heats," Yvette suggests. "FHI heat gloves are lightweight with the fingertips coated. You can work with ease, without the bulk, and protect your hands from burns."

Figure 3.41 FHI heat gloves

Blow Dryers

"Another important piece of equipment is the blow dryer," says Yvette. "What you use in the trailer or on set has to work efficiently. Since there are so many choices, use a blow dryer that works with your environment and the style being created. For example, I have a blow dryer that is quiet, as actors do request from time to time a hair dryer that is made specifically to run quietly. A Centrix Q Zone blow dryer is both reliable and quiet. It's a great dryer to have in small areas or in a hair and makeup trailer where people are trying to work and actors might be running their lines. Another recommendation is a FHI Heat Platform blow dryer. Other suggestions are Sedu blow dryers." She advises, "Attachments for a blow dryer can vary from brand to brand. Make sure attachments you buy or go to replace are parts made for your dryer."

Blow Dryer Facts

Ionic Dryer

This type of dryer reduces static electricity, and dries faster, with a sleek effect.

Ceramic Heating Elements

Ceramic units heat evenly without getting too hot.

Tourmaline

Tourmaline is a gemstone used in the heating elements of some hair dryers. A tourmaline dryer is said to produce negative ions.

Diffuser

A diffuser is a blow-dryer attachment that reduces and cools the airflow for a slower drying time.

Concentrate Airflow

An attachment that concentrates the airflow to a specific spot for faster drying.

Combs and Brush

An attachment for blow dryers, allowing the stylist to dry the hair without the use of brushes or combs.

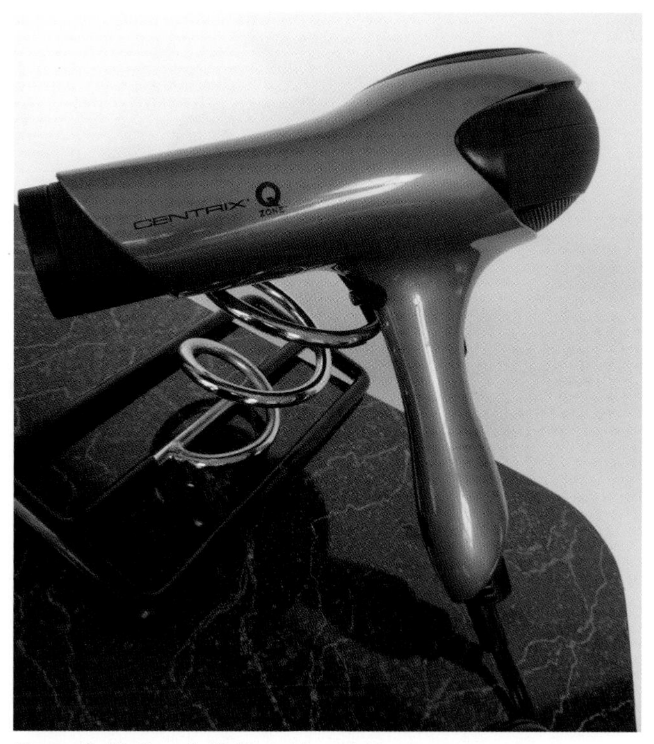

Figure 3.42 Centrix Q Zone blow dryer

Figure 3.43 FHI Heat Platform blow dryer

Figure 3.44 FHI blow dryer attachments

Portable Hair Dryers

Portable dryers are popular in the hair and makeup trailer and they can be used on location for myriad things. For example, if a perm needs to be set, or if wigs that have been treated with color or perm solutions need setting.

While an actor is under a portable dryer, it's possible to apply makeup at the same time.

Hot Curlers

Yvette says, "Hot curlers have come a long way. Curlers heated by steam are not used very often now. Many of the hot curlers today are heated up with a heating element housed within the base. InStyler has clamps, referred to as clam shells, that are heated. FHI Hot Rollers are heated by clicking the curler onto the base. When ready, you'll hear the click again."

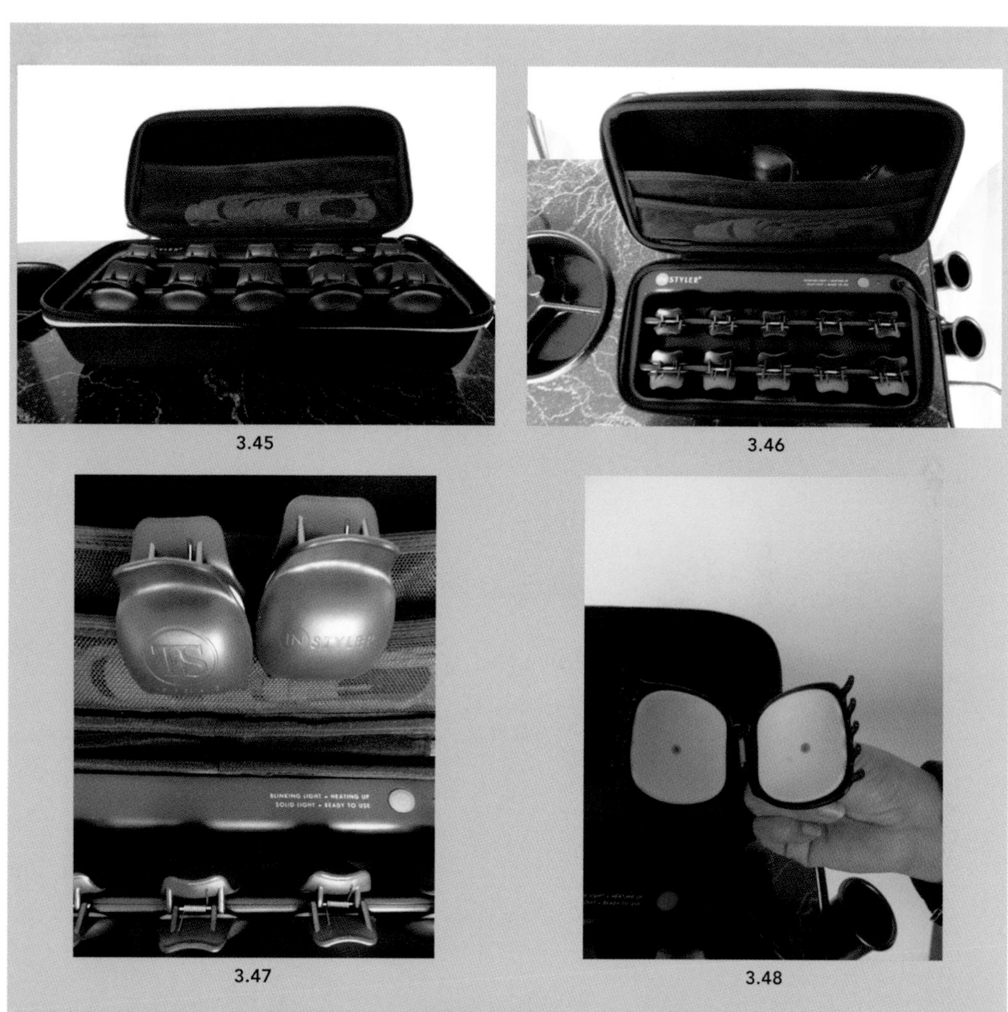

3.45 3.46

3.47 3.48

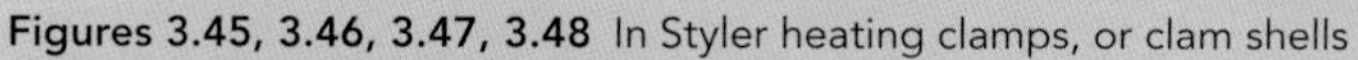

Figures 3.45, 3.46, 3.47, 3.48 In Styler heating clamps, or clam shells

3.49 3.50

Figures 3.49 and 3.50 FHI hot rollers

Hair Curlers

Hair curlers are a matter of choice. Non-heated curlers work best when wrapping hair that has been warmed up in some way. The hair will cool down with the curler in place. Curlers without clamps help to keep the hair from creasing. Their rough edges secure them into the hair. When you are doing several things at once, with the hair set in curlers you are free to move onto another actor for the time being.

Figure 3.51 Curlers

Fun tip: If you cut sponge curlers in different shapes, you can use them to create stipple sponges for effects work. They are used with Illustrate products to give the actor different shapes as well as sheer colors and patterns.

Hair Ties

"Smoothies are used often by hairstylists for their reliability," says Yvette. "Recommended Smoothies for shoots are head bands, thick ties in size large, thin ties in sizes large and small. The most versatile colors to have are black, brown, blonde, and color combos. It's best not to use hair ties of any kind that have metal connectors. The metal can rip out hair. Blax ties are great for blending in the hair, and won't damage or slip out of fine hair. Great hold! You'll want to use hair-tie colors black, brown, and clear in widths thick and thin. Also No Crease Hair Ties by Kenz Laurenz, and Hair Ties Multi colors on a ring."

Figure 3.52 Smoothies

Figure 3.53 Hair ties

Bobby Pins

Yvette explains, "Sta-Rite Bulk Matte Toy Pins are one half the size of a bobby pin. This pin works well on finer-textured hair. It also hides well. The Sta-Rite Blend Rite Matte Bobby is a pliable bobby pin, easy to bend or shape to your client's head. Matte pins hide well in the hair, and are often used for stunt actors, wigs, and wig preps, as there is no slipping out of the hair. Recommended colors are black, blonde, dark brown, medium brown, light brown, and white. Frends Matte Black long and short hair pins and Frends Matte Blond long and short hair pins are another good choice. Ripple Premium hair pins won't slip in the hair and are rust resistant. The matte finish of these pins ensure there will be no shine that can be seen by camera on any film set or photo shoot."

Figure 3.54 Sta-Rite Blend Rite bobby pins boxes

Figure 3.55 Different-colored bobby pins

Figure 3.56 Frends Blond short hair pins

Figure 3.57 Frends Black long hair pins

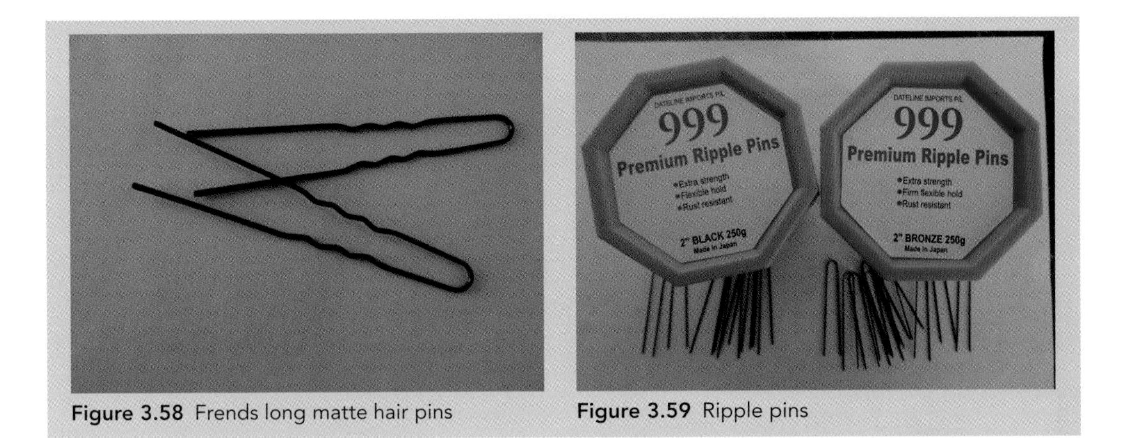

Figure 3.58 Frends long matte hair pins

Figure 3.59 Ripple pins

Gator Clips

"Gator clips hold sections of the hair when styling," explains Yvette "These clamps should be used in thick hair. More than a few times clients will tell me, 'Those clips will not hold!' It tells me there are hair stylists who have not learned how to put up hair with clips. When done properly, Gators will stay put with no creases left in the hair."

Figure 3.60 Gator clips

Gator No Creases slip onto clips and pins to help protect the hair from creasing.

Figure 3.61 Ricky Care No-Crease clips

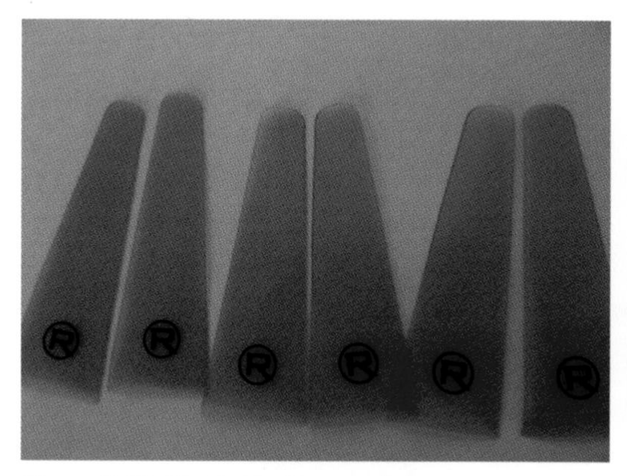

Figure 3.62 Plastic No-Crease pinks

Figure 3.63 Selection of Ricky Care clips

Atomizers

Atomizers are used in makeup and hair for all sorts of things, from lightly spritzing hair fibers, dust, or powders over an effect, to filling in hairlines or thinning hair for a voluptuous full head of hair.

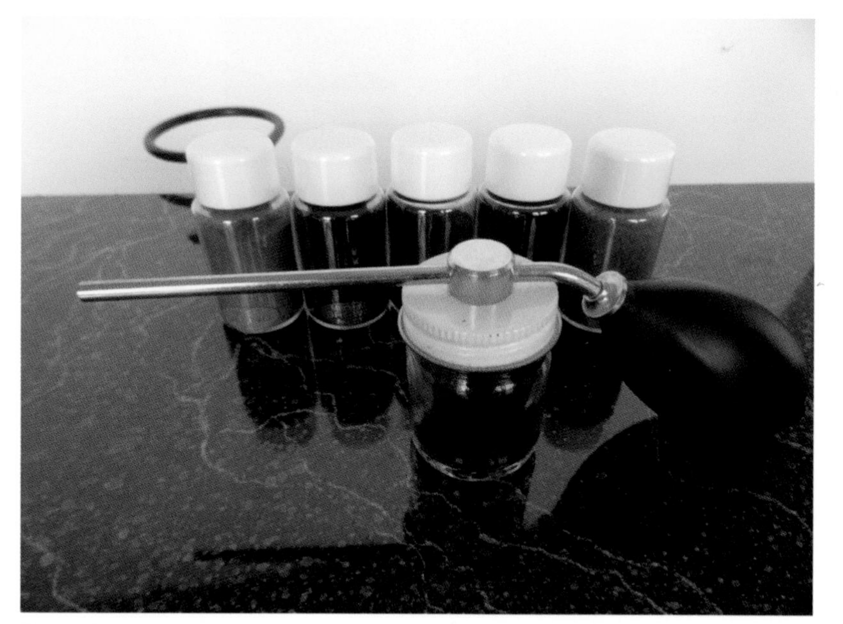

Figure 3.64 Atomizer

Figure 3.65 Atomizer with hair fibers

Airbrushes

Figure 3.66 Air Brush Temptu Air with rechargeable battery

Airbrushes are used on the hair and on the face and body. You can create crisper lines at the edges of facial hair, fill in bald spots, or alter hair color if that's what is needed. Airbrushes can also add variations of color to hair, hairpieces, facial hair, and body hair. Airbrushes are also used to tone down (fade) or bring up tattoos that are used on or around the head, face, and body.

How to Keep Your Equipment Clean

Every tool has specific directions on how to maintain it. It's important to keep all your equipment in good working order. Read each manufacturer's suggestions. Clippers, trimmers, and shears must be cleaned and stored after each use. Brush out any hair with a stiff brush. Wipe or spray down these items with a sanitizer followed with any lubricating oil. Take heed of every part of the clippers, trimmers, or shears. Keep blades sharp. Store equipment until the next time you use it in a good container or a pouch specifically made for that item.

Brushes and combs can be cleaned with an antiseptic shampoo and a stiff wood-handled brush. (Be sure to remove hair from the bristle of the brush first.) Rinse and wipe dry with a soft cloth. Use an antiseptic spray, then put away. If working in one place, like a salon, you'll have antibacterial solutions available to soak your combs and brushes. Brushes and combs can be bought in bulk, especially for a larger show, and if there is a lot of dust and dirt on the project, don't hesitate to toss out a comb and use a new one if you need to.

Credits

Airpod Foundation by Temptu
www.andis.com
www.beauty.com
Centrix Q-Zone
www.cricketco.com
www.fhiheat.com
www.folica.com (Compare hair dryers)
www.frendsbeauty.com
www.hottools.com
www.instyler.com
www.joewell.com
www.kamisorishears.com
www.masonpearson.co.uk
www.miragehairfibers.com
www.monroebrush.com
www.osterstyle.com
www.scissormall.com (Shear Technology)
Shisato
Silkomb Combs
www.temptu.com
www.totalbeauty.com

CHAPTER FOUR
Men's Grooming

One of the most common situations you'll run across while working as a hair stylist or makeup artist in the entertainment industry is establishing or maintaining haircuts and facial hair. Facial hair alone can define an actor's character, giving an impression of grief, hardship, prosperity, happiness, or illness, for example. Facial hair can also change throughout the film or TV series to reflect moods as well as time periods. Sometimes your character will travel through decades and you'll have to change his hair and makeup to reflect his transformation. Continuity thus is huge. To keep track of haircuts, hair styles, and facial hair you should use copious and specific notes and pictures. This is crucial, because many productions don't shoot scenes in progressive segments, i.e., the '70s, '80s, '90s. One week your character may be a hippie in the '60s, the next week, a grandfather in the '90s. Hair stylists are responsible for keeping haircuts looking exact, which can be challenging for styles that have exact hairlines that need to be kept tight. Generally, makeup artists are responsible for all facial and body hair on an actor, and that includes anywhere on the body. So a good makeup and hair team should work together and create an overall look. With male clients it is particularly important because head hair and facial hair needs to blend together seamlessly. Even though most of us are not barbers, correctly addressing barbering and grooming issues will be a big part of your job. Have the proper equipment for the task at hand. These days it's no longer acceptable to have one portable shaver if you're going to correctly groom your clients: Groomed facial hair and clipper cuts have never been so popular.

Figure 4.1 Lennotch Taplet

Lennotch Taplet specializes in traditional barber services, haircuts, and shaves. He's from New Orleans, now lives in San Francisco, and is the owner of Details Barbershop. He's been barbering for decades and explains:

"A clipper cut is a haircut performed with a machine. Clippers are used to get close to the scalp for easy shaping and outlining the hair. About 85 percent of my clients, both male and female, request clipper cuts. There will also be times that hair designs require shears and clippers. After a cut it's important to maintain the look on a regular basis. Don't let my good work go ragged.

"I get a lot of requests for straight razor shaves as well as beard detailing. Any beard, moustache, sideburns, or stubble can be created with clippers, straight razor, shavers, or scissors over comb."

Since facial hair is often grown shaped or trimmed to reflect a character, it is important to know what different styles look like in order to create period pieces or to update an old style for modern day.

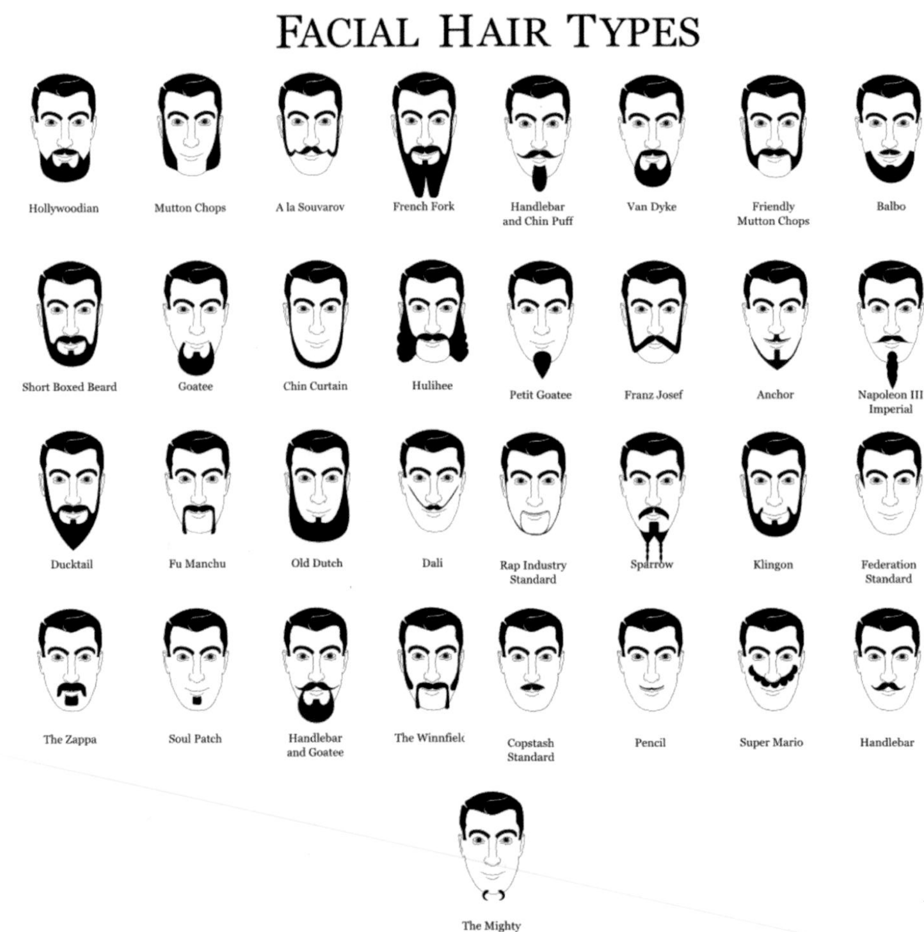

Figure 4.2 Facial Hair Chart, image courtesy of Jon Dyer/dyers.org

Facial Hair Terms

Brett: Hair covers the entire chin in this style, but does not connect to the sideburns.
Chin beard: A beard that comes forward under the chin connecting to the sideburns. The chin curtain is the same, except that the beard covers the entire chin.
Circle beard: A smaller chin beard that connects in a circle to the moustache.
Fu Manchu: A full moustache that starts at the corners of the mouth.
Full beard: A full beard that might or might not connect to the sideburns. It is left natural or styled.
Garibaldi: A full beard that is rounded at the bottom.
Goatee: A short or long patch of hair on the chin.
Handlebar moustache: A long moustache that flips upward at the ends.
Junco: A goatee that extends upward to the outside corners of the mouth but does not have a moustache.
Meg: A goatee that extends to the moustache.
Mutton chops: A shaved chin with long chop sideburns connected to the moustache.
Neck beard: The jaw and chin are clean shaven, with the beard grown on the neck.
Reed: A beard and moustache that do not connect to the sideburns.
Sideburns: Hair that is extended down the sides of the face.
Soul patch: A small patch of hair centered in the middle of the chin right below the lower lip.
Stash: Large sideburns that extend down the face, connecting to the moustache.
Stubble: This looks so easy to maintain on film. The rough exterior is purposely groomed that way. Edgers are used to create the crisp outlines often seen with a stubbly face. Be aware that not all stubble will look good. For example, if the actor's own hair has an uneven color or growth pattern, it won't register well on camera.
Van Dyke: A goatee and moustache.
Verdi: A short, groomed beard and moustache.

Figure 4.3 Lennotch with clippers

Clippers

Clippers are used for haircuts such as fades and crews, etc., and also for facial hair. Your clippers should be well maintained, with clean, sharp blades. Clippers such as Andis have a clipper line with a side lever that allows you to set the clippers at different settings. For most facial hair trims, haircuts, or close shaves this is ideal. Clippers can also come with different-size guards that snap on. This gives you an array of settings to choose from. The bigger the motor in an electric clipper, the quicker they can become hot. Aileen Nunez, International Manager of Education and Style for Andis, gives this advice:

"Keep clippers cool by spraying your clipper blades top and bottom with Cool Care. Cool Care is a lubricant by Andis that cools, lubricates, sanitizes, and prevents rust on the clippers. It's also a good idea to have another set of clippers ready to go that can be switched out with the hot clipper."

Immediately after you are done with the clippers, clean and sanitize them using various products made for clippers. Wipe the clippers down with a soft towel, rag, or cloth baby diaper. Clippers should be cleaned after every use.

Figure 4.4 Andis Cool Care

How to Remove the Blades

Periodically you'll want to remove the blades from the clippers for extra cleaning and sharpening. Follow the manufacturer's directions for those particular clippers.

Unscrew any of the screws that hold the guards into place. I usually keep six or seven different sizes of screwdriver in the trailer. You never know when you are going to need them. Have a dish at your station for the loose screws so they won't be lost. After all the screws are removed, clean, oil, sanitize, and, if needed, sharpen the blades. Also clean with a brush any residue or hair that is trapped under where the blades sit.

Lennotch: "I use Wahl 5 Senior for detail work, Oster 111 for bulk cutting and fading, and an Andis outliner for edging. I also use Wahl 5 Super Shaver for building tapers and fades. These are all reputable professional brands set to industry standards. Clippers should be held as though you are shaking someone's hand. Palms should face in with knuckles out.

"Clippers tend to get hot when overused. It's a good idea to use different clippers for various tasks at hand. Oster 111 or 76 Turbo have carbon brushes and a fan that will help reduce overheating. This clipper in particular is designed to do heavy cutting with speed. Whatever clippers you use, have the right clippers for your workload."

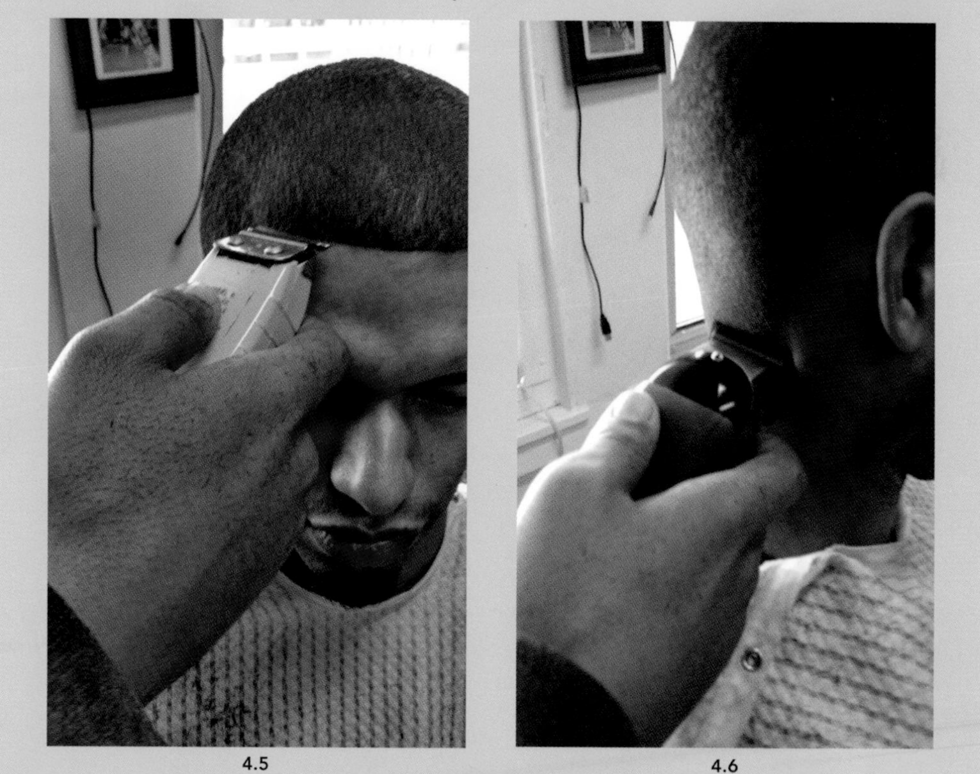

4.5 4.6

Figures 4.5 and 4.6 Lennotch performing a clipper cut

Kinds of Clippers

There are so many good, reliable clippers, trimmers, and edgers on the market. A few models are used often in the hair and makeup trailer. The following can handle any situation you'll find yourself in.

Andis Masters

Several different clippers come under the Master series. Andis Masters use magnetic motors that can handle big jobs in cutting and tapering. There is a controlled side switch, and a single-lever clipper-blade adjuster. The Fade Master SR is used for fades, low fades, tight fades, and blow-outs.

Figure 4.7 Andis Masters

Andis Pivot Motor Combos

Great for general cutting of all hair types, these can be used on wet or dry hair. The lower speed makes this clipper perfect for a new stylist. A good clipper for flat tops.

Figure 4.8 Andis Pivot and SpeedMaster

Andis Supra Cordless Clipper

This cordless clipper, with adjustable blade, is lightweight and easy to clean. The Andis Supra has a detachable battery that recharges in about an hour, with two-hour usage. Aileen suggests, "Have an extra backup with fully charged battery on hand to exchange clippers."

Figure 4.9 Andis Supra

Ceramic BGR and Professional Detachable Blade Clipper with Sensa Charge

This is a powerful cordless rotary motor clipper.

Important suggestion: You should always have handy cordless clippers, trimmers, and shavers. You might have to work on set or where power outlets are hard to come by.

Andis GTO T-Outliner

An edger with a motor that runs at a high speed, this is fantastic for crisp edges and light fading. Its housing is grey.

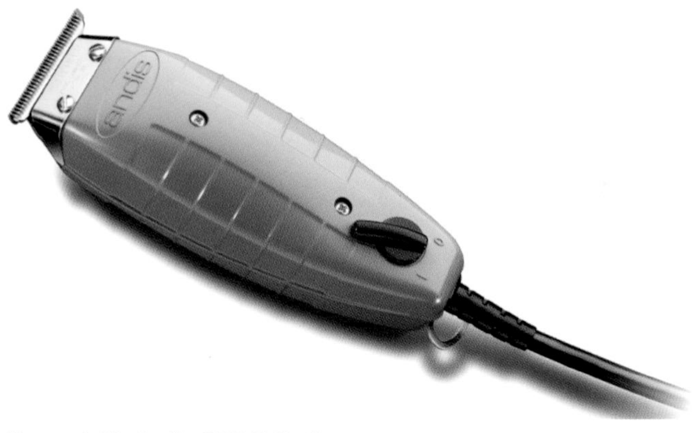

Figure 4.10 Andis GTO T-Outliner

Andis GTX T-Outliner

The deep-toothed blade on this clipper helps to anchor the hair down, allowing removal of the hair on the first pass. It is housed in black.

Figure 4.11 Andis GTX T-Outliner

Figure 4.12 Andis GTX T-Outliner

Andis US Envy

This is a hybrid, with the best of all the motors, and can be used wet or dry, with smooth transitions of hair techniques. It has a quiet whisper.

Figure 4.13 Andis US Envy

Guard Sizes

Lennotch: "There are different types of guards, from plastic, metal, and magnetic. Guards are used on clippers to determine the length of hair when cut. Interchangeable blades can be used, or a plastic snap-on. Use guards that are consistent with the clipper brand you are using. This will ensure a proper fit. Watch guards sold as compatible: They do not always fit securely. This can leave room for a guard to slip while cutting: major problems for a barber."

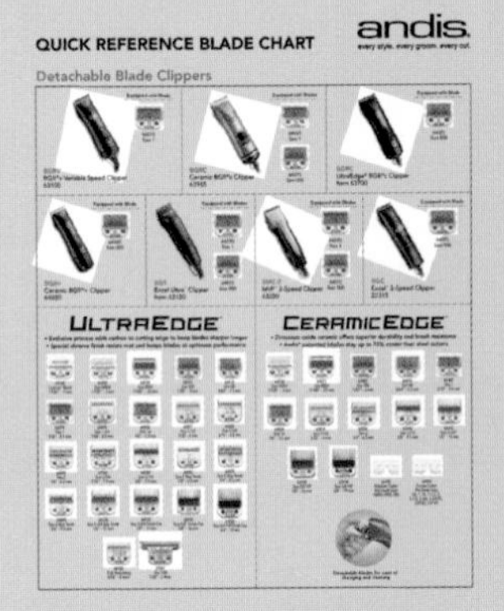

Figure 4.14 Andis Quick Reference Blade Chart

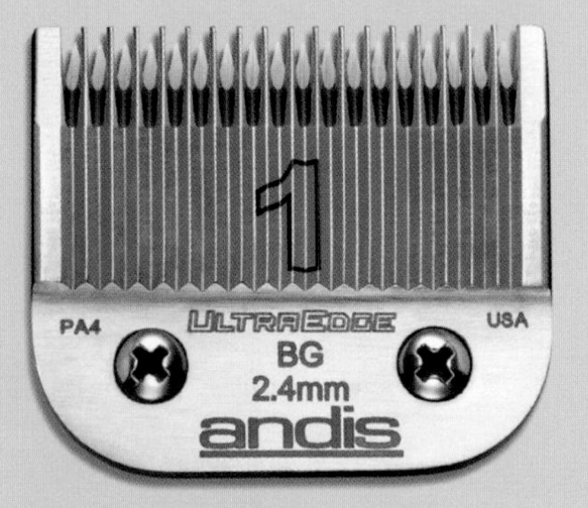

Figure 4.15 Andis 1

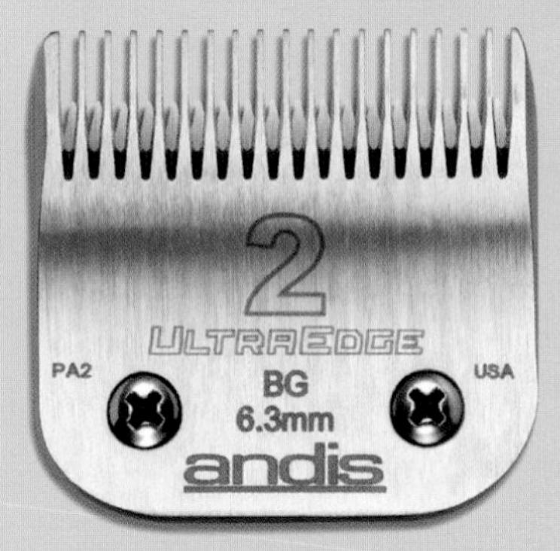

Figure 4.16 Andis 2

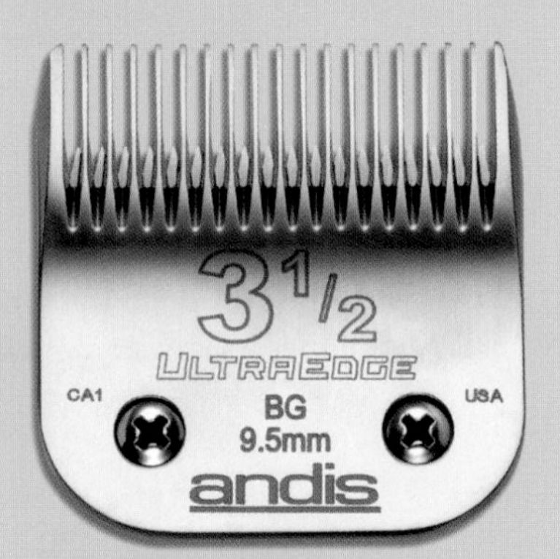

Figure 4.17 Andis 3½

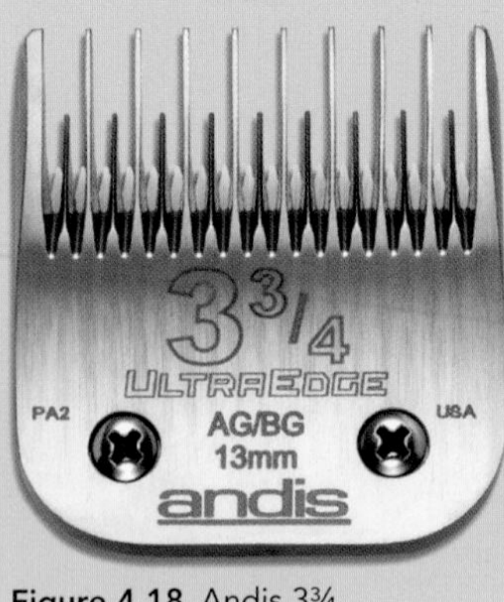

Figure 4.18 Andis 3¾

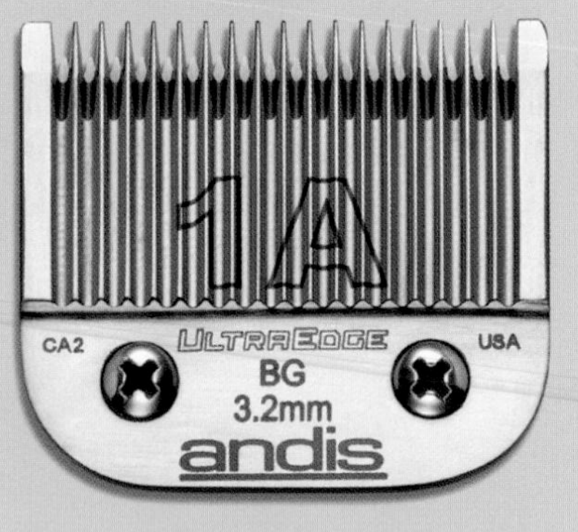

Figure 4.19 Andis 1A

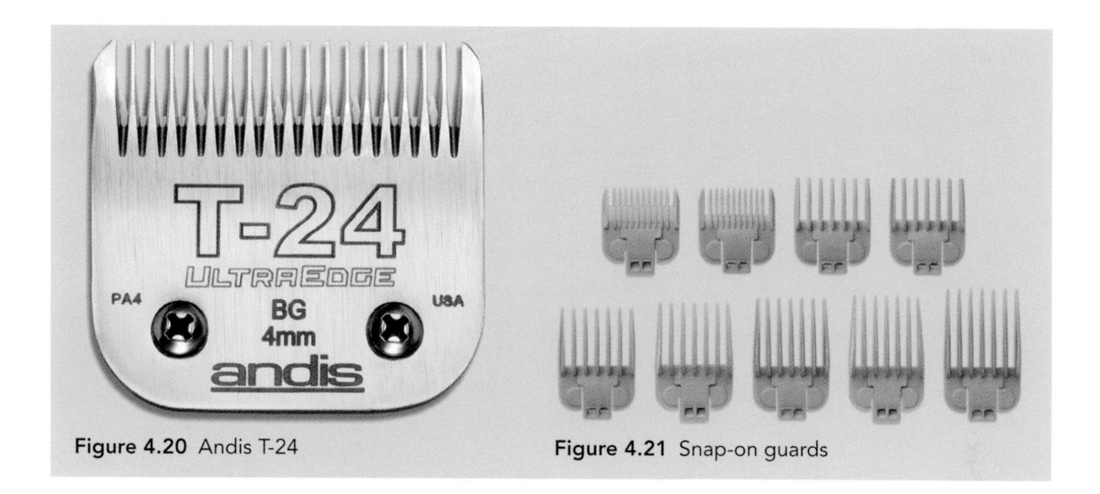

Figure 4.20 Andis T-24

Figure 4.21 Snap-on guards

Oster is also a popular brand of clippers. The Classic is used for a variety of styles.

Figure 4.22 Oster Classic

Lennotch: "Bald fade, taper, comb over, and faux hawks are popular cuts. These cuts all start off cutting from bottom to top using short upward strokes. For a bald fade start an Oster 111 using a 00000 blade at the base of the neck around the ears and work up to a 1½ blade to the top of the head. Follow with a Wahl senior to do detail fading. Andis finishes off the look lining the edges with an Outliner. I suggest Ruezel Pomade, Fiber Grease, Fiber Tech, and Suavecito Pomade to polish off a clipper cut."

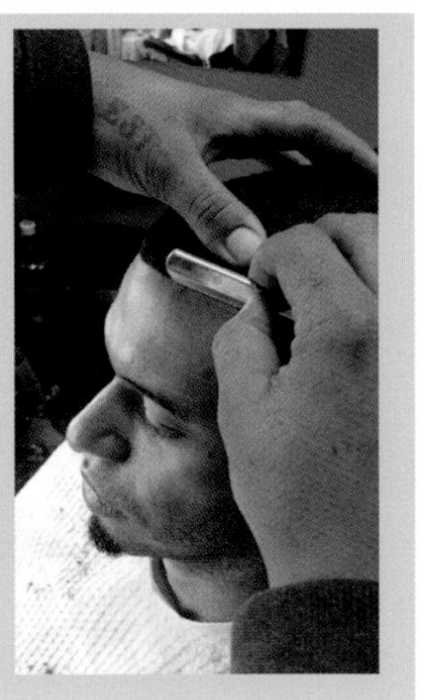

Figure 4.23 Lennotch working on the hairline

Haircut Terms

Arch: The hairline above the ear.
Bald: All the hair is removed.
Bangs: The hair over the forehead.
Blocked nape: A square straight hairline across the nape.
Bowl cut: A haircut like the shape of a bowl.
Brush cut: The hair is cut like a crew but slightly longer at the top, brushed upward.
Burr: The entire haircut is done at one setting.
Business or graduation cut: This is tapered on the sides and back with hair left longer on top, then parted.
Butch: A short haircut with tapered sides and back.
Caesar cut: The sides are evenly cut, with longer hair on top pushed forward onto the forehead, creating short bangs.
Crew cut: The hair is cut all the way around, with the top rounded to the contours of the head.
Fade: A haircut with a very tight taper on sides and back.
Faux hawk: A tapered haircut that is styled in the center for the hair to stand up.
Flat top: The hair is cut like a crew, except the top is cut flat across the head.
High and tight: The sides and back of the head are cut short. The top is cut with a higher number on the clipper or guard.
Horseshoe: Clipper cut this style as a flat top, then clipper a U-shape into the middle of the flat top.
Induction: The shortest cut you can have, for which the hair is clipped without a guard.
Ivy League: The same as the crew cut but with the blade several numbers longer.
Landing strip: An extreme take on the high and tight, it is also close to the style of the Mohawk.
Mullet: This is short on the front and side, but longer in the back.
Pompadour: There are many styles and creativity for this hair style. A pompadour has hair styled upward at the front.
Regulation: A short military cut.

Taper cut: This is shorter on the sides and back, and longer on the top. The hair on top can be parted, pushed forward, or slicked back.
Taper fade: A taper cut that has a fade cut to blend seamlessly into the nape and sides of the head.
Temple fade: A fade at the temple that blends into the longer length at the top.

Scissor over Comb

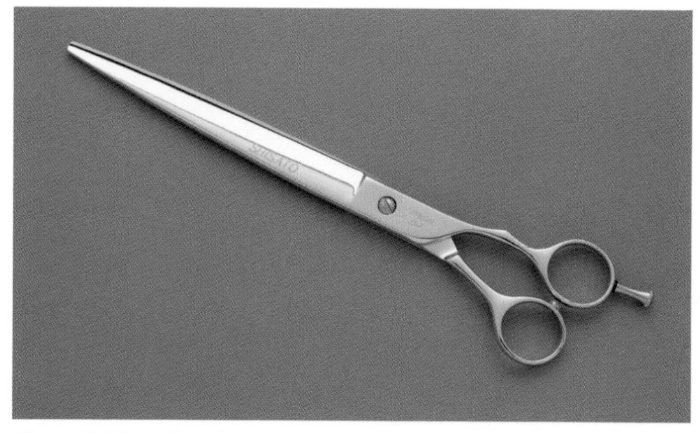

Figure 4.24 Barber shears

Scissor over comb is a method of cutting hair and facial hair. The technique is very effective in shaping beards, brows, and moustaches before using any trimmer. In many cases, using the scissor-over-comb technique can stand alone.

Men's Shaving

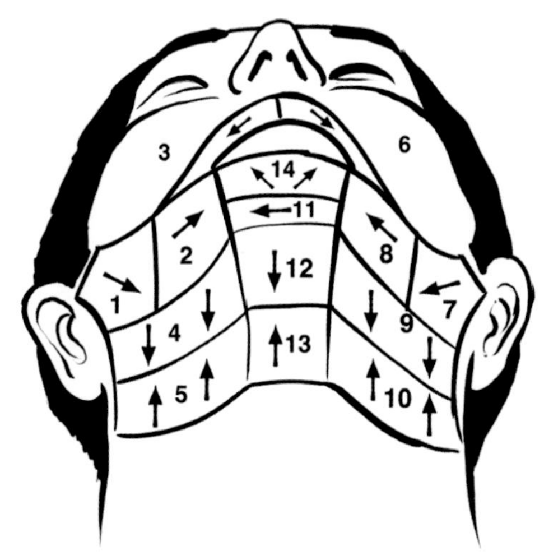

Figure 4.25 Chart of direction of hair growth

Lennotch tells us, "Straight razor shaves and beard detailing is a part of grooming. It's important to remember there is a proper way to do this. We use a hot towel to open up the pores. Follow with a pre-shave oil to protect the skin. Hot lather is applied next to keep the beard hair soft, plus it helps to minimize razor drag and pull. Go for one pass with the razor in the direction of the hair growth to get a close shave. Apply a lavender-infused cold towel wrap to close the pores, and soothe the skin. Finish with an aftershave balm to moisturize the skin."

Lennotch suggests the following products: The Art of Shaving, Bevel Shave, and Favorite Razor Gillette Fusion.

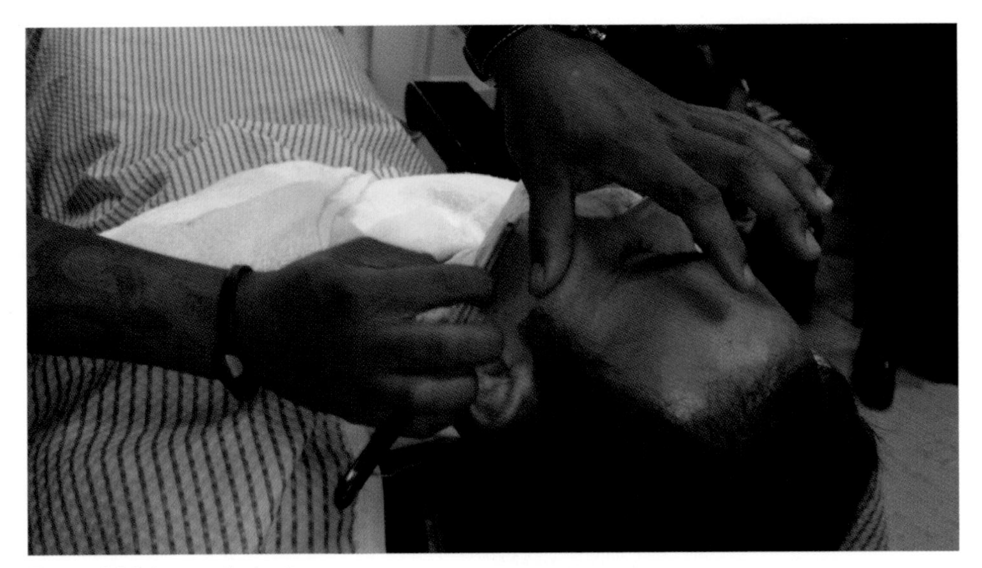

Figure 4.26 Lennotch shaving

Disposable Single-Blade Razor Shave

For quick shaving in the hair and makeup trailer, I would not recommend using a single-blade razor. But there will be actors who will want to be shaved or shave themselves with a disposable single-blade or removable-blade razor. Also hairlines, between clipper cuts, can be tightened up using a single-blade. Have everything you will need in the trailer for a seamless positive shave using a straight single, double, or disposable razor. Keep straight razors that can be used several times over in a ziplock bag with the actor's name on it. Put it in a visible place (like a bulletin board) for the actor or yourself to pull out for use.

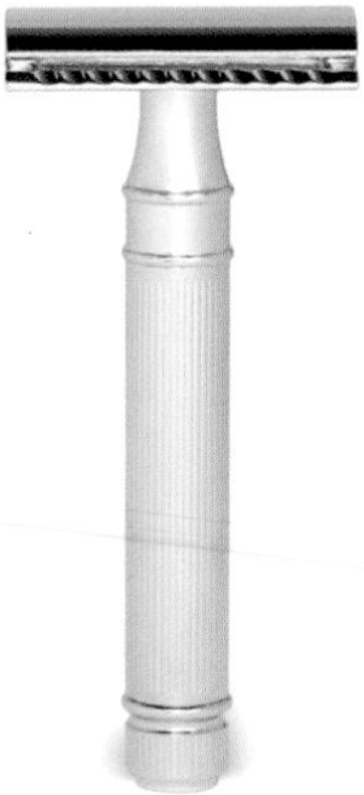

Figure 4.27 EJ lined razor

Steps

1. Turn on the hot towel cabinet. Dampen your towels and apply any treatment products to the towels of your choice. In this case a small amount of oil cleanser would work nicely. Roll the towels and stack them in the hot towel cabinet. Prep your station. Have everything you will need to start shaving. Lay down a hand towel with set towel on top. Have one or two cloth baby diapers for removing any water or product on the face. (Yes: Baby diapers have a good amount of thickness, no shred, and are gentle for the facial area.) Have one dampened towel ready rolled in a bowl. Have a pre-shave and aftershave toner or tonic of your choice, a few small bowls to pour toners into, some large square no-shed cotton pads, and a palette to put down any creams or gels. Have ready your shave product of choice, and your razor of choice.

Suggestion: Paper palettes work great as a quick cleanup, as you can simply throw everything away in one swoop.

Suggestion: Put several towels in a plastic ziplock bag. Add water plus your treatment product. Close the ziplock and shake the bag until the towels are evenly damp. Remove the towels and put them in the hot towel cabinet. Don't throw away the bag. You can also put dampened towels already in a ziplock in a microwave to heat up.

2. Have your actor sit comfortably in a chair, draped. Tilt the chair slightly back. You can also adjust the headrest for maximum comfort. If the actor is chilled, add another layer of protection with a thin blanket or another drape. Small pillows can ease any neck strain.
3. Take a hot towel from the steamer. Carefully unfold. Check the temperature. You should see steam raising from the towel, but it shouldn't burn your hands. Stand behind the actor, draping the towel across the face. Press the towel gently into the face and neck with the palms of your hands. Keep doing this until the towel starts to cool off. Remove the towel.
4. Massage a pre-shave oil into the face and neck. Just a few drops rubbed into the palms of your hands will do.
5. Follow with a shave product of choice: gel, shave soap, oil, or cream. If using a shave soap or shave cream, you will be using a bristle shaving brush. In fact you can use a brush to apply any of these products except the oil. The oil you will massage into the face and neck with the palms of your hands.
6. Ready to shave! Start shaving in a comfortable pattern. For example, cheeks, sides of face, neck, and then chin and lip. Shave with the grain of the hair. The razor should slide right over the face with very little pressure. The razor should be kept clean of hair and product during shaving. Swipe the razor over the dampened towel in the bowl. Reshave any areas of the face that need extra attention. Be aware that the more often you go over the same area, the more irritation can occur.
7. Rinse by once again using towels from the hot towel cabinet. Press the towels into the face. Massage with the towel with small strokes, starting with the neck, removing the shave product.

8. Follow with an aftershave lotion or toner. Apply using a saturated large shred-free cotton pad. This removes any excess product and hair. It also helps to tamp down any possible irritation that might occur with shaving.
9. Apply a small amount of moisture product to finish.

Recommended products: Barbasol Thick and Rich Shaving Cream, Kiehl's Facial Fuel, Kiehl's Blue Astringent Herbal Lotion, Mario Badescu Seaweed Cleansing Lotion, Tend Skin, Mario Badescu Aloe Moisturizer SPF 15, Mario Badescu After Shave Moisturizer.

Electric Shave

Figure 4.28 Fellow Barber Shave Brush; **Figure 4.29** Musgo Real; **Figure 4.30** MCM beard oil; **Figure 4.31** Bevel shave products; **Figure 4.32** Art Of Shaving products

Shaving with an electric razor is common in the hair and makeup trailer. It's quicker, very efficient, and some brands are portable. The trick with an electric is having your equipment in tiptop order. Cleaned, sanitized, oiled, and charged. A good electric like Braun charges and cleans at the same time. You also will get a really close shave. A trick to a comfortable close shave is to start the process with a clipper like the Andis, at its closest setting. Go over the beard area, then follow with an electric, like the Braun. If possible, have the actor come into the trailer with his face already washed. I then use a toner that helps to lift the facial hair and prep/protect and condition the beard area against ingrown hairs.

Set-Up

Have ready your electric shaver, clipper, set-up towel, Face Saver powder, aftershave or toner, prep toner, small bowls, large square no-shred cotton pads, moisturizer.

1. Sit your actor in the chair and drape.
2. Apply Face Saver powder all over the area that will be shaved. You can use the stick directly onto the face or apply with a makeup powder brush.
3. Start shaving the sides of the face, cheeks, neck, then chin and upper lip. Shave in a downward stroke or with the grain. Then repeat, moving upward or against the grain. Do not apply a heavy hand. After the majority of the shaving is done, look for any areas that have been missed. Gently, with the tip of the shaver go back and forth until the desired effect is reached.
4. Saturate a cotton pad with toner or aftershave and remove any unwanted Face Saver powder and hair.

Important suggestion: Be sure to write down each actor's personal settings on shavers and clippers to maintain the exact trim each time. If facial lengths change, take pictures and write down the scene, day, and time of day. Keep these on hand for yourself and anybody else in the trailer who might end up working on the actor.

5. Follow with a moisturizer.

Recommended products: Braun series 7 self-clean and charge, Andis Master, Eltron Shave Stick, Kiehl's Facial Fuel, Kiehl's Blue Astringent Herbal Lotion, Mario Badescu Seaweed Cleansing Lotion, Tend Skin, Mario Badescu Aloe Moisturizer SPF 15, Mario Badescu After Shave Moisturizer.

Shaving a Head Bald

Lennotch: "A grooming tip specifically for men who shave their heads consistently is stay on a regular schedule. This encourages a consistent growth pattern. In turn you will reduce irritation. Don't let the hair grow out too much. This gives a sloppy appearance. Using aloe vera, preferably directly from the plant, helps reduce irritation, treats blemishes, moisturizes, and relieves ingrown hairs, a problem especially seen in men of color. My favorite razor is the MD Dragon Straight Razor with Dorco blades. Dome Shine-Absorbing Anti-Aging Finishing Serum leaves a shaved head smooth and satiny. Dome Shave Gel is clear, won't clog blades, and is not messy, the perfect scenario for clients who need to be done fast and out the door.

"If you have a request or an actor's character calls for a bald head, for maintaining a shaved head, or matching a stunt double, have the actor come in the day before shooting. It's a simple process, but if not done properly can be a terrifying and uncomfortable service for everyone involved. Be sure you are set up properly. Drape your client securely, so no hair drops down the neck. Cut with clippers with a guard. Go through the whole head front to back. Take a clipper with no guard at all. Repeat the process. Before shaving, rub the head with a warm damp towel.

This will help the hairs stand up for a cleaner less evasive shave. A clear shave gel like Dome Shave Gel allows you to see what you are shaving. Use the straight razors of choice and shave in the direction of the hair growth. Glide the razor without too much pressure, rinsing the blade often. Check all areas for a clean uniformed look. Apply an after-shave product to reduce irritation and give a smooth, silky appearance."

Figure 4.34 Dome Care products

Skin Problems Due to Shaving

Alopecia, dandruff, ingrown hairs, and acne are common skin problems found in men and women. Men experience ingrown hairs, irritation, acne, and nicks from shaving. To combat this, listen to the actor and what he has to say about his shaving routine. Use all possible means for a comfortable shave using the appropriate products. Follow up with a regular treatment regime. Products like Murad and Proactiv can be used alone or combined with another treatment routine. Don't apply makeup such as concealers over areas that are broken out unless it's an antibacterial product. Makeup could make the situation worse. Never cross-use makeup with several people. It will be very hard to keep skin from breaking out if you do so. Men can benefit greatly from facials. If there is an actor who needs facials, schedule him once a week, for example, for a treatment like the SenSpa Gentleman's Life Style Facial. This customized 60-minute treatment exfoliates, massages, hydrates, and protects the skin from ultraviolet rays. It uses LED lights to reduce redness, antioxidant applications, and masques for targeted skin issues. Treatment products are suggested for use at home or in the trailer.

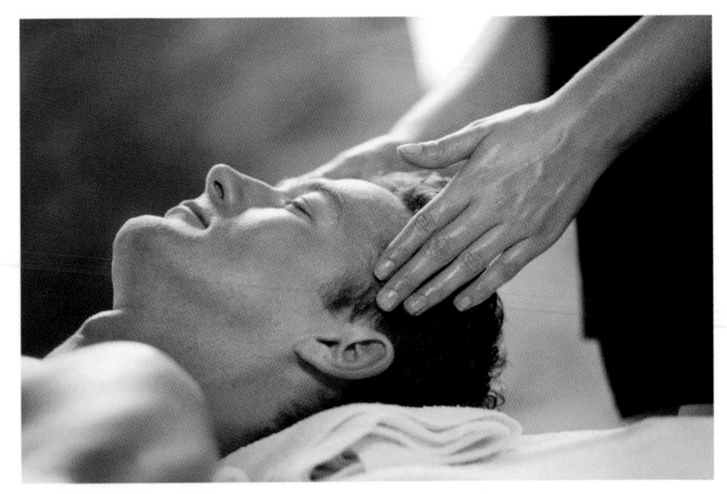

Figure 4.35 SenSpa Gentleman's Lifestyle Facial

Figure 4.36 Murad Acne Treatment Concealer stick; **Figure 4.37** Murad Acne Treatment Concealer medium; **Figure 4.38** Murad Razor Burn Rescue; **Figure 4.39** Murad Face Defense

A Man's Intimate Grooming Utensils

Groomers for ears, nose, brows, and back come in a variety of brands. Most have one house with exchangeable heads. Women also like to use these smaller portable groomers.

Coloring and Filling

Another situation that comes up in makeup and hair is adding color, filling in hairlines, adding hair, and building up existing hair for a period piece. There are so many ways to do this. Here are some reasons why you might add lace hairpieces to existing facial hair: Hair growth, color patterns in the facial hair, or bald patterns are not always ideal. Grooming might include filling in with makeup or lace pieces to achieve a uniformed look. What's funny is, if done right, no one will know you've added anything.

Figure 4.40 Temptu Hair Dura palette

How to Maintain Haircuts, Beards, Moustaches, and Stubble for Continuity

Yvette adds an important note: "Right after you are done with a haircut, beard trim, or establishing facial hair lengths, write down the date. Take up-close pictures of the front, back, and both sides of the head for haircuts. Facial hair only needs the front and sides unless the neck has been worked on also. Write down any relevant notes that pertain to the haircut. Pictures, notes, and the dates will be your guideline and continuity. Every head of hair grows differently. If the hair grows faster in the front, then you'll need to trim the actor's bangs between haircuts. A fade clipper cut requires a touch-up every two days. It will be your responsibility to keep any haircuts or beard trims looking the same throughout the show. Schedule haircuts, clipper cuts, beard trims, and so on before a shooting day; if not, then after shooting is completed."

The actor's own schedule is tied up with the other schedules involved in the show, and characters' looks often come straight from the director. Any changes in an actor's appearance therefore have to be discussed between the director and the department head. Unless changes are approved, do not let anyone talk you into any different haircut, no matter how small that request seems. Haircuts are part of the character being played. As a department head, you need to pass this rule along to your crew.

Credits

www.andis.com
www.badgerandblade.com
www.braun.com
www.domecaresolutions.com
www.dyers.org
www.kentbrushes.com
www.mariobadescu.com
www.masonpearson.co.uk
www.mcmcfragrances.com
www.murad.com www.kiehls.com
www.royalshave.com
www.senspa.com
www.temptu.com
www.tendskin.com
www.theartofshaving.com
www.topnotchbarber.com
www.westcoastshaving.com

CHAPTER FIVE
Design

Technique has everything to do with good design. Hair design becomes second nature once you become familiar with hair and how to work with it. You will always be challenged to create a character using only what's in front of you. In Chapter 3 we showed you what tools to use for curling or flattening hair. What simple bobby pins to use. What combs or brushes our industry uses. All of these types of things bring you to the next step: knowledge and execution. I'll give you an example. Take the cover photo. How would you approach this look if a director, art director, photographer, or the hair department head requested it? How could you, on a limited budget and with little time, achieve your goal and complete this task? We'll help you in this chapter, which concentrates on techniques to construct any hair style.

Jill Glaser is the owner and founder of Chicago's Makeup First School of Makeup Artistry. Jill is an Illinois state-certified makeup artist, specializing in commercial media applications. Jill is also an expert in makeup and hair styling for high-definition television, film, web series, video, and print. At the start of her career she had a passion to open up a school offering formal training in makeup and hair skills.

Dave Bova resides in New York City and is an instructor in theatrical makeup and hairstyling. He's also an expert in wig construction. As a makeup designer, Dave has worked on Broadway shows such as *The Real Thing* and *Wicked*, and Cirque du Soleil. A designer with a long history in theater, Dave has given his time and knowledge to teach up-and-coming makeup and hair artists. Both Jill and Dave lend their knowledge to the following.

Words of the Experts: Jill Glaser and Dave Bova

"Adding volume, flat iron, or curling to hair all uses some kind of heat," says Jill, "even if the heat comes from a hair blower, except when hair is being formed and set. A simple rule to remember about hair is that cold means working without heat, like a dry set. Hot means heat is added to the hair by means of irons, blow dryers, steam, etc. When using a curling iron, for example, hair will hold its memory from heat after the hair has cooled. Brushing or finger styling hair before the heat has cooled will give you poor results.

"It's important to work the cuticle of the hair correctly, like creating a curl pattern that might not be what the natural hair does. When using any cold or heat elements, if the hair is not manipulated right the outcome will be less than desired. Texture and curls can be created with a number of tools, for example, curling irons. Firstly blow dryers are used to dry, straighten, or add volume. Before you start blow drying hair, have all the right products, combs, and brushes for the desired effect. Curling irons can be used in a number of ways. Each technique will give you a different curl and texture. Apply these techniques to create many different styles. You can wrap the hair around the inside barrel, wrap around the entire curling iron, or slide the hair down the barrel and then curl upward or backward, to name a few."

"For flat irons take one- or two-inch sections of hair. Clamp the flat iron down at the root and slide down the hair."

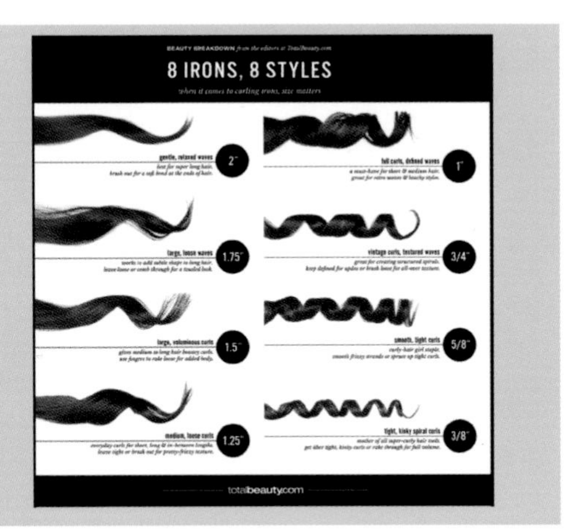

Figure 5.1 Curling-iron curls (TotalBeauty.com)

Jill goes on to explain the basics of using rollers:

"Hot or cold rollers are rolled into the hair in different patterns to give you styles that can work in different time periods, or to recreate an old style with a modern twist, although hot rollers will give you quicker results. For example, you could apply larger rollers to the top middle section, rolled away from the face, continuing with medium and then small, reaching the back of the neck, and all other rollers rolled to the side. As long as you know the direction and outcome, the possibilities are endless."

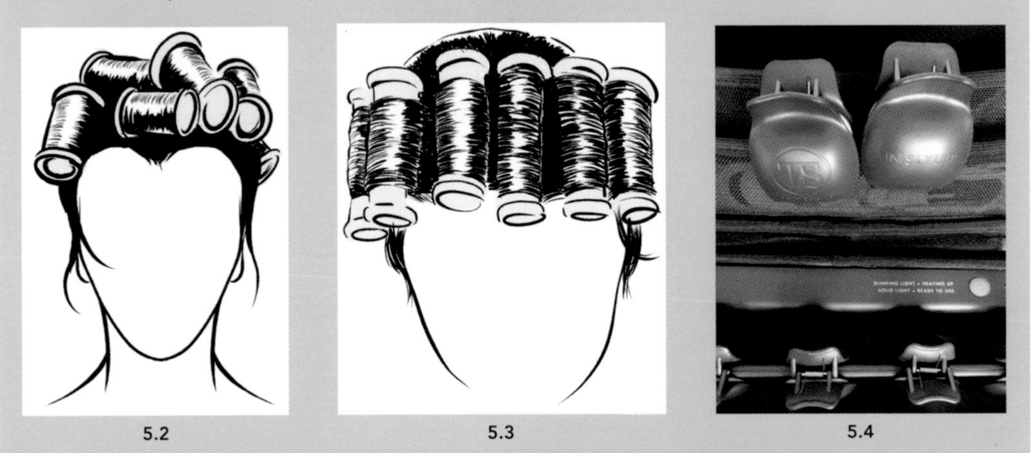

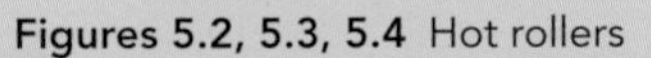

Figures 5.2, 5.3, 5.4 Hot rollers

Dave: "Pin curls are used to create volume, for wrapping hair under wig caps, and especially for period hair styles. The direction a pin curl is set dictates the style. For example, a curl can be forward or rolled backward. Staggering pin curls also gives a softer effect. Stand-up pin curls give the curl a lift from the scalp. Period hair styles can have very specific directions of the pin curl. Pin curls can be set the day before to style the next day. This is especially helpful for large scenes in film or theater, with background actors who must look period. Hair stylists will only need to style hair on the day the scene is filmed if the background artists pins and curl their hair the night before. Pin curls are created by sectioning the desired hair. Comb the section of hair smooth, applying any hair product of choice. Wrap the hair around the finger. When fully wrapped, place the curl flatly against the head and clip in the center of the curl."

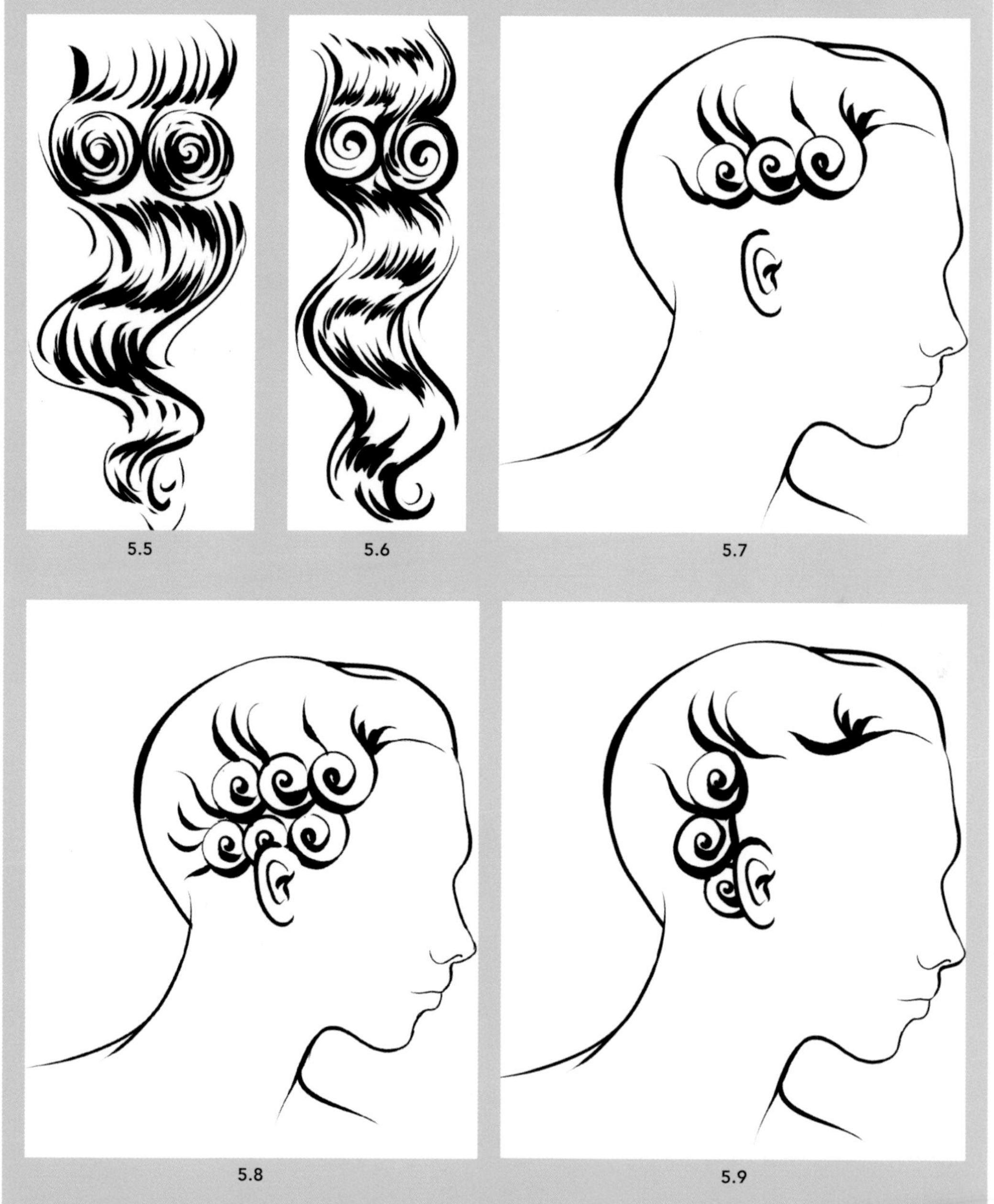

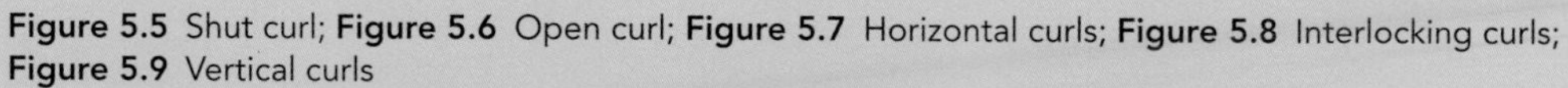

Figure 5.5 Shut curl; **Figure 5.6** Open curl; **Figure 5.7** Horizontal curls; **Figure 5.8** Interlocking curls; **Figure 5.9** Vertical curls

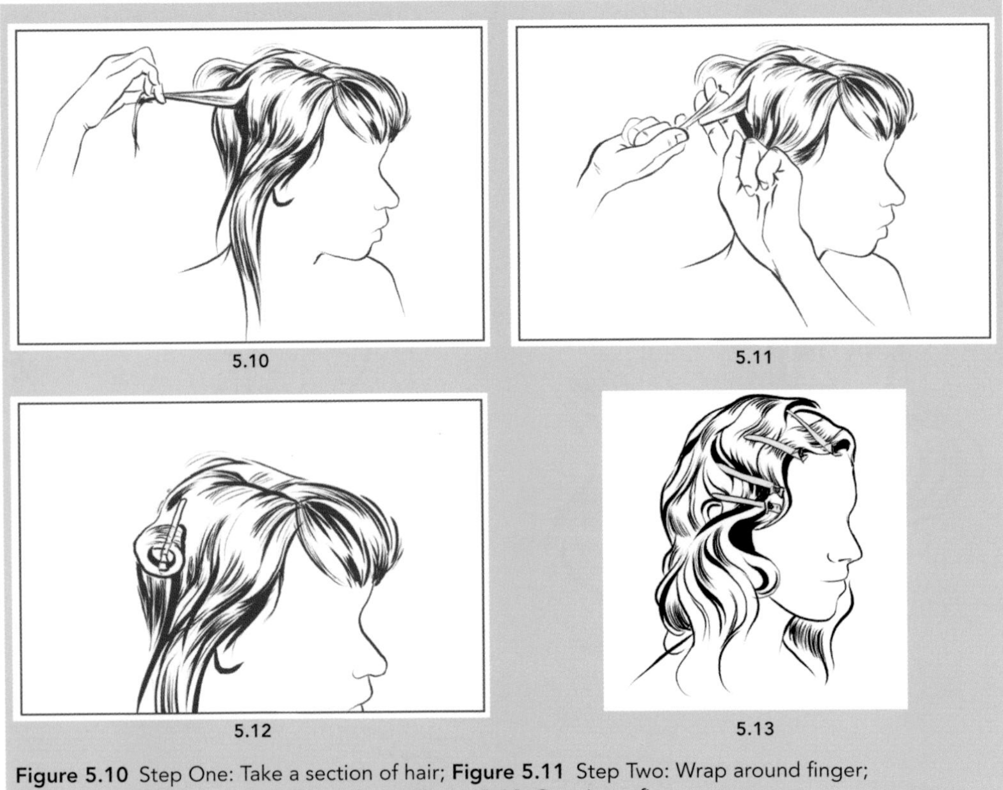

Figure 5.10 Step One: Take a section of hair; **Figure 5.11** Step Two: Wrap around finger; **Figure 5.12** Step Three: Lay flat and pin; **Figure 5.13** Creating a finger wave

"Finger waving is the shaping or molding of the hair while wet into 'S'-shaped curved undulations with the fingers and comb."
Jill Davis, *The Art of Finger Waving* (Paul Compar Bramcast Publications).

Dave: "Finger waves today can be formed on dry or wet hair clips, or no clips at all. Sometimes you need to mimic the style with very little time to do it.

"Finger waves are usually done on washed, clean hair. Products are applied on damp or dry hair to help create the wave. The hair is then set and let to air dry, or dried with a heating element such as a hair dryer or blow dryer. To recreate the finger wave, start with damp hair. Part the hair into one-inch pieces, with the heavier side treated with a styling product. Take a one-inch section, using your middle finger to create a ridge, then with a comb, lift hair and comb up and back. Pinch between your two fingers the ridge you've created, rest, then roll your fingers backward. Start again with a new wave, do the exact same things, but this time roll the fingers toward the face. Insert the clips in the middle of your wave."

Hair Styles for Inspiration

Illustrations of hair styles can be a great resource to quickly remind yourself of a period look and how it's styled. One of the fascinating things about historical hair styles is that techniques used long ago can still be applied today, although modern-day tools are much easier and safer.

Figure 5.14 '30s-style braids

Figure 5.15 Braids

Figure 5.16 '40s-style hair

Figure 5.17 '90s braid up-do

Figure 5.18 Jane Austen style

Figure 5.19 Flapper-style hair

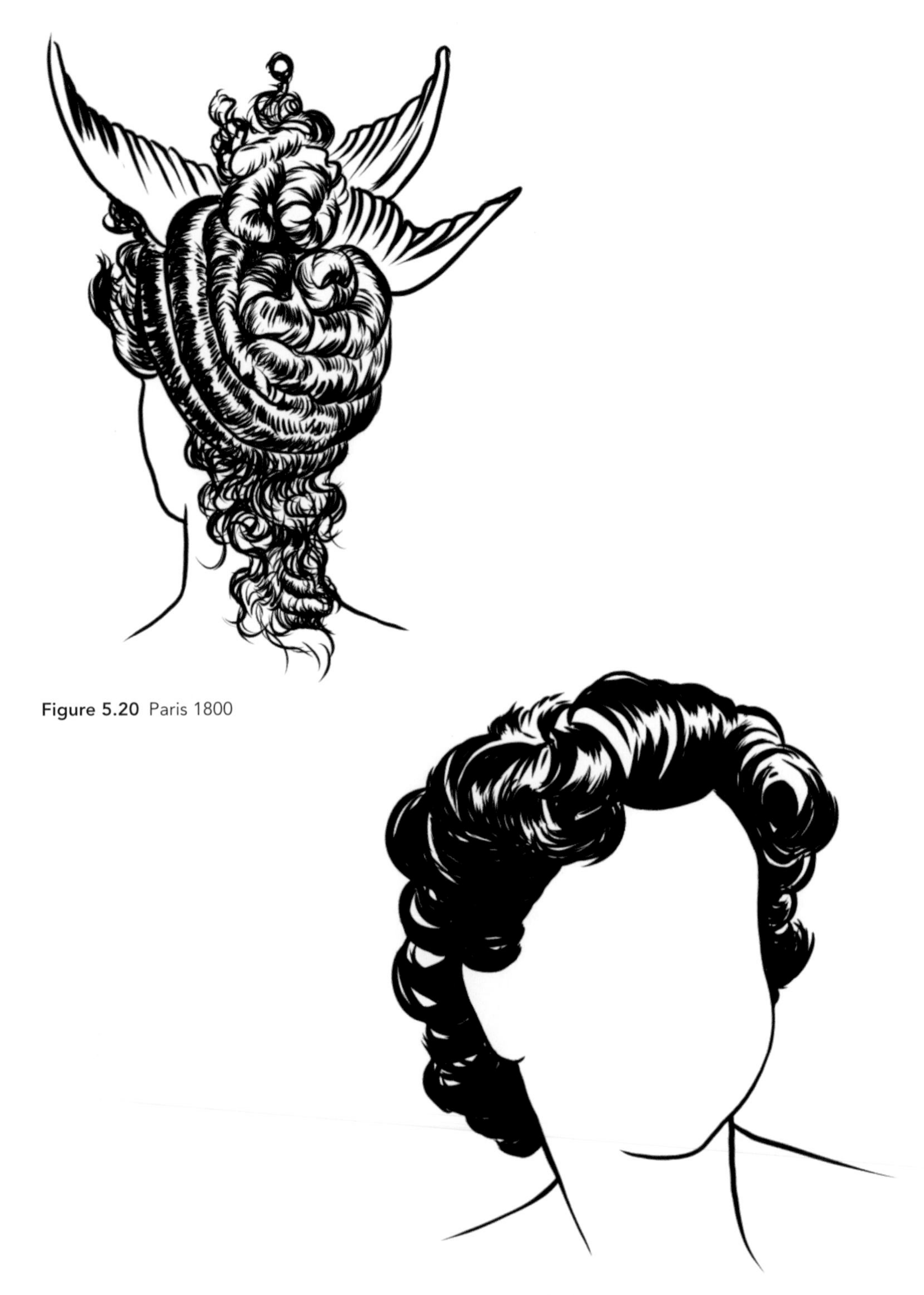

Figure 5.20 Paris 1800

Figure 5.21 '50s-style hair

Figure 5.22 Braids from the 11th century

Figure 5.23 Early Egyptian

Figure 5.24 Mohawk

Figure 5.25 Dreads

Figure 5.26 '60s-style hair

Figure 5.27 Gibson

Figure 5.28 1835

Examples of Period Design

Jennifer Stanfield is a makeup artist and hair stylist with a rich history of working on films such as *The Hobbit: An Unexpected Journey* and, most recently, *San Andreas* and *The Daughter*. Jennifer knows the importance of mixing old with the new:

> "Period pieces have their challenges. I've never done a job where there isn't the use of some, or all, hairpieces, extensions, wigs, facial hair, groomed beards, brow and lash tinting, hair color, highlighting, or contouring. This can all be very expensive. It helps to hire on your team experts in these areas."

Costume design has a huge influence on what the makeup and hair department creates, and will often dictate what class or position in society the character is portraying. The condition of the costumes can reflect any changes the character might be experiencing. Through makeup, hair, and wardrobe, we follow the actor's journey throughout the story.

Testing is important for period pieces. Tests can be done in several stages: one for the overall look, and another to see if those looks work with camera and lighting. Wigs or facial hair are all part of the costume, and must be realistic. Testing takes time, but is important, in order for decisions to be made. Once approved, measuring, ordering, or creating these final looks can begin. After testing, when everything is locked in, chart the final makeup/hair for reference and continuity.

Jennifer describes an example of '40s-style hair and makeup, in the film *Voyage of the Dawn Treader*:

"Research is important for a period character. I find as many images that I can. For the character Susan, Lauren Bacall's image from the '40s had a big influence. When the actress arrived, her hair needed to be trimmed. We were able to do this in pre-production.

"Setting up hair for a look like this, you will need rollers, plastic pins, an end tail comb, setting lotion, water spray, and a hood dryer. You'll also want a soft-bristle brush (such as Mason and Pearson), hair serum, or smoothing cream. The hair is set first, so that makeup can be done while the hair is drying. Use setting rollers approximately ¾ inch in diameter. Set the rollers, starting with the middle section from the hairline to the nape of the neck, all directed off the face. Take the sides and set the rollers toward the face. Spritz the hair lightly with setting lotion and water. Do not make it too wet, or the drying time will be too long. Position the hood dryer over the set rollers, leaving room for the makeup to be done. When the makeup is done, take a roller out and check to see if the hair is 100 percent dry. If not dry yet, leave the roller in the hair a bit longer. This will save you time in the long run.

"To style the hair, remove the curlers. Brush through well. Add a small amount of serum or smoothing creme through the hair as you brush it. Encourage the hair into waves. Part the hair on the left. Brush down so there is not too much volume at the part line. Brush lightly up at the front hairline, creating waves that lift off the face. Secure with a kirby grip if required. On-set maintenance is crucial, so roll the hair up into five or six loose pin curls and secure with a single-prong metal sectioning clip. (Make sure the clip has no teeth, or it will mark the hair.) Tie a scarf or loose hair net to keep the hair from becoming messy while waiting to shoot. Let the clips out and brush the hair into place just before shooting. Don't use hairspray unless you absolutely have to. It's better if the hair can move and be brushed easily. Roll the hair back into pin curls any time your actress has time off.

"Makeup comes next. Brows and lips will be the focus for the '40s . To complement the hair I used a red lipstick by Mac and a matte rose pink blush dusted onto the apples of her cheeks. This gives a healthy glow. Anna's complexion was already a perfect pale for the '40s. When this is the case, conceal only where needed. Start with a primer, following with your foundation. Taupe browns define the eye shape. Use very fine eyeliner painted right at the lash line on top lid only. Black or black brown mascara rounds out the look. Don't forget the nails. File and paint if required. If there is any brow shaping to be done by tweezers, wax, or any hair-removal system, try and do this at least the day before. I was able to tweeze Anna's brows into a '40s-period style the day before. After grooming the brows, paint in individual hairs throughout the brows with a fine brush to define the shape."

Recommended products: Mac red lipsticks, Chantecaille Future Skin Foundation, Skin Illustrator Brow Pallet, Hourglass Primer, Tweezerman Tweezers.

Hair Extensions and Artificial Dreads

> "Hair extension: a synthetic or real swatch of hair that is attached to make longer, fuller, hairstyle." dictionary.reference.com

Extensions

Figure 5.29 Hair extensions

Film and TV stylist Yvette Rivas tells us:

"Working with hair extensions or any synthetic hair, especially in the beginning, can be a daunting task. For one, there are several ways to apply hair extensions. It helps to approach and problem-solve your immediate situation at hand. What technique will you apply? What kind of hair will you use? What colors? What system? How much time do you have? What elements are you in? How fast is removal? And what is your budget? In film you will not always have the luxury of advance preparation, so thinking on your feet goes a long way. You only need to use your imagination. Hair extensions that are sewn in, glued in, clipped in, braided in, sandwiched in, and taped in will give you a variety of choices. It's smart to keep all your different systems

Figure 5.30 Numbered hairpieces

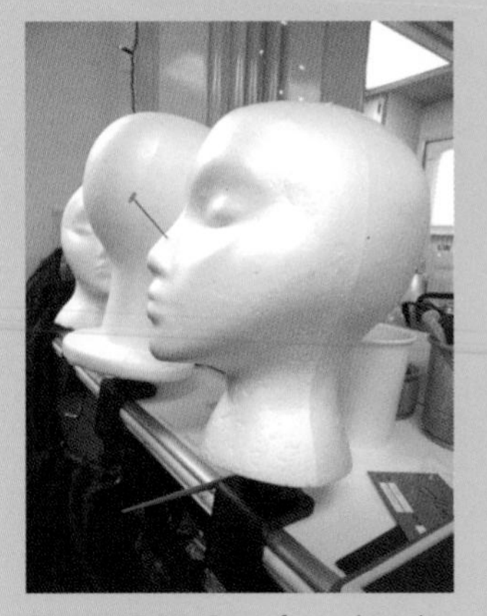

Figure 5.31 Styrofoam head

separated. Not only is it much more organized, but less time is taken trying to find what you need in a pinch. Clear plastic set bags are a great way to organize your tools and extensions. Also you can make and stockpile your own extensions by cutting sizes of hair wafts that you will need, and dipping the end into melted keratin. Gently roll the treated end between your thumb and finger to cool. Although there are keratin pots on the market today, it's just as easy to make your own. Labeling your custom or store-bought extensions is another way to help the application to go smoothly, especially for complicated hair styles. For example, 'top sides' or 'bottom row middle.' Not only will hair styles go quicker, but your continuity will be consistent."

Applying Extensions

Before you start applying the hair extensions, lay them out on a clean dry work surface like a towel or cloth or styrofoam wig head. If your extensions are labeled, set them out in the corresponding patterns. Hair should be washed with a clarifying shampoo to remove any oils and residue.

Aluminum extensions come in different sizes and colors. The beads used to attach the hair extension are matte: black for darker hair, brown for medium, and blonde for lighter hair.

Figure 5.32 Aluminum beads

Section hair to where you want to start. For example, do you just want to fill in areas to make the hair fuller? Do you want to add length? To add length, start at the bottom and move your way up. Keep in mind that a full head of aluminum extensions can be heavy and appear too much like a wig.

Figure 5.33 Sectioned hair

Position the aluminum bead with the hair.

Never position an extension directly on the scalp. Extensions should be able to bend and move naturally.

When hair is positioned correctly, press the bead flat.

Give a little tug to make sure the hair is secure.

Remove the extension by using the flat side of the pliers to reshape the bead for removal.

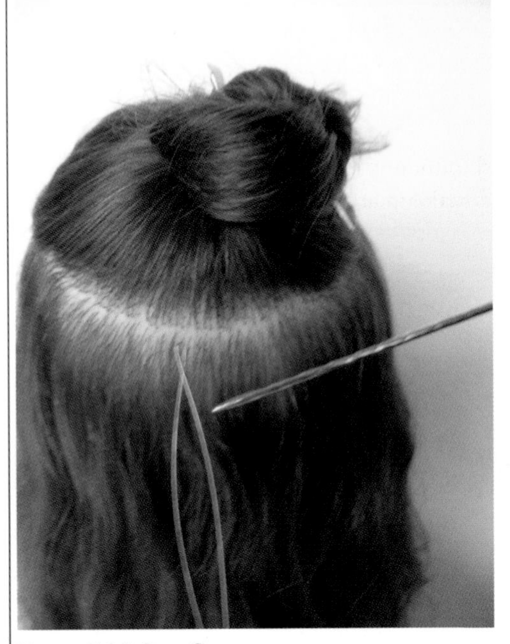

Figure 5.34 Step One

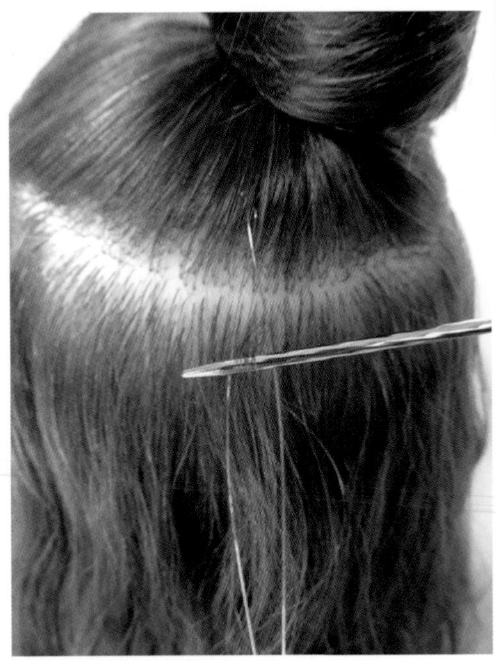

Figure 5.35 Step Two

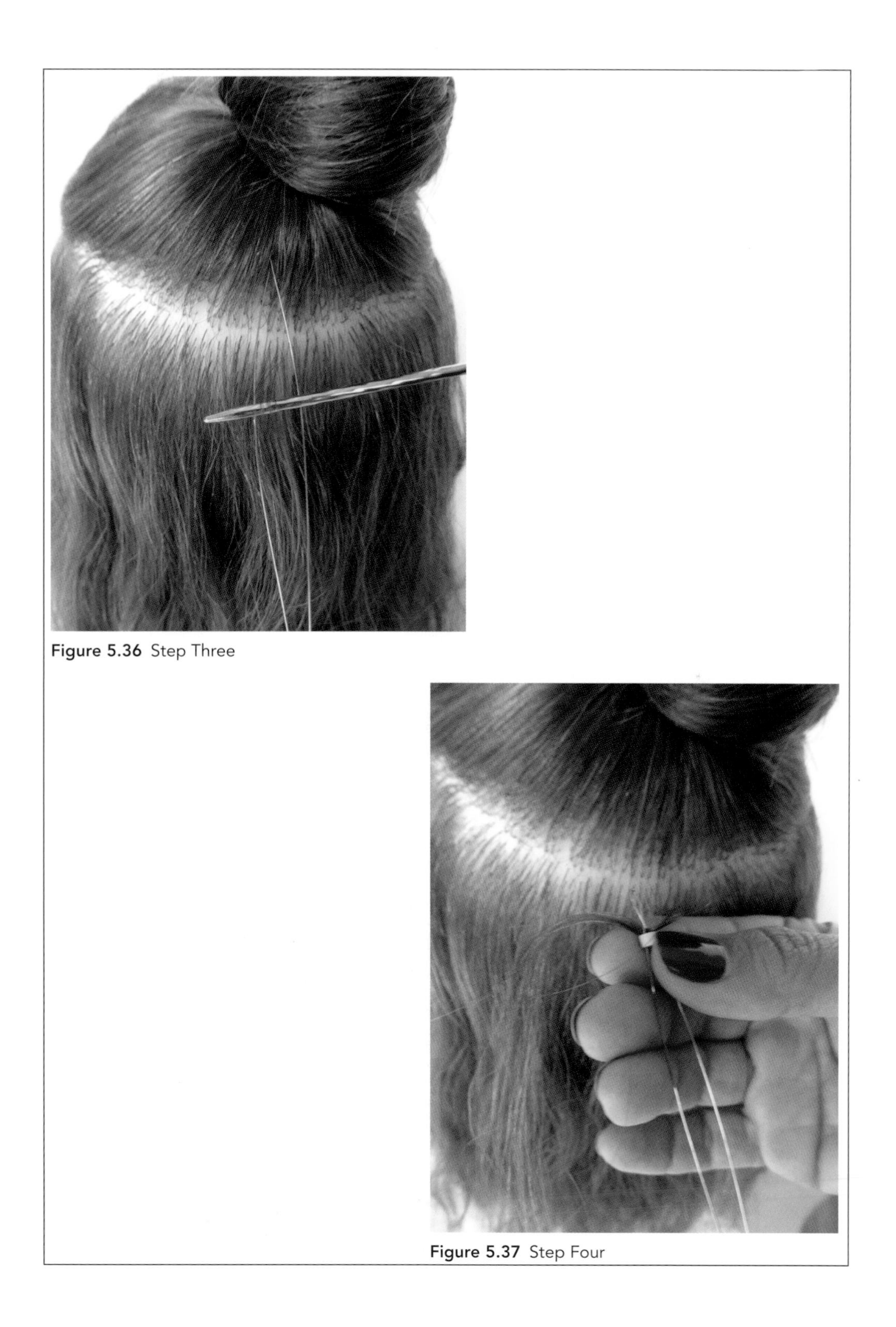

Figure 5.36 Step Three

Figure 5.37 Step Four

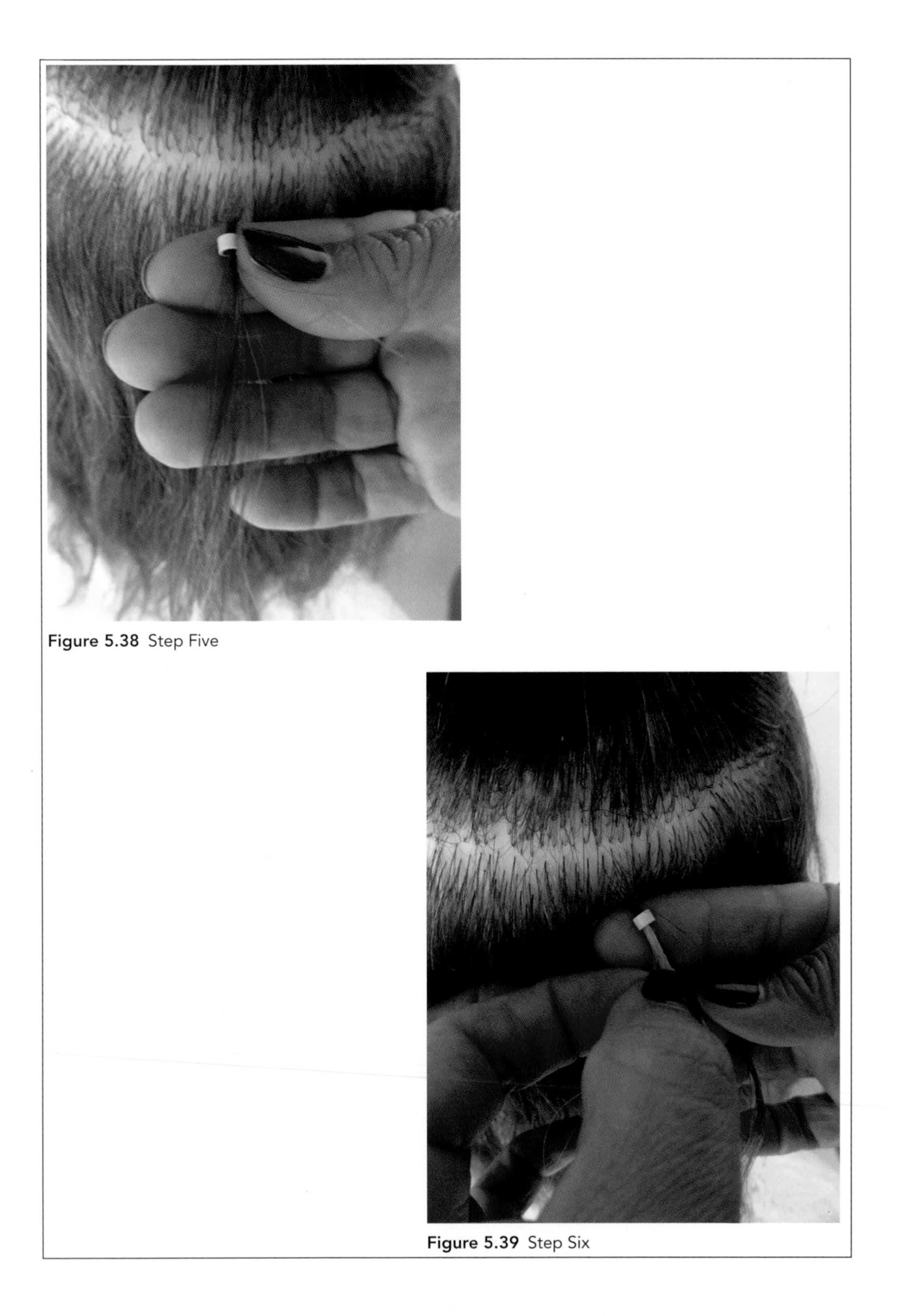

Figure 5.38 Step Five

Figure 5.39 Step Six

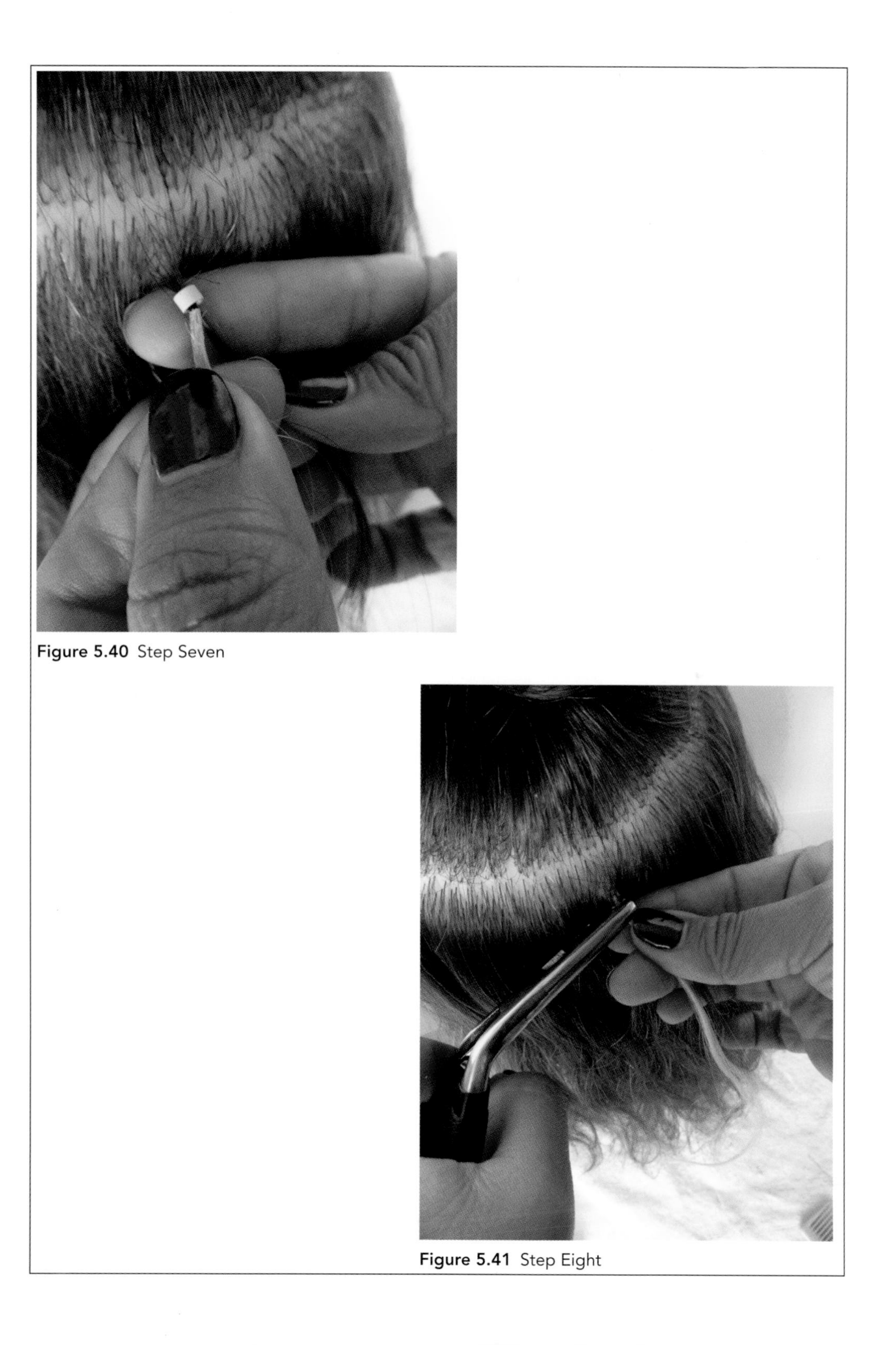

Figure 5.40 Step Seven

Figure 5.41 Step Eight

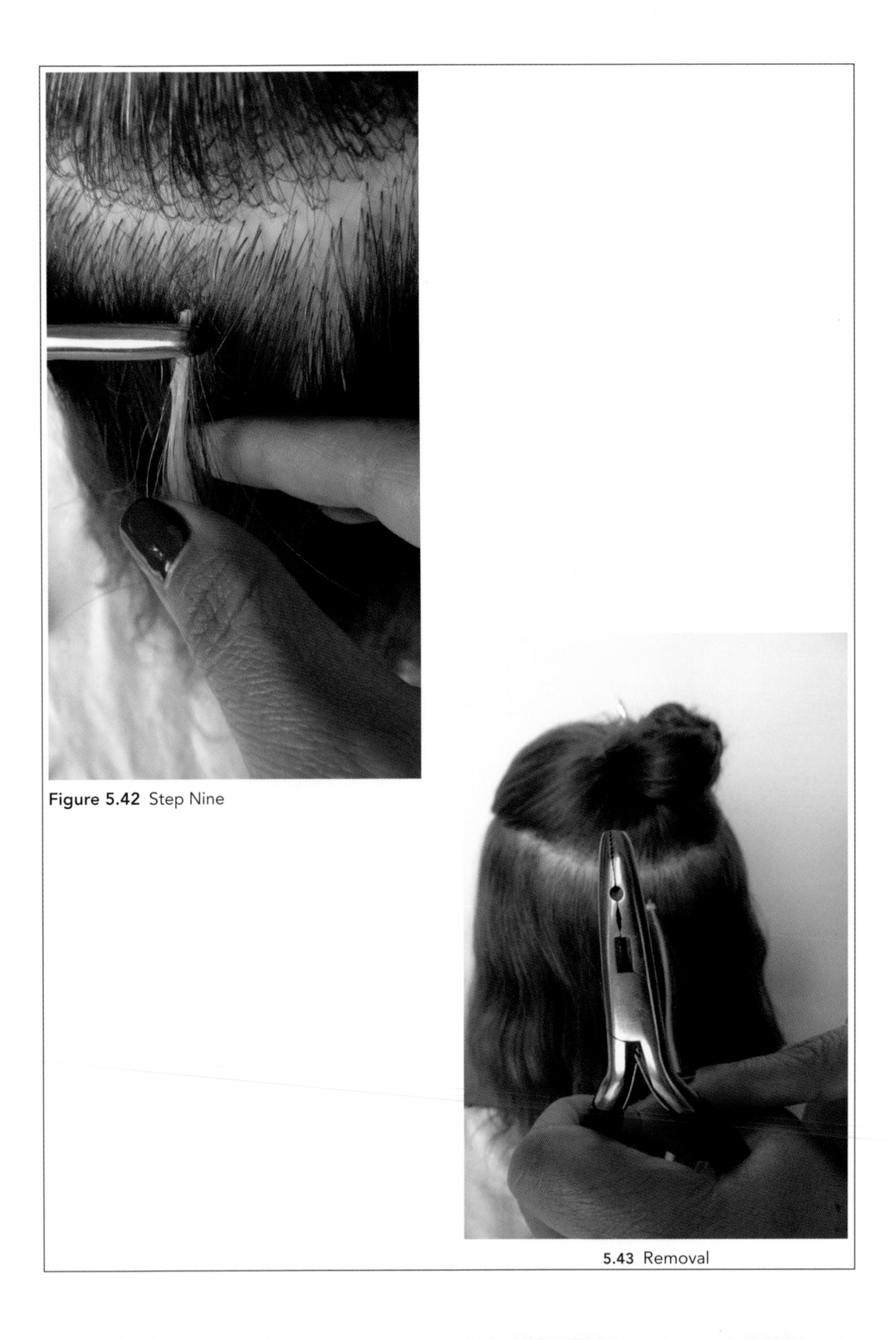

Figure 5.42 Step Nine

5.43 Removal

5.44 Removal

5.45 Removal

5.46

Figures 5.43, 5.44, 5.45, 5.46 Aluminum bead removal

Keratin links are applied with a hook utensil that can be loaded up ahead of time.

Start with the bottom of the nape and work your way up.

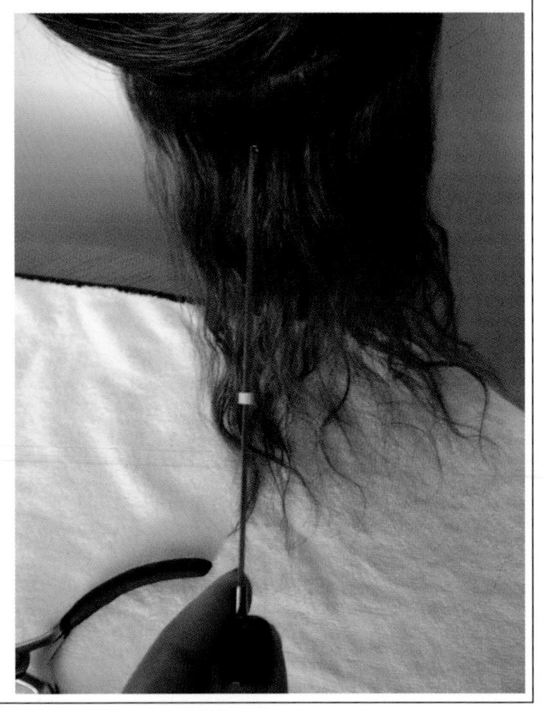

Figure 5.47 Loading a bead

Grab a section of hair with your hook and pull through the loop.

With extensions and tubes on, apply heat with an iron to seal. These extensions are transparent, which makes them impossible to detect.

Extensions do not have to be lined up in a neat little row, but can be applied slightly off center or just where hair is needed. It's better to break up the pattern by alternating or filling. That way, when hair parts or flies around, you won't see a straight line of extensions. Off center is always best.

Figure 5.48 Loaded bead

Figure 5.49 Loop hair through bead

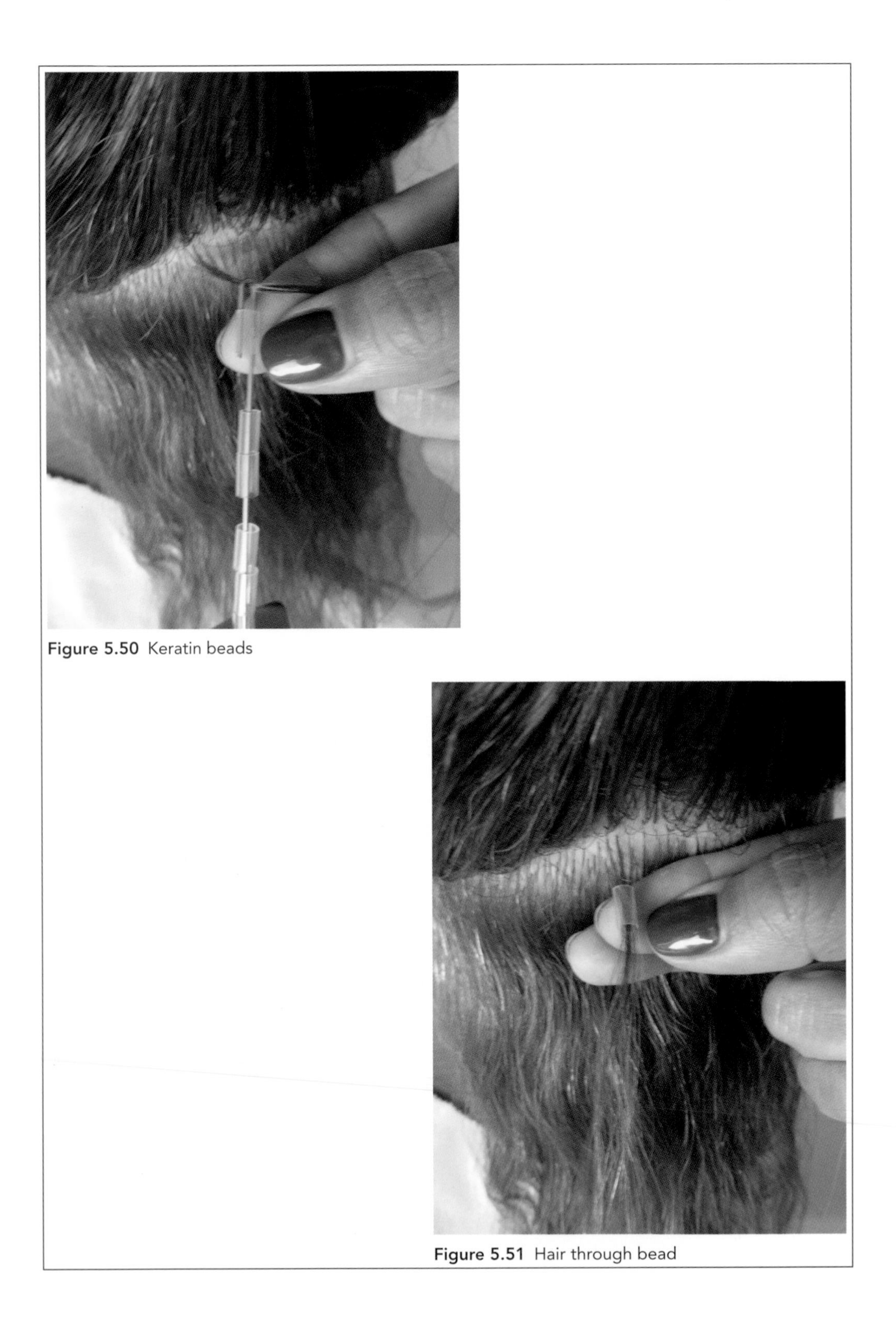

Figure 5.50 Keratin beads

Figure 5.51 Hair through bead

Figure 5.52 Extension through bead

Figure 5.53 Heat the keratin

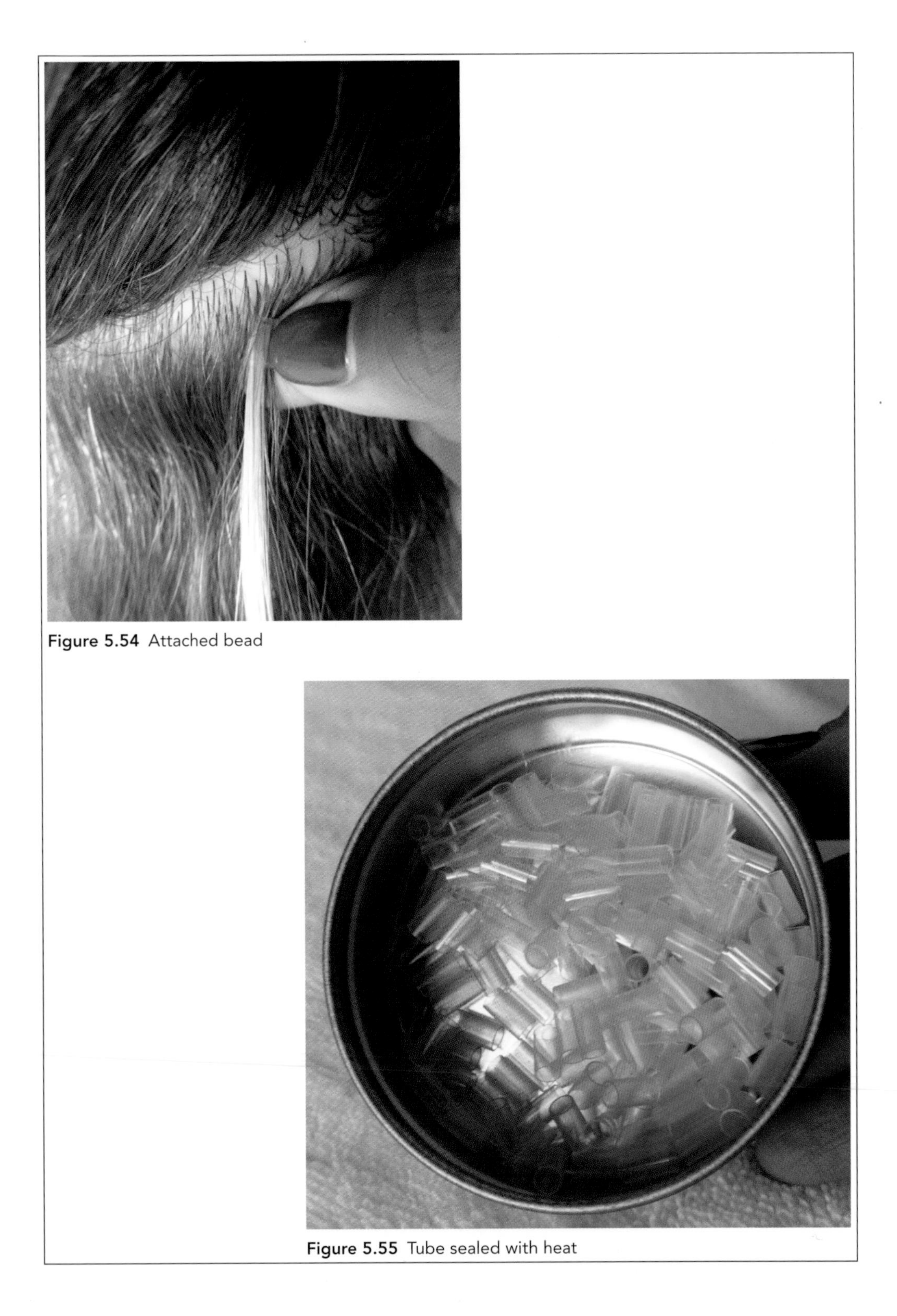

Figure 5.54 Attached bead

Figure 5.55 Tube sealed with heat

To remove the extension, use heat with an iron, applying pressure while sliding the bead down. Follow with hair oil with a small bristle brush (or find a brand that sells keratin-removal products). Gently work the oil into the hair, brushing the residue away. Hair can then be washed with a clarifying shampoo. The removed hair extensions can be cleaned further with 99 percent alcohol.

Figure 5.56 Small-bristle brush

Mark Berrington is a company that knows all about the keratin system, and you must be certified in order to use their system. They also supply one of the most recommended tape-on extensions. Pink tape is for temporary and green is for permanent.

Figure 5.57 Green tape

Figure 5.58 Pink tape

Recommended tapes you can find at beauty-supply stores include Ultra Hold and Lace.

Figure 5.59 Ultra Hold and Lace

Tapes can be cut in different sizes, easily labeled ahead of time, and placed where you think they should go. Don't apply the tapes directly onto the scalp at the sectioned part. You want them to move. Tapes can also be sandwiched between the hairs, taped on both ends.

Figure 5.60 Different tape sizes

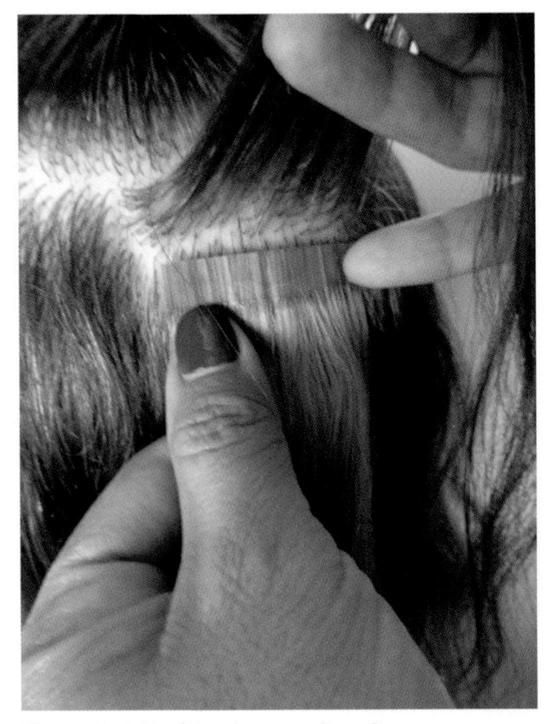

Figure 5.61 Position the tape: Step One

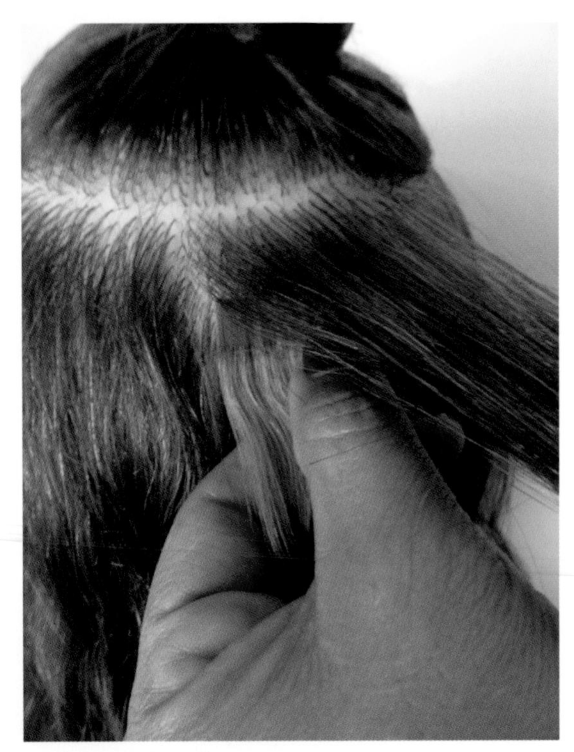

Figure 5.62 Step Two

Figure 5.63 Step Three

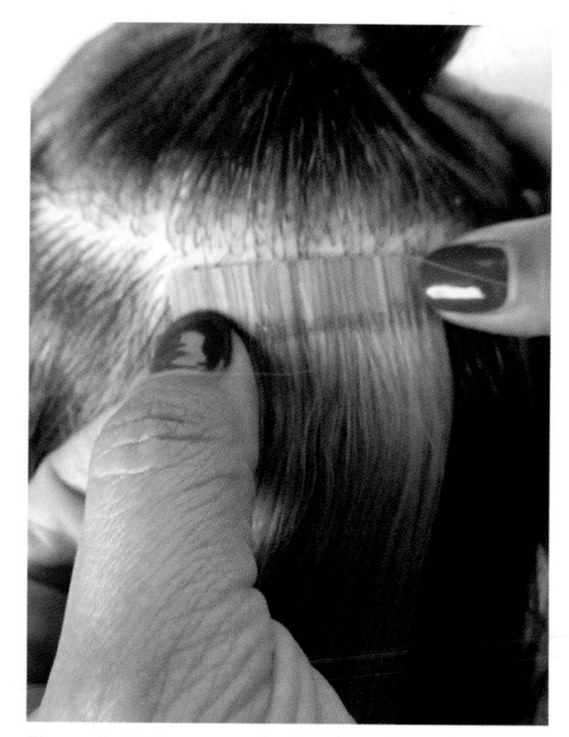

Figure 5.64 Do not apply directly to the scalp

Tape-removal systems such as Lord & Cliff can be found at beauty-supply stores.

Figure 5.65 Lord & Cliff tape remover

Sewing Extensions into the Hair

Sewing extensions into the hair starts with braiding a track of cornrows where you want your weft to start. You can make a pattern with the cornrows, all depending on what the final style will be, for example curves or an S. It's a misunderstanding that the tighter the cornrow, the longer the extension will last. This is not true and has caused a lot of problems with hair loss and scalp problems. The cornrows should be firm but not uncomfortably tight.

Figure 5.66 Thread and needles

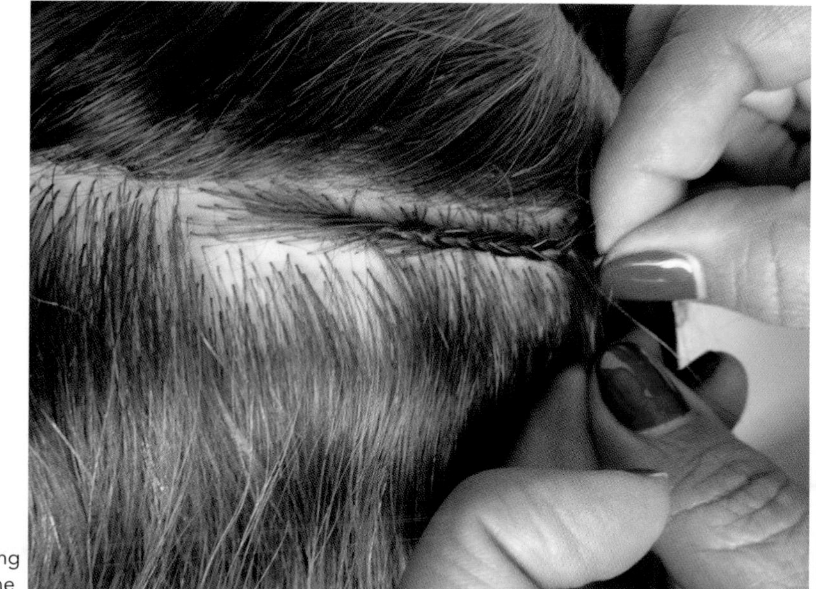

Figure 5.67 Making cornrows: Step One

Figure 5.68
Step Two

Figure 5.69
Step Three: Sewing extensions to cornrows

Figure 5.70 Step Four

Figure 5.71 Step Five

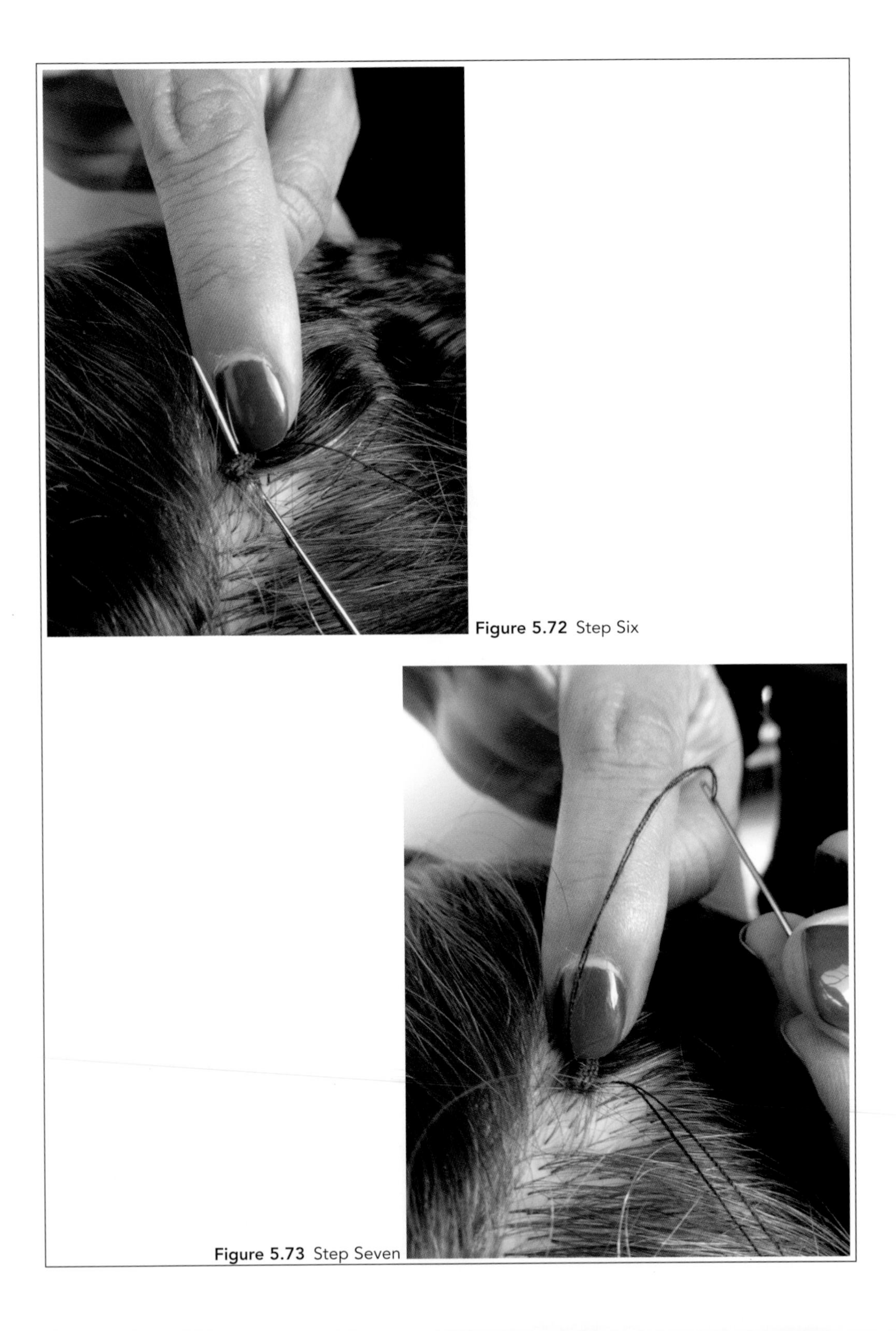

Figure 5.72 Step Six

Figure 5.73 Step Seven

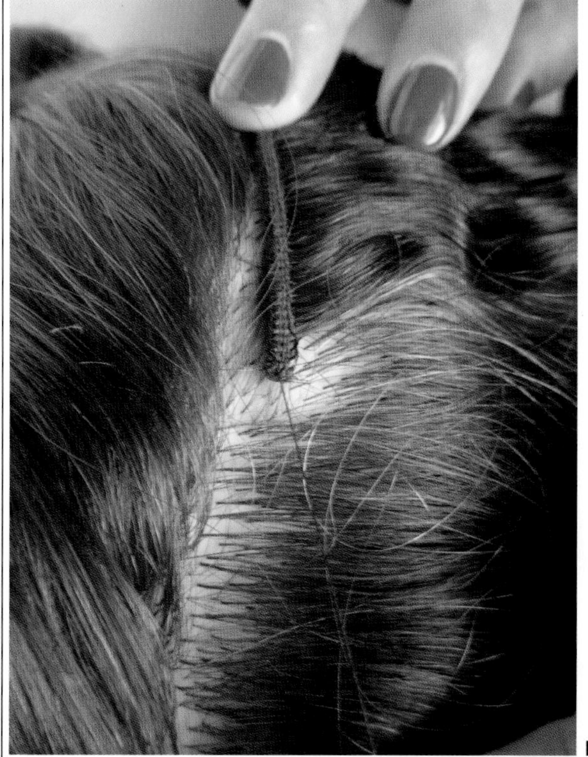

Figure 5.74 Step Eight

Down and dirty means getting the job done with what time and product you have on hand. In film, you must be able to be creative at the moment. One way is to cut off the top of a tape extension. Square off the hair with scissors. Braid a small section of hair, with the cut hair going halfway down, and sew the end of the braid.

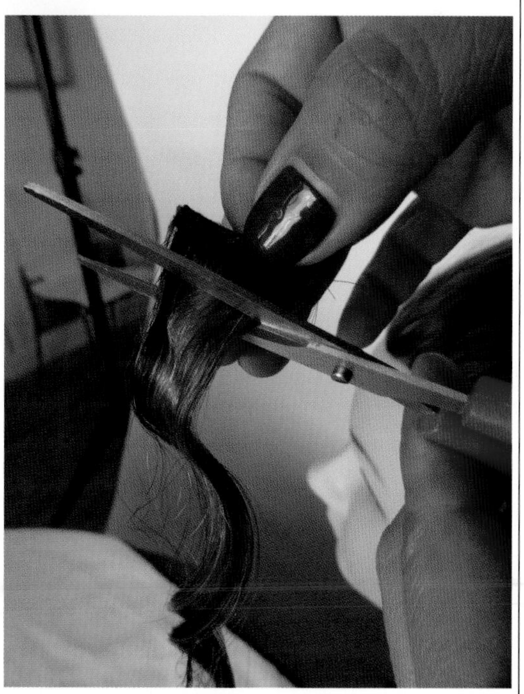

Figure 5.75 Step One: Square off the hair extension

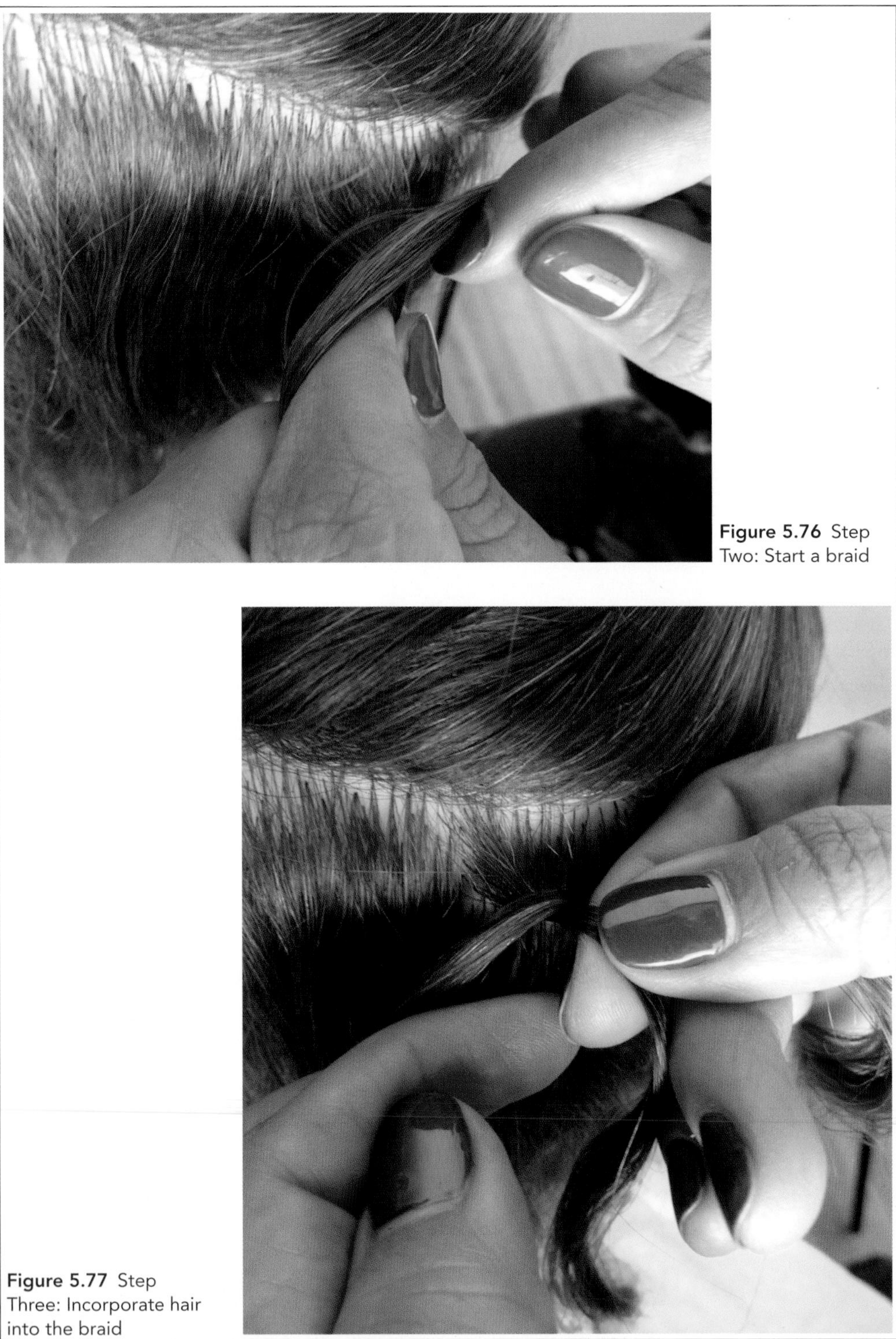

Figure 5.76 Step Two: Start a braid

Figure 5.77 Step Three: Incorporate hair into the braid

Figure 5.78 Step Four: Braid in extension

Figure 5.79 Step Five: Braid in extension to ends of hair

Figure 5.80 Step Six: Sew end of braid

5.81

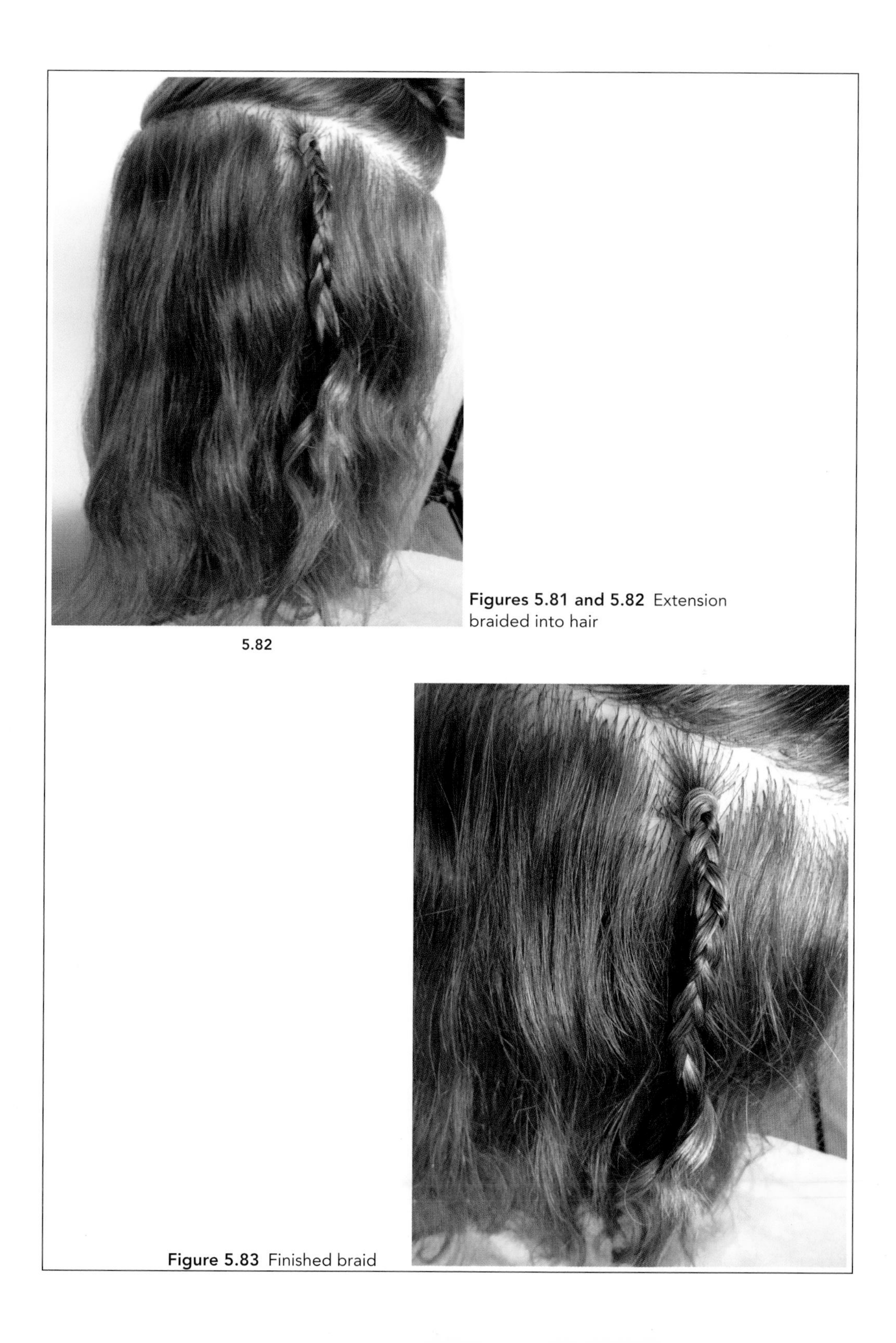

5.82

Figures 5.81 and 5.82 Extension braided into hair

Figure 5.83 Finished braid

You can also use toupee clips to secure the wafts into the hair. Slide the hair into an open toupee clip and snap shut, then clip into the hair. You can also buy premade wafts with clips.

Figure 5.84 Toupee clip

Figure 5.85 Hair inserted into toupee clip

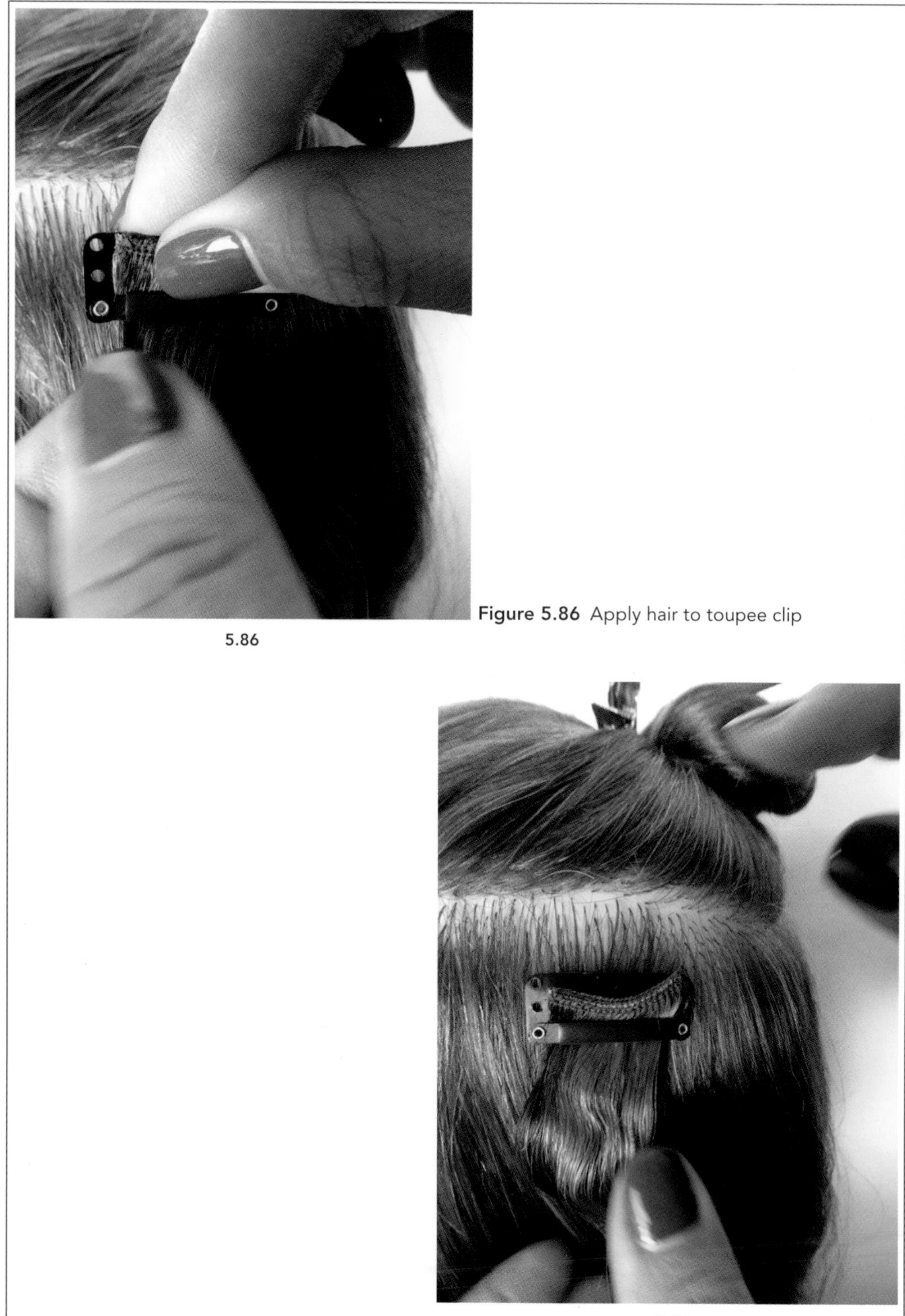

Figure 5.86 Apply hair to toupee clip

5.86

5.87

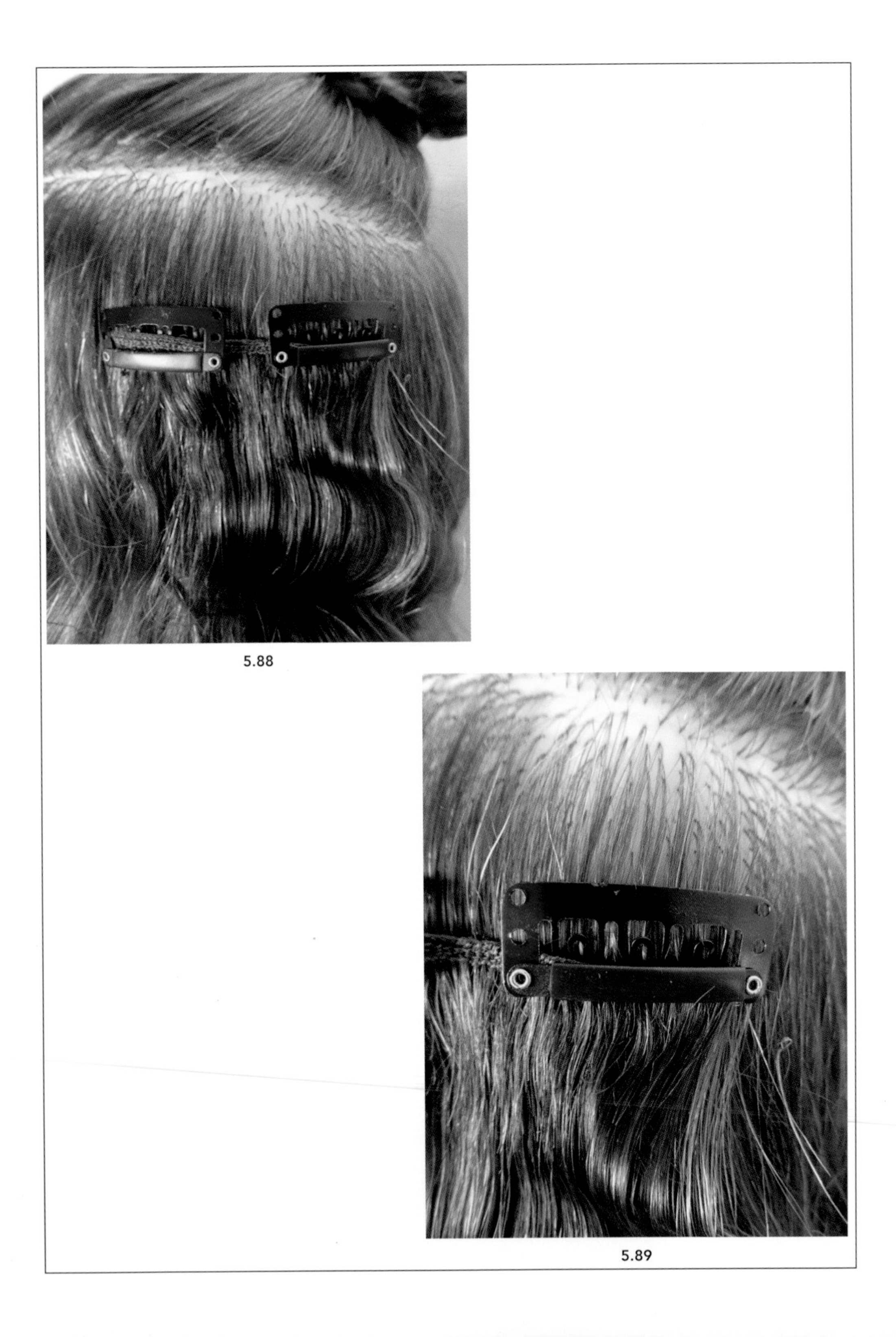

5.88

5.89

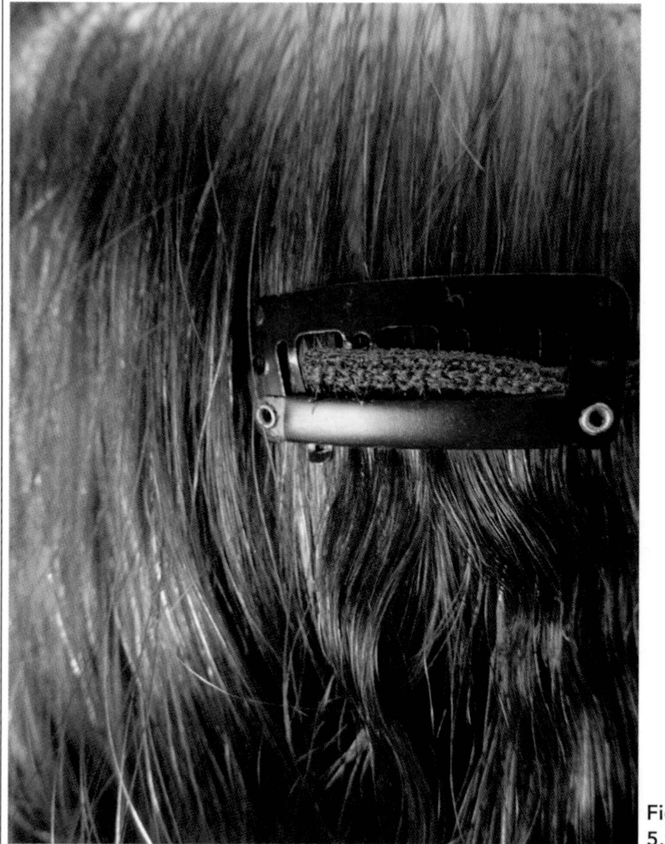

Figures 5.87, 5.88, 5.89, 5.90 Toupee clips in hair

5.90

One full piece with clip-ins is used in large sections of the hair. Backcomb the hair first with a rattail comb. Attach the hair, with the clips on top of the backcomb to help anchor the piece in place. You can also pull the hair through the piece in sections. Comb the hair down in place.

Figure 5.91 Whole piece with clips

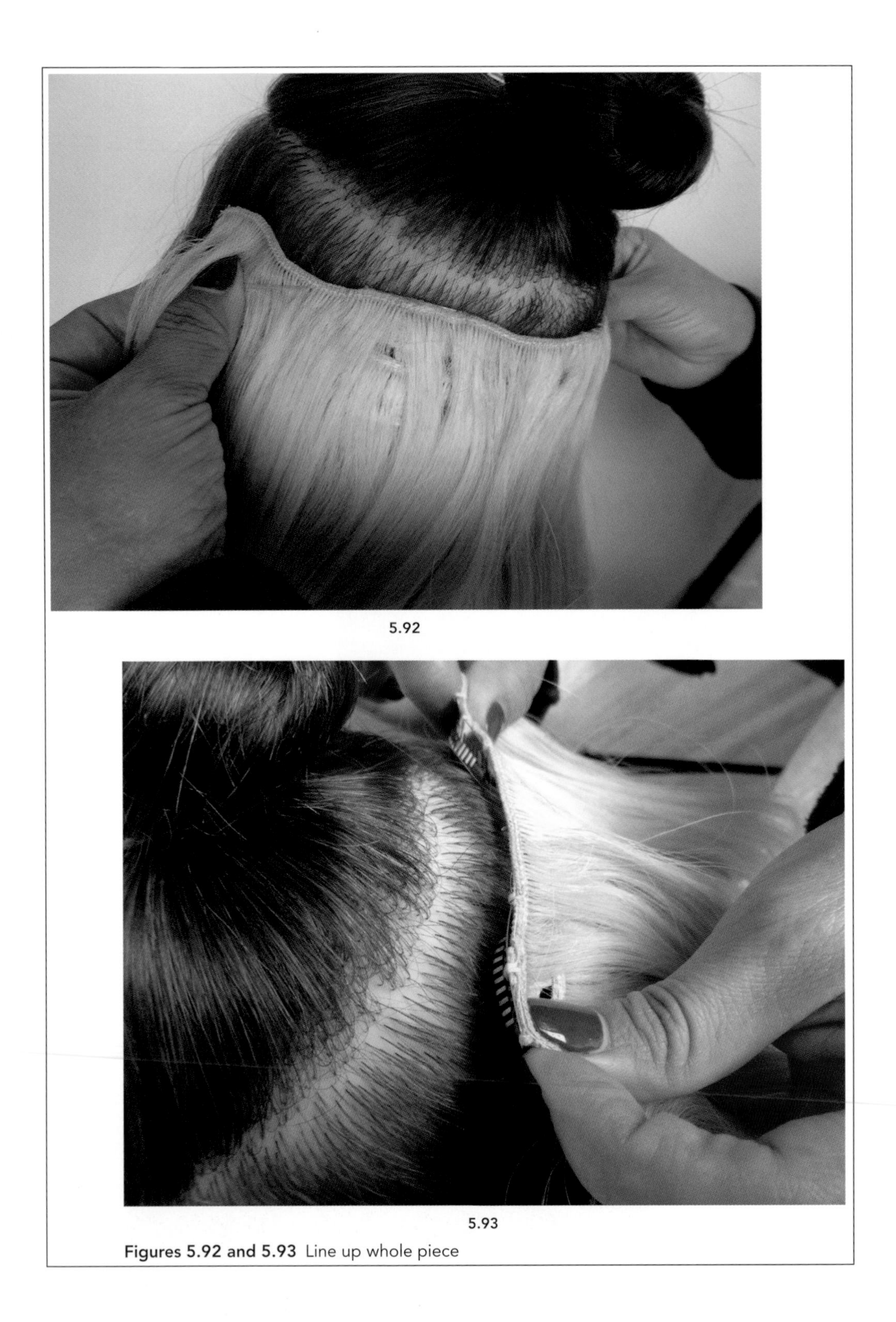

5.92

5.93

Figures 5.92 and 5.93 Line up whole piece

Figure 5.94 Section the hair

Figure 5.95 Back-comb the hair

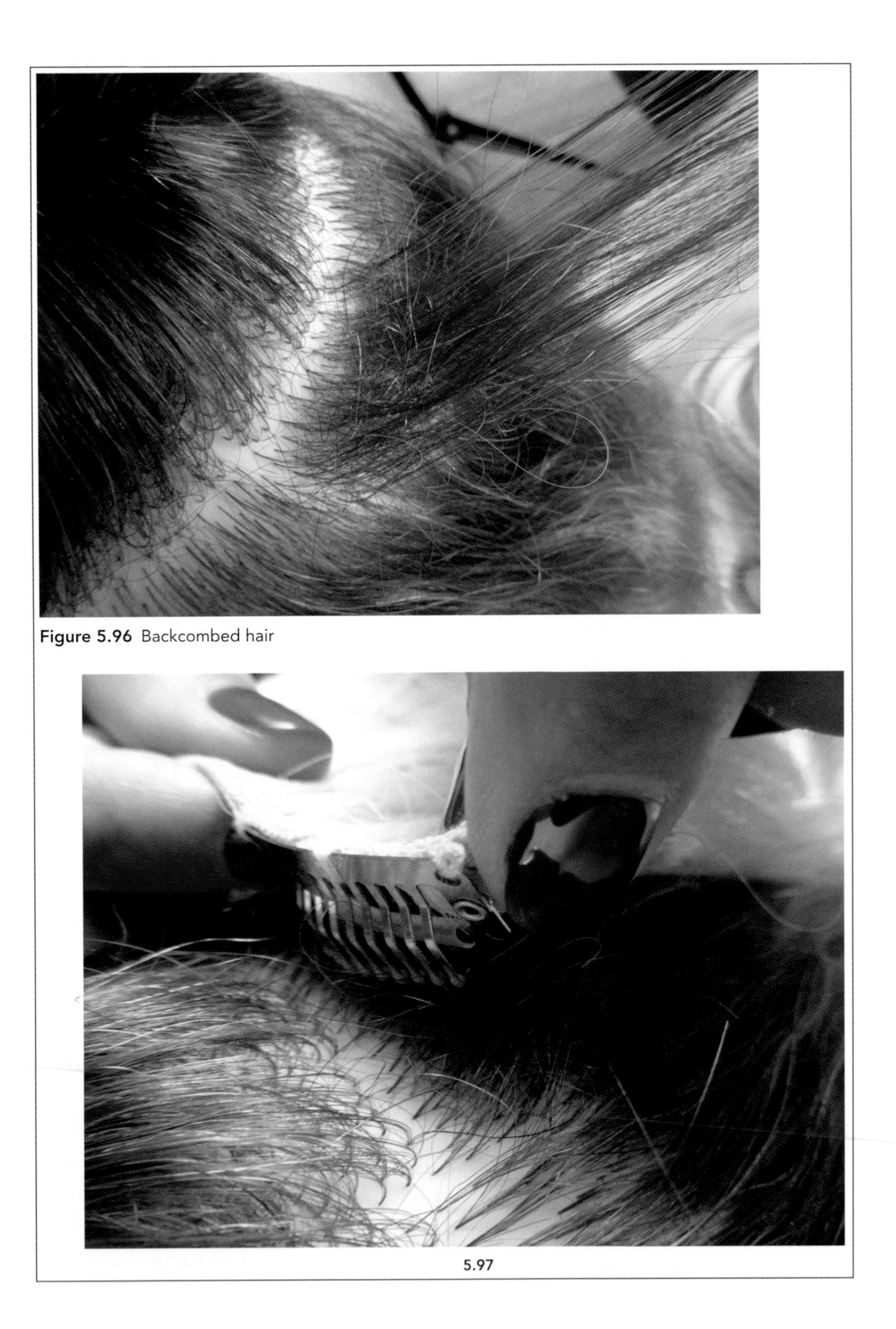

Figure 5.96 Backcombed hair

5.97

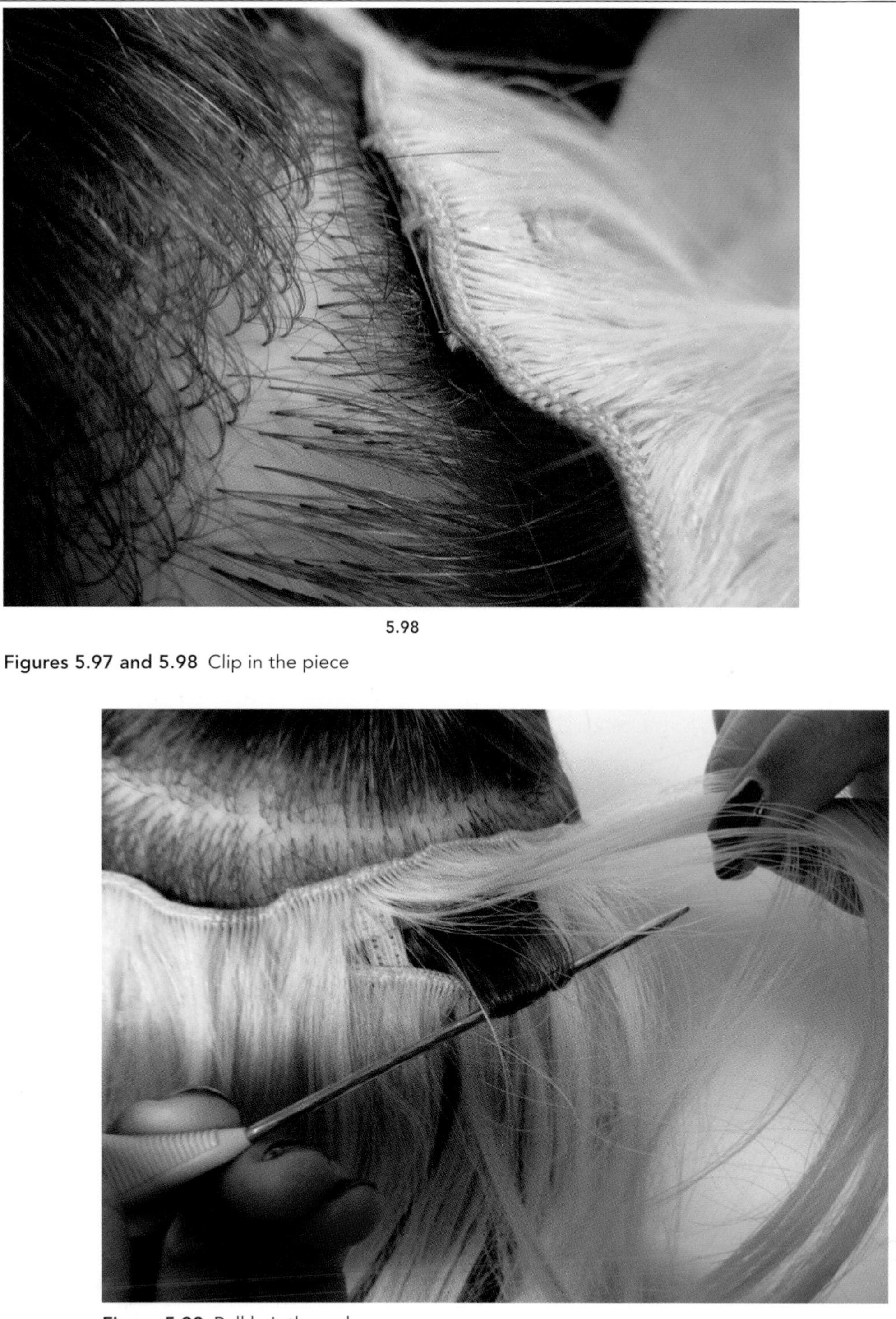

5.98

Figures 5.97 and 5.98 Clip in the piece

Figure 5.99 Pull hair through

Figure 5.100 Hair pulled through

Figure 5.101 Comb through

Fusion hair systems are keratin-based systems that melt the protein, attaching it to the hair. An iron is used, such as the Lord & Cliff Fusion Iron. Wait 24 hours before shampooing after applications. If you need to remove the extensions early, use the heated iron, following with a hair-oil remover. If a few months have gone by, using the remover alone will be fine.

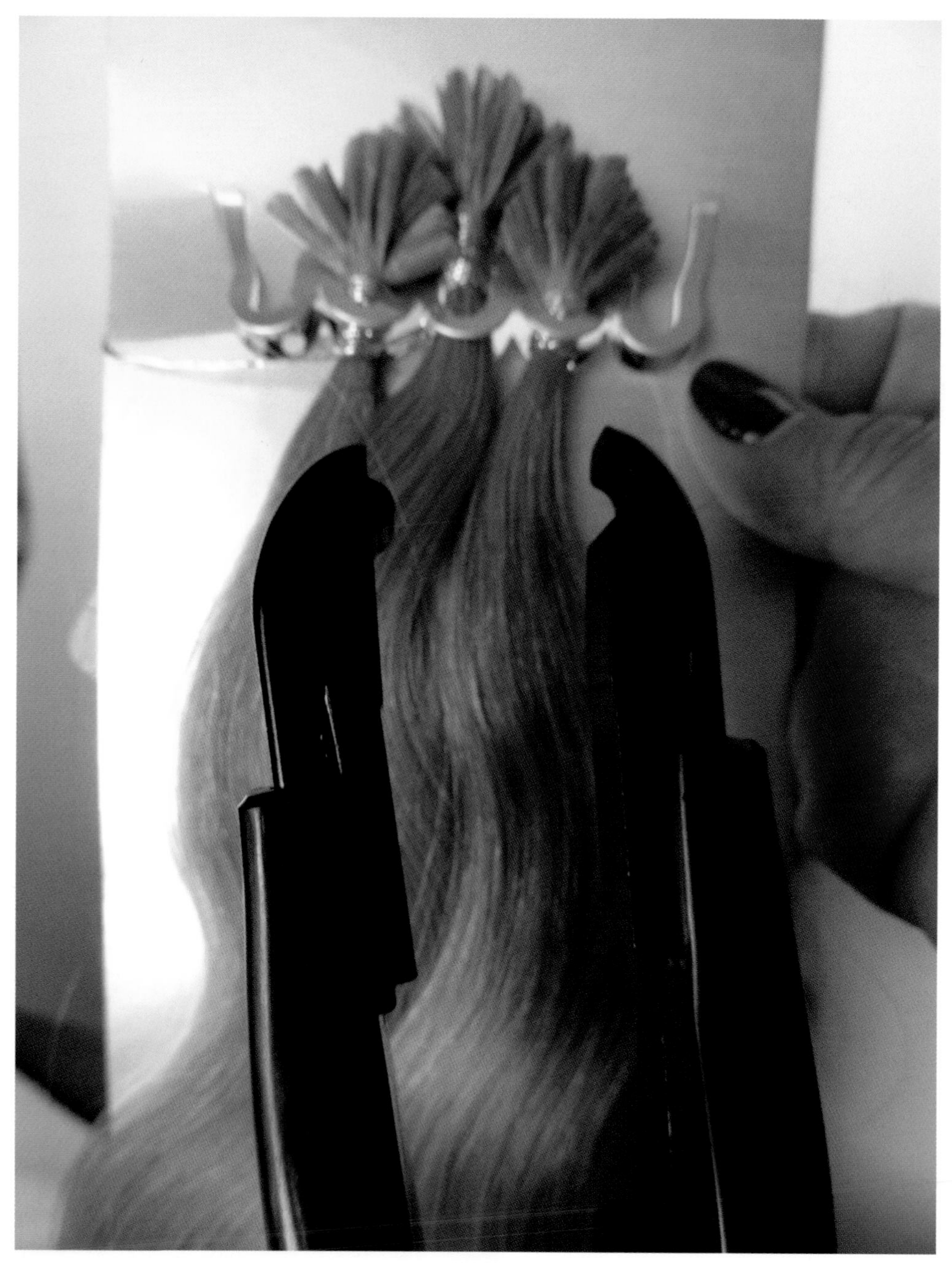

5.102

5.103

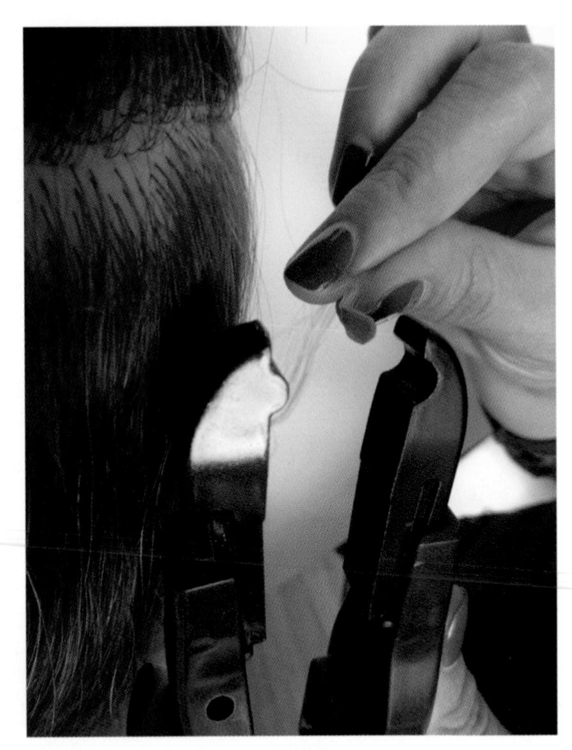

5.104

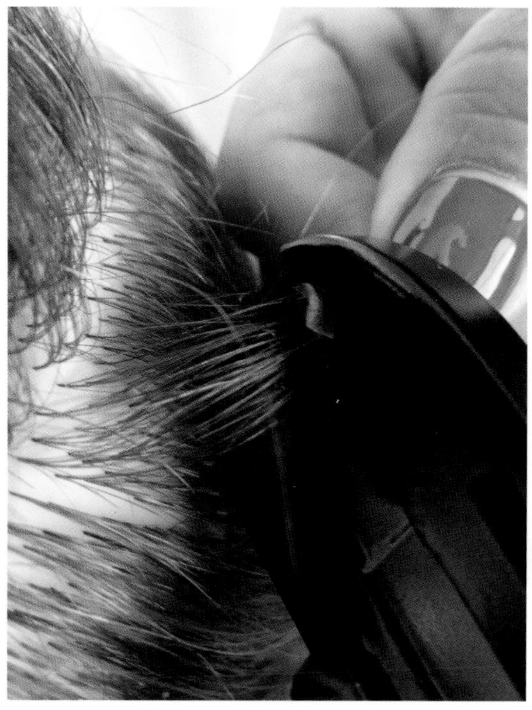

5.105

Figures 5.102, 5.103, 5.104, 5.105 Fusion system

Figure 5.106 Applying heat

Figure 5.107 Fused hair

Dreads

"Dreads," says Yvette, "is a common hair style and lifestyle in films, web series, and television. Dreads are not an easy thing to do, especially where they look full, not flat. You can use human hair, synthetic hair, or cheap bagged hair like 'Kanekalon.'" Yvette explains the process here:

Creating Dreads

Start by anchoring your hair to something sturdy. This leaves both hands free to work. Take a section of hair the size you would like the dread."

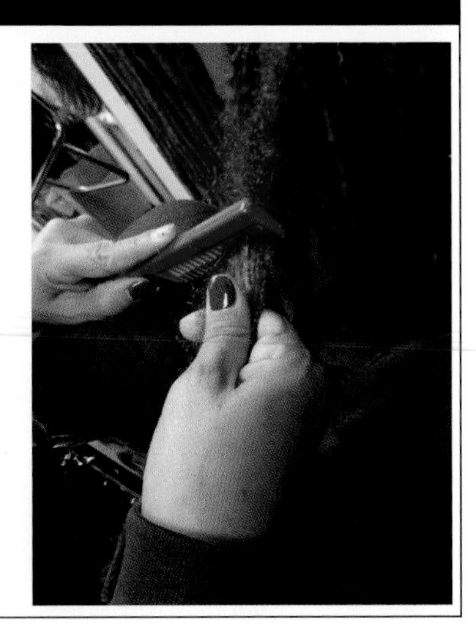

Figure 5.108 Backcomb hair

Use a sturdy comb or backcombing brush. Start backcombing at the base and work your way down the dread. The dread will start to form. You can do this tight or loose.

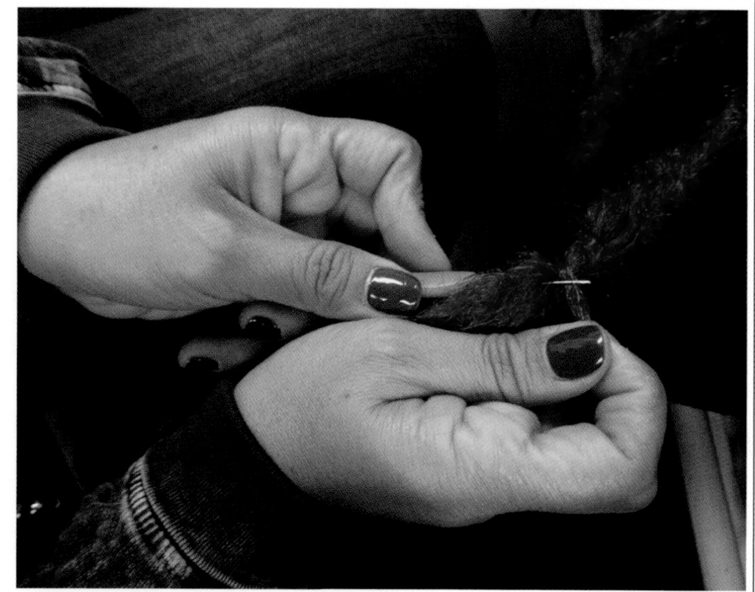

Figure 5.109 Push needle through

For tight dreads use a crochet hook: Size 5 works well. Start moving the hook up and down, sideways, back and forth. Work this knot from the inside of the dread.

Figure 5.110 Roll and steam knotted hair

If using synthetic hair, steam the dread. This will shrink the hair together. Another way to work with a synthetic is to apply to the dread a strong hairspray followed with a blow dryer on high heat. This also shrinks the synthetic hair to a tight lock.

Keep your dreads all together on a string. There are so many ways to use them. Wrap around a pony tail, or sew individually into cornrows.

Figure 5.111 Hairpieces to be worked on

5.112

5.113

Figures 5.112 and 5.113 Hairpieces hanging on a string

Figure 5.114 Finished hair

Measuring the Head

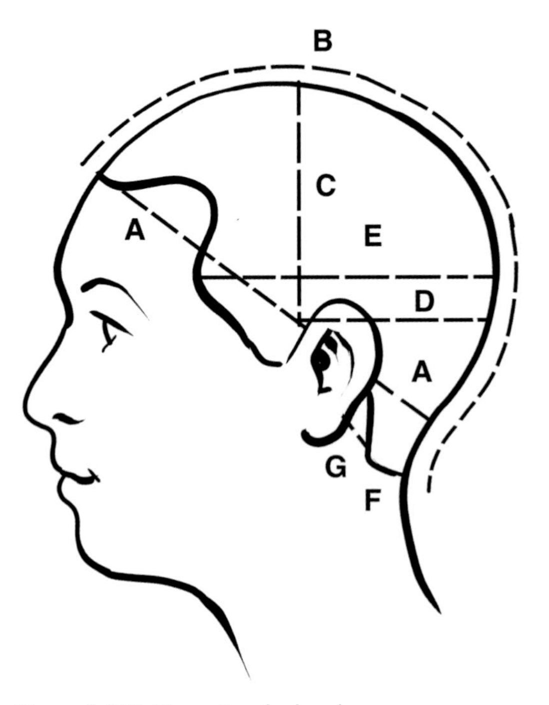

Figure 5.115 Measuring the head

The head of your actor should always be measured for anything that needs to be an exact fit. This includes bald caps. The closer the fit, the better the look will be. Measuring for the face and head can be a really extensive process, but a quick down-and-dirty way is to measure the circumference of the head, ear to ear and front to back. In a pinch these measurements will help the wig maker ventilate pieces to fit. On a bigger budget the actor will be scheduled for an appointment to make a cast of his or her head and neck. Often a wig maker or ventilator will come directly to the hair and makeup trailer to cast or measure the actor for any hairpieces or wigs that actor will be wearing for the show. So, instead of sending the actor to the shop for this service, the wig master will come to us. Sometimes we will do these measurements ourselves and send the finished measurements to the shop or to whoever is making the wigs and hairpieces. Once the measurements or a cast have been taken, a head is then made, which the hair stylists, makeup artist, or ventilator can work off of.

Ventilating

Learning to ventilate, or knowing someone who ventilates, is invaluable. Not only might characters within a story need elaborate beards, moustaches, sideburns, etc., but their photo doubles and stunt men will need to match. It might also be written into the script that the character has no facial hair or a different hair style, only to flip back in a reshoot to a previous look.

Sometimes only a very small ventilated piece is needed to fill in a hairline or bald spot in a beard, or to reshape or fill an eyebrow. Facial hair and wigs ventilated on good film lace are without a doubt the most realistic. There are many techniques for prepping the lace used and the actual knot count of the hair being ventilated. One knot (how the hair is tied to the lace) works well for film or any media of higher quality.

Lace can be bought already tinted, although some artists prefer to tint the lace themselves.

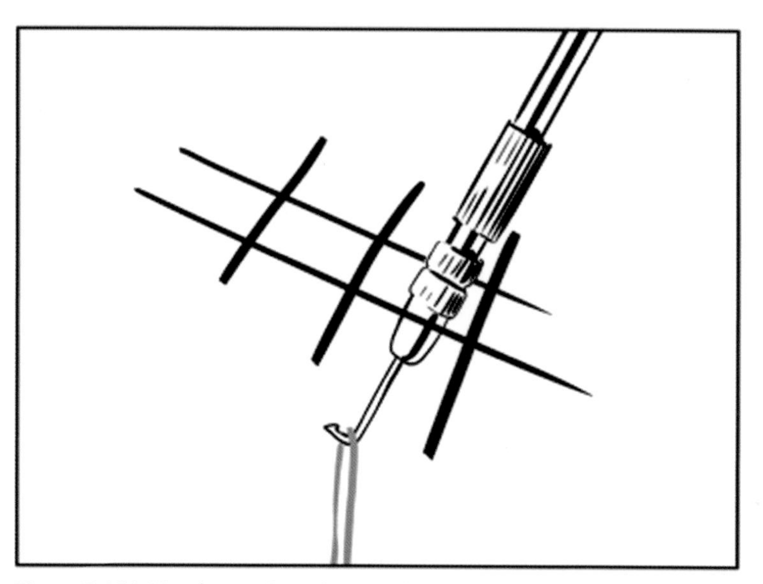

Figure 5.116 Ventilating: Step One. Grab a strand of hair on loop

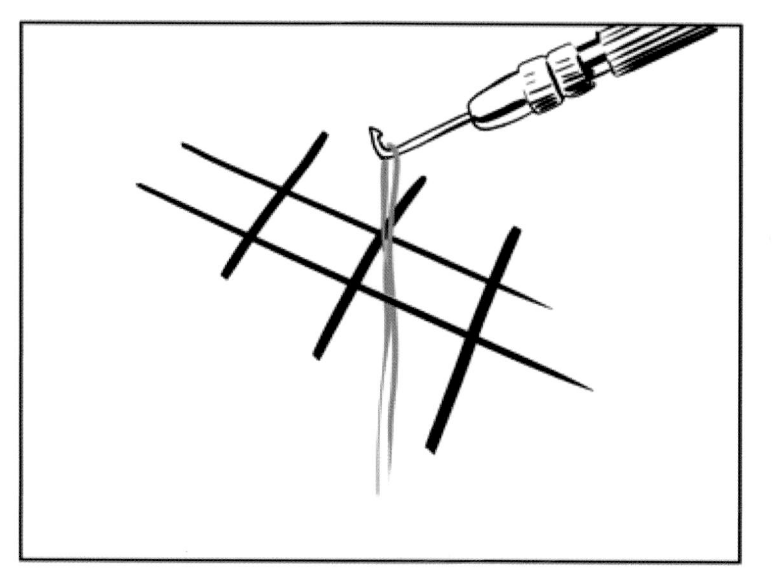

Figure 5.117 Step Two. Pull hair through lace

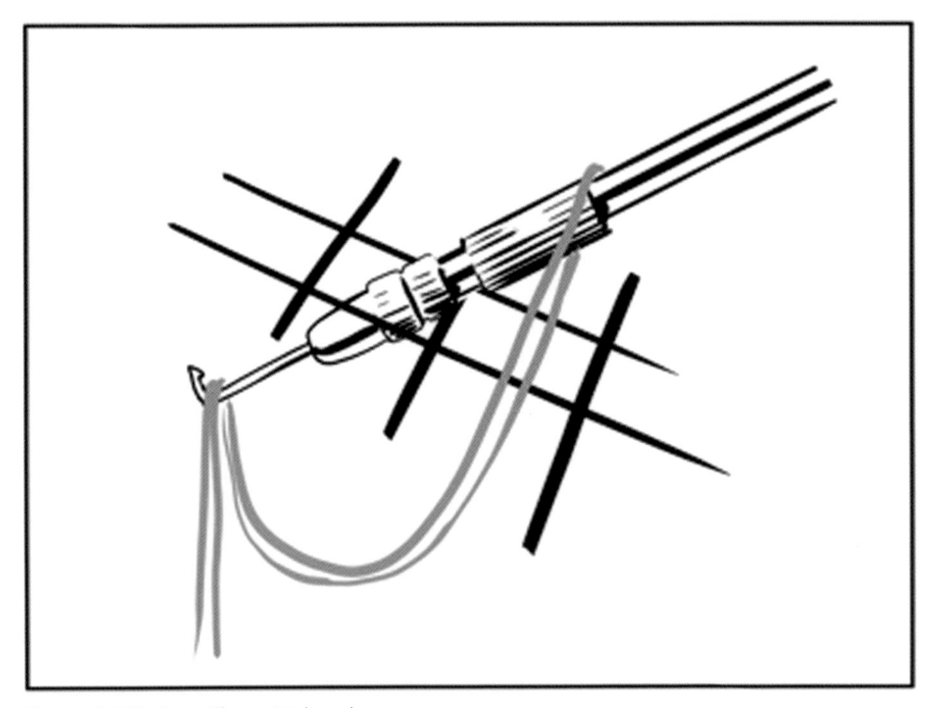

Figure 5.118 Step Three. Make a loop

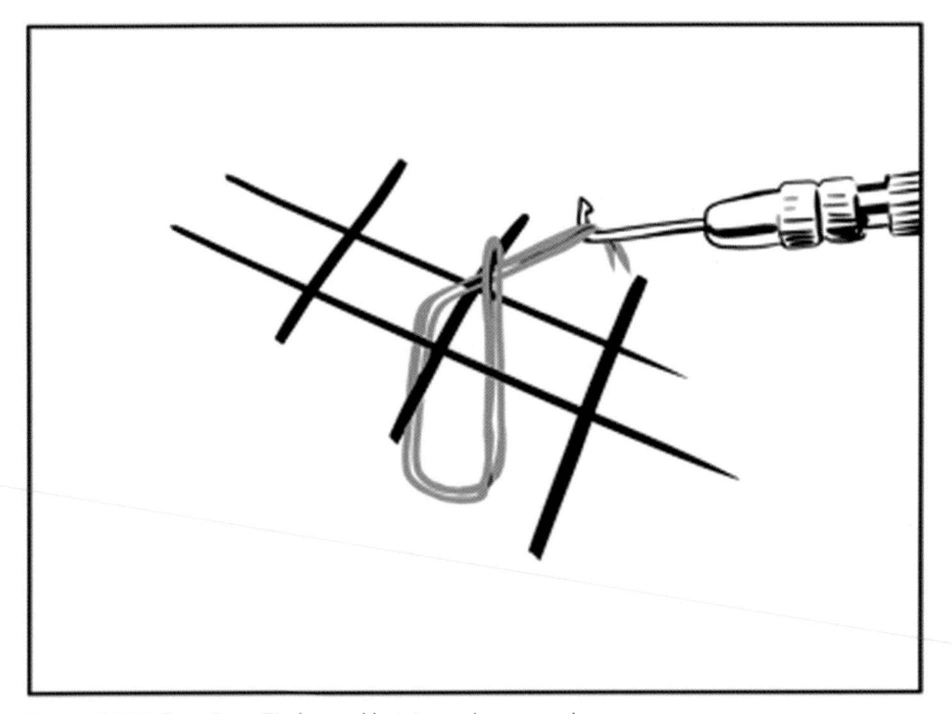

Figure 5.119 Step Four. Tie looped hair into a knot onto lace

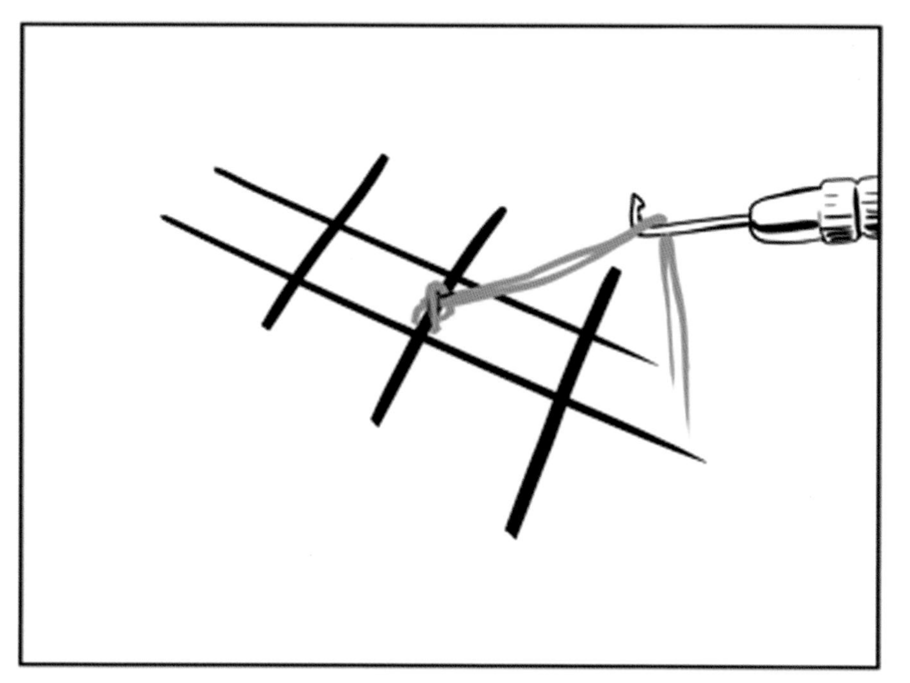

Figure 5.120 Step Five. Hair now secure on lace

Applying a Wig

For every show, work on wigs can be applied a little differently. There is really no wrong way as long as you can see a part through the wig after it's applied, the lace melts into the skin undetected, and the wig stays secure without any lace lifting. (A list of bald caps and related material will be listed at the end of the chapter.) Adhesives are a matter of opinion, and we will go into a number of adhesives and their removers used in films later on.

Working over the years with so many different and talented artists, one thing I am aware of is that wigs, even the best wigs, are not fool proof. You must be vigilant on set: Lace can lift! Be prepared with a set bag that contains tools for any wig-related emergency.

A side note about wigs: If renting wigs for a show for film or television, make sure they are not theater wigs. The lace edge for theater will be too large. Renting wigs mean you cannot cut the lace. If you do, you've bought it. This is a very strong argument for always having wigs made for the actor wearing them, for a perfect fit and the appropriate lace.

You need to know how to prep hair for a wig cap. First, flatten and secure the hair under the cap. The least amount of bumps and lumps the better. Another reason is to control sweat, and you may want to use a barrier spray to help with this. Wig caps can also help to anchor pins to the wig. Film wigs are always applied to look as real as possible. Sometimes in film wig caps are not used. Bald caps are used instead.

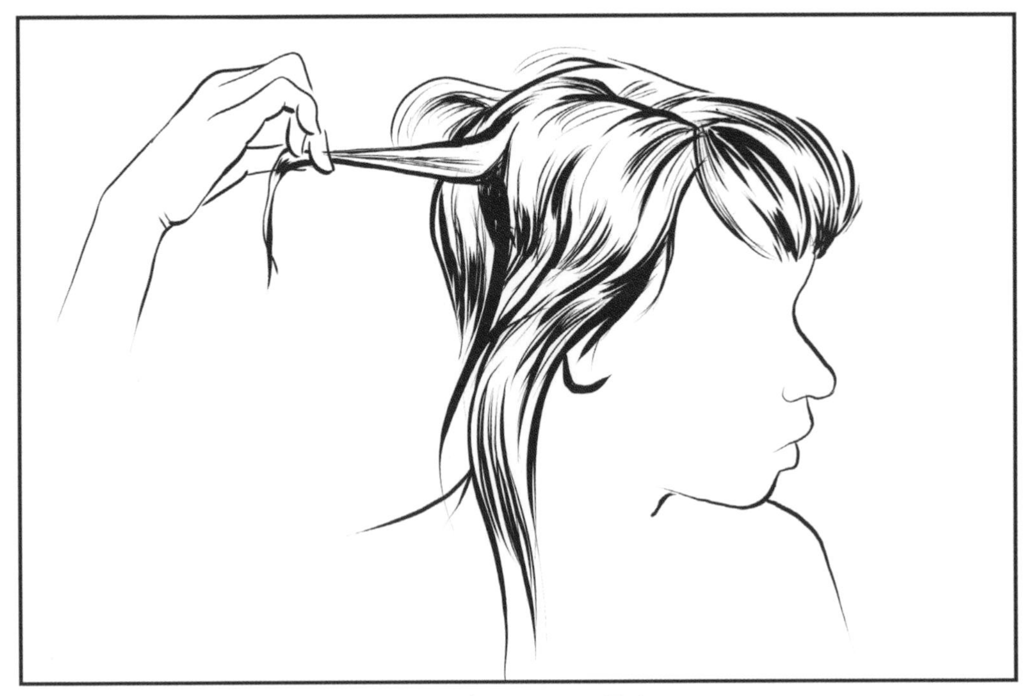

Figure 5.121 Applying a wig cap: Step One. Take a section of hair

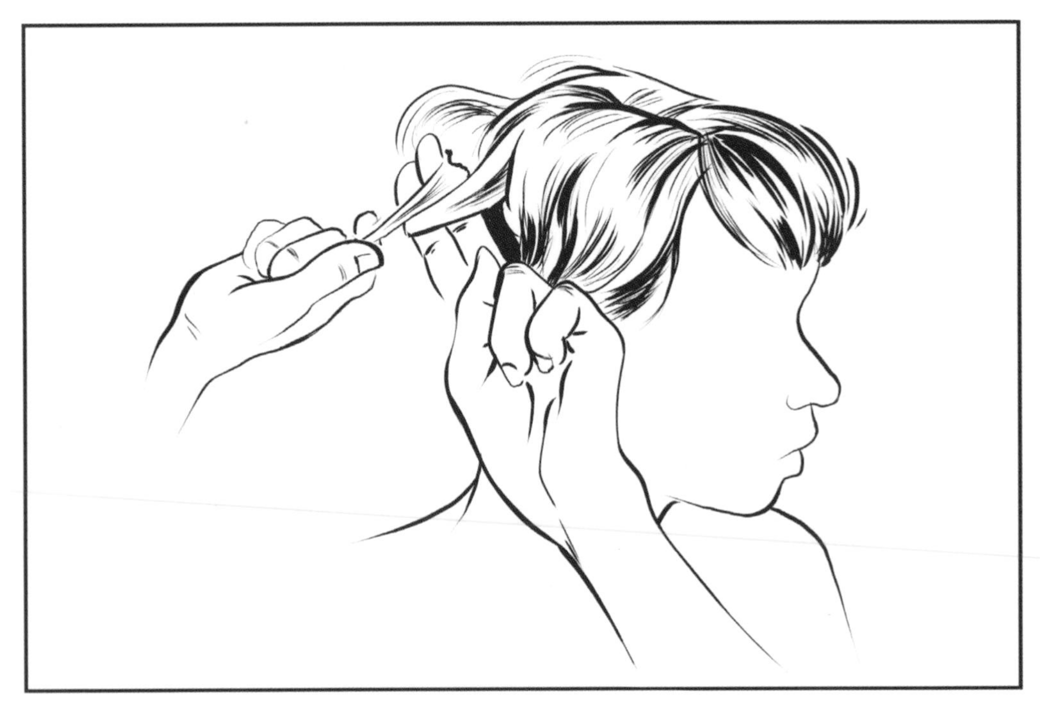

Figure 5.122 Step Two. Wrap the hair around your fingers

Figure 5.123 Step Three. Remove sectioned hair from fingers and secure flat to the head

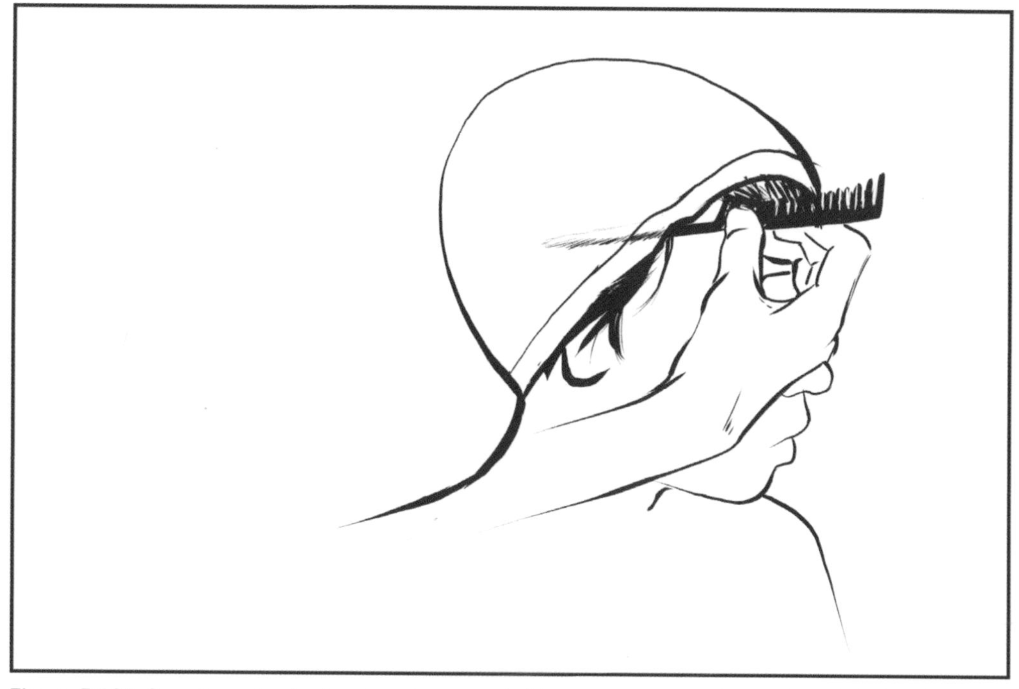

Figure 5.124 Step Four. Apply stocking wig cap or bald cap over prepped hair after whole head has been wrapped. Secure to head.

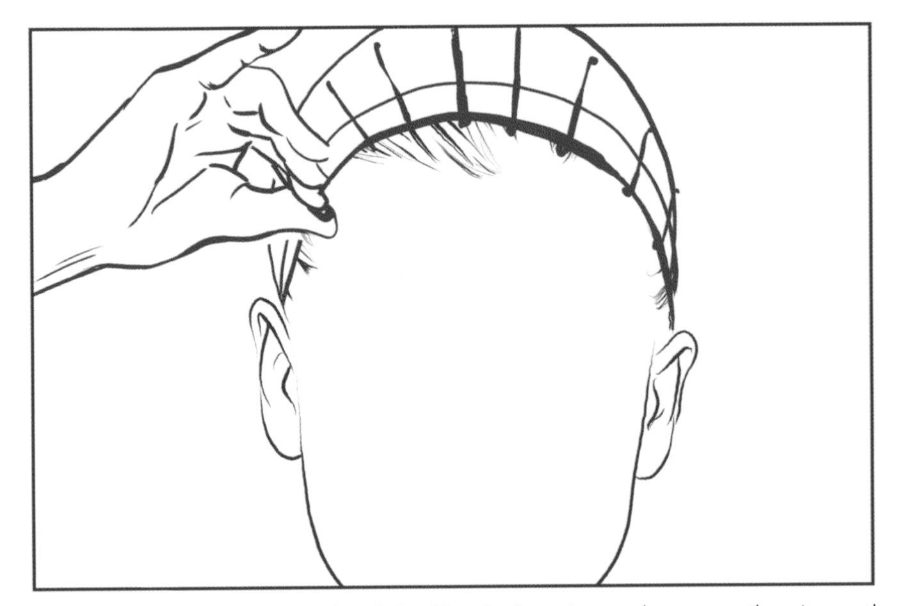

Figure 5.125 Step Five. Secure to head. For film, the less pins used to secure the wig cap the better.

If the hair you are dealing with is long, really curly, thick, or you want to save time, there are other options to prepping the hair for a wig cap. One way is to divide the hair in two at the back of the scalp. Make two loose braids starting from the ear downward. Wrap one braid loosely around the head. Secure with bobby pins. Take the other braid and repeat, but not overlapping the first braid.

Prepping the hair without a wig cap is another option. One way is to approach the prep as if you are applying a bald cap. Use a product like Aveda Flax Seed Sculpt Gel, as not only does this product have a strong hold, but it doesn't stay wet.

Blocking a Wig

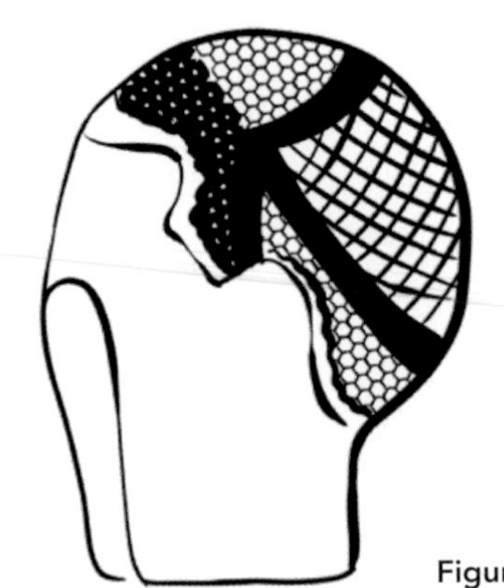

Figure 5.126 Wig block

Susan Stone, Wig Master of the San Francisco Opera, explains, "Blocking a wig is the process of attaching a wig to the canvas block in order to set and style the wig. This is especially important for any lace front wig. Lace front wigs, if handled improperly, rip easily. Blocking lace properly also ensures that the lace lies close to the face without any gaps." Here, Susan explains the process:

How to Block a Wig

To block a wig for theatrical lace fronts you will need a canvas block, ¼- or ½-inch twill tape (bias tape or ¼-inch grosgrain ribbon are other options), bank pins or two-inch corsage pins for the back, 1¼-inch ballhead pins for the front lace, and a rattail comb or brush.

Items you need for blocking film lace fronts will be a canvas block, two-inch corsage pins to block the back, silk pins to block the front, and a rattail comb or brush.

Your first step is to choose the correct size block for your artist's head size. Canvas blocks generally range in sizes from 19 to 25 inches, and sizes increase by half-inch increments. Many wig stylists opt for a canvas block half an inch bigger than the artist's head size, to leave room for the wig prep.

Some companies and artists like to have individual blocks sized for a specific actor by measuring the actor with a head tracing taped onto the block. Often the head tracing is stuffed with cotton batting or paper towels to fill it out so that the canvas block follows the exact contours of the artist's head. Once you have chosen the correct size, you are ready to pin the wig to the block.

Place the wig on the block, making sure the hairline is in the proper place and no edges of the foundation are turned under. Take the rattail comb or brush and smooth any hair peeking out from the lace behind the hairline. Be sure to check the wig in the mirror for symmetry. Blocking a wig properly ensures the lace will lie closely to the face when it's next applied.

Dampen the twill tape and stretch it over the edge of the lace so both edges of the tape cover the lace edge. Pin both edges of the lace every inch with the 1¼-inch ballhead pins. Be sure to stretch the twill tape smooth around the corners. Use the bank pins at each corner of the nape and on the foundation edge just behind the ear. Note: If you are blocking a film lace front wig, use silk pins to block the lace front.

At the end of the show or at the end of a shooting day, all the wigs should be placed on the blocks properly, checking that no edges of the wig are turned under and no hanging hair gets caught under the wig. A moment of care at the end of the show will make your maintenance duties much easier. If there is time, laces can be cleaned and blocked before the next show.

Suggestion: In film, all facial hairpieces and wigs will need to be cleaned of all glues, washed, and blocked to be ready the next day.

Upkeep includes cleaning the lace, making sure the wig is blocked properly, and redressing as necessary. Before you redress wigs, the lace front is cleaned with 99 percent alcohol and a lace-cleaning brush. Natural-bristle dye brushes from Frends Beauty Supply are very good tools for this job. I have also seen stencil brushes and shoe-dye brushes used for cleaning lace. Put a paper towel between the front lace and the block, and gently rock the brush to remove the glue and makeup residue. Do not scrub. It's important to use the proper solvent for cleaning. For spirit gum, use 99 percent alcohol Telesis Super Solv.

Suggestion: There are several ways to clean a lace-like facial hairpiece. The more people you work for, the more methods for cleaning lace you will see, all good tips for developing your own style. One way is to pour 99 percent alcohol into a shallow pan. Soak the piece for a few minutes. Transfer the facial hair to a paper towel and brush the glue off from the front of the piece. Check your work as you go along, and when done, block the facial hairpieces to hold their shape.

Redress wigs with curling irons or hot rollers for quick touch-ups. Smooth away any flyaway hair with a light-working hairspray such as Paul Mitchell Super Clean Extra.

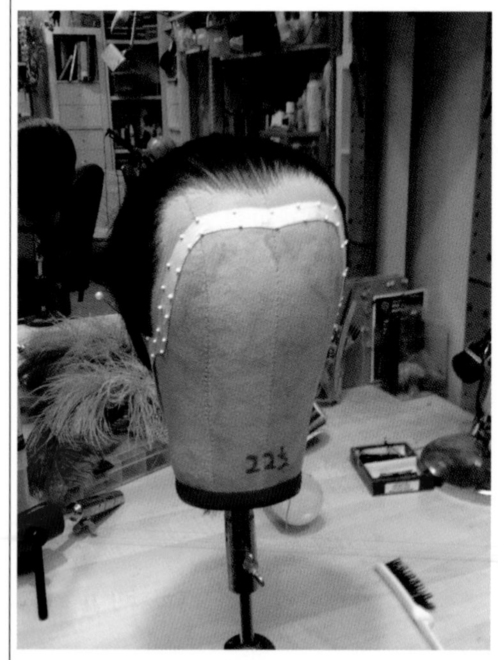

5.127

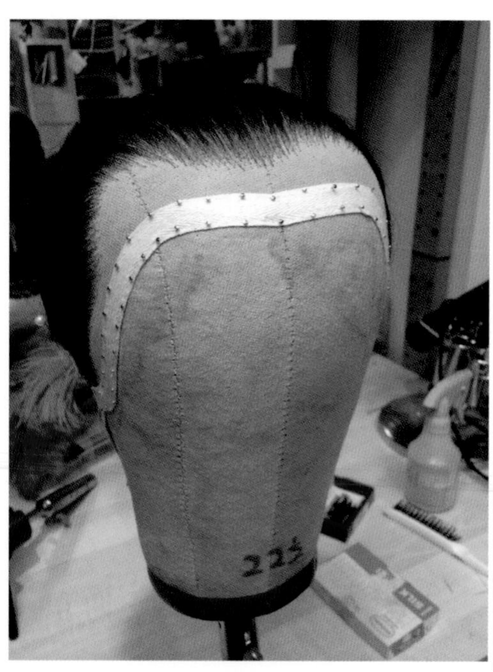

5.128

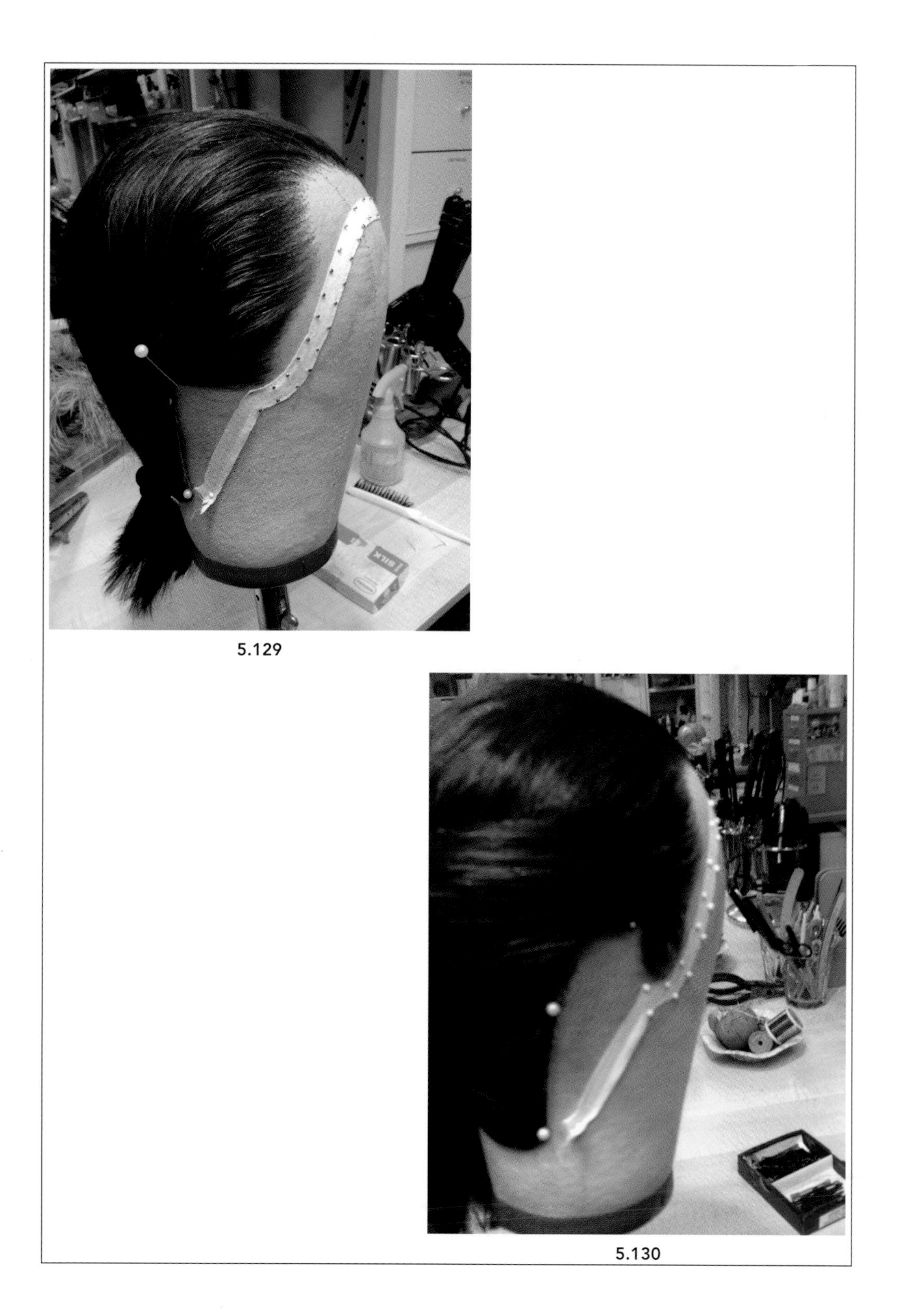

5.129

5.130

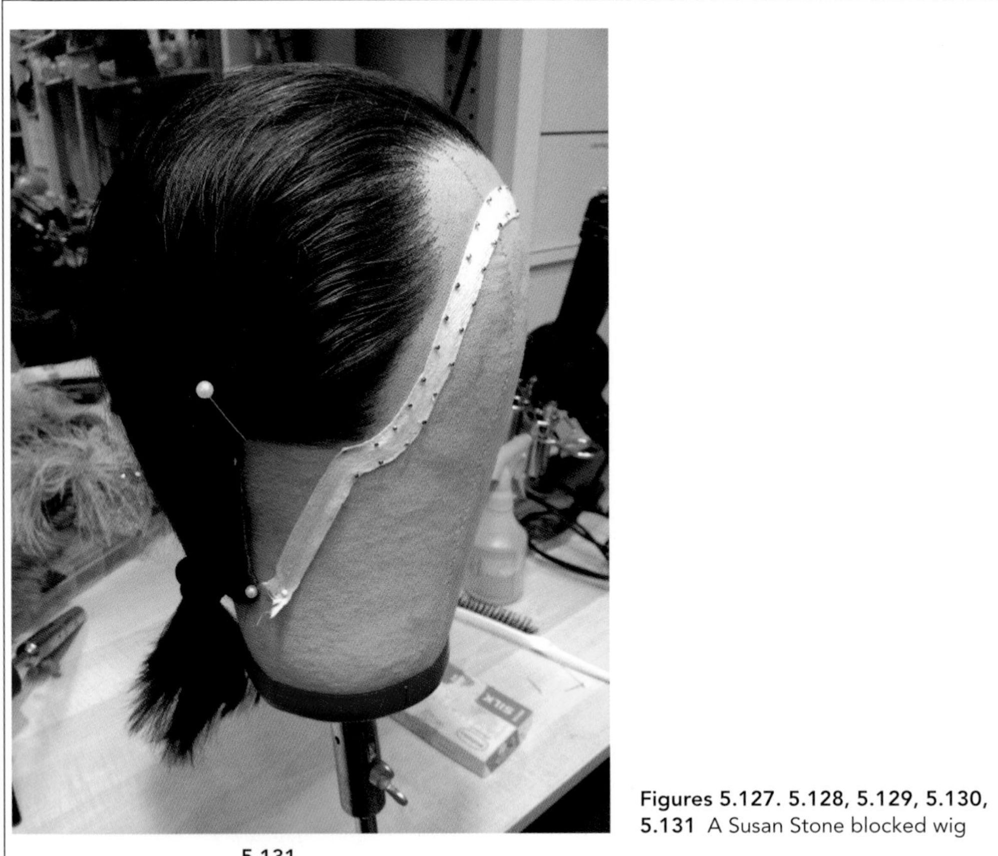

5.131

Figures 5.127. 5.128, 5.129, 5.130, 5.131 A Susan Stone blocked wig

Tattooing on the Scalp

Kentaro Yano designs and produces tattoo transfers for the film industry, and anyone else who needs his services. Tattoo transfers can look amazing or not work at all, and applying them to the actual head can present a few challenges.

Kentaro says, "Clients often ask for designs to be drawn up. Today custom tattoo transfers are a given. You want your character to have a variety of tattoos that reflect who they are. Airbrushes are a tool used to fade or add color to tattoo transfers. When I make transfers for round surfaces like a head I reshape the design for the tattoo transfer on the computer by cutting the images in pieces. This allows me to create a proper fit. If you have an actor who needs tattoos placed on the top and sides of the head, here are a few suggestions."

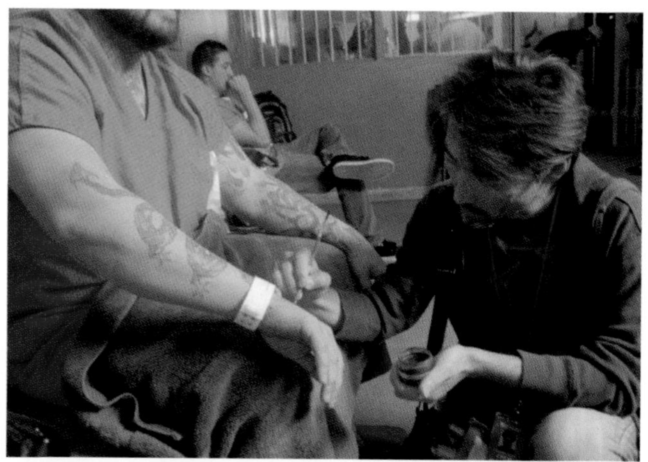

Figure 5.132 Kentaro Yano

Applying Tattoo Transfers to the Head

Prep your station: Every station is individual, but you should always have a towel on hand to keep your hands dry while applying tattoos.

1. Shave the head. This process can be done the day before shooting. (See Chapter 4, Men's Grooming.)
2. Prep the tattoo transfer. Prepping transfers is up to the individual, but a good system is to cut out all the tattoos on the transfer sheet, leaving 1 to 2 mm of white space from the edge of an image. Use an X-Acto blade for an even, smooth cut. If a tattoo you are creating is a bit more complicated, draw markings or trace parts of the image to use as a guide to where to place the tattoo transfer exactly.
3. Prep the area the tattoo is to be applied to with alcohol.
4. Press the tattoo transfer, design side down, onto the skin. The head has different shapes and nuances. Take care to press the transfer firmly all around.
5. Take a small towel that has been dampened with water, pressing against the transfer. When the tattoo starts to slide or float, lift an area of the transfer and check to see if the tattoo has been transferred. If not, lay back down and apply the dampened towel again until all has transferred onto the skin.

Suggestion: Use a small or medium dampened towel for larger tattoos. For smaller tattoos, a damp set-up towel folded into a square works well.

6. Let the tattoo sit a few minutes to dry.
7. Follow with a sealer of choice that dries matte, like Blue Marble.

Maintenance: For emergencies and touch-ups on set, use PPI's tattoo wheel or K.D. 151 tattoo pens for filling in areas that might lift. If the tattoo is looking too dry, apply a small amount of Dermalogica's Active Moist, as this will keep the transfers flexible.

Figure 5.133 Wet hair design (Jenny Boot Photography)

Wet Hair

Working in film and television, there are various options for creating wet hair styles. Yvette suggests using Davines Oil Non Oil, as this product is workable, holds memory, is anti-frizz, and has a wet effect. Yvette uses Davines Oil Non Oil to keep hair that's wet in its original shape, looking like the actor just stepped out of a shower. If you just use a spray bottle with water, you'll end up with a continuity miss: As hair dries, it moves. You also don't want to end up having to rewet the hair too often, annoying or needlessly soaking the actor. To use the Davines Oil Non Oil for this effect, wet the hair, then apply the product to the hair, shaping the desired look. Right before the actor is ready to shoot, spritz the hair lightly with an Evian spray. Your style will maintain a wet look, and will not change from the start of the shot.

Adhesives and Removers that Can Be Used in Hair

Aqua Bond

An acrylic-based adhesive that works well for lace hairpieces and wigs. Aqua Bond has strong holding power and can be used with Top Guard Skin Barrier. Remove with Super Solv or Super Solv Plus.

Beta Bond

This polymer acrylic daily-wear adhesive dries clear and can be removed with Beta Solv.

K.D. 151 Extra Strength Ultra Matte Lace Adhesive

A spirit gum adhesive with a strong hold. Excellent for lace fronts, and laid facial hair.

Prime Bond Plus

A professional adhesive made from natural latex, Prime Bond is used for a permanent adhesion.

Prime On: Professional Use

This removes all the buildup from multiple products in synthetic hair.

Shaving Cream

Have a dozen of the small travel sizes for all your peeps in the trailer and in BG (background). Keep one large can at each station. Shaving cream will gently remove most residues from hair. Follow with a warm damp towel from the hot towel bin.

Sigma Bond

An acrylic-based bond designed for lace fronts. This gives long-lasting adhesion, and can be used with Top Guard Skin Barrier for extra holding power. Remove with Super Solv, Super Solv Gel, or Super Solv Plus.

Silicon-Based Adhesive

This dries quickly with a permanent attachment quality. Use with silicon adhesive thinner for less attachment, and remove with Super Solv or EZ-Off.

Telesis 5 Silicone Matte Lace Adhesive

An adhesive formulated to work well with laying hair or applying lace fronts. The adhesive stays matte when dry.

Telesis Makeup Remover

This product removes adhesive residues, and is safe to use around the face, eyes, and lips.

Unlace-Wig Adhesive

This adhesive remover is used to remove lace fronts and delicate hair systems.

W.M. Creations, Inc. Xtra Hold Spirit Gum

An extra-strong matte adhesive for lace fronts, facial hair, or prosthetics.

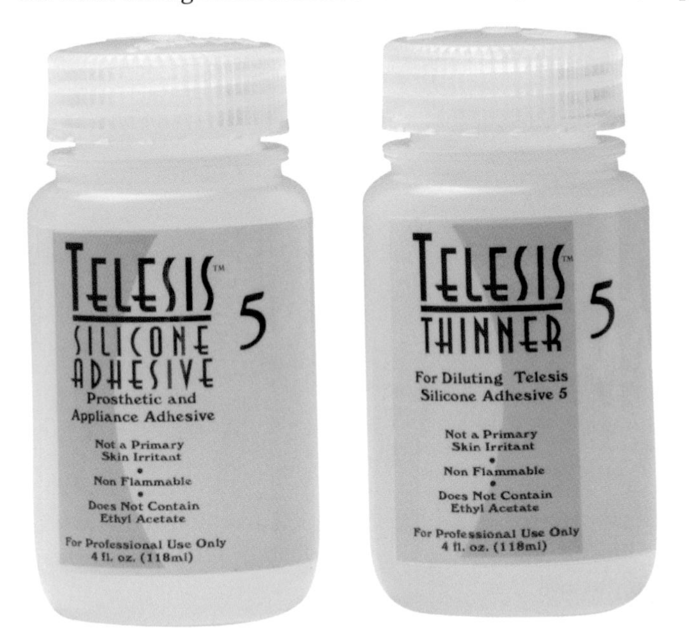

Figure 5.134 Telesis products, Silicone Adhesive and Thinner

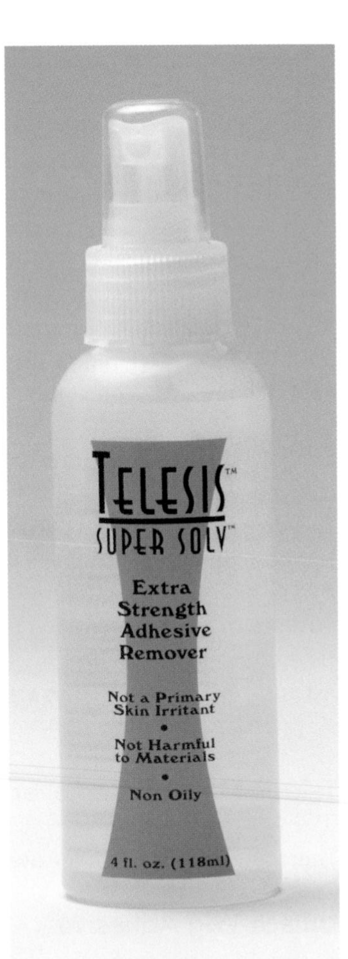

Figure 5.135 Telesis Super Solv

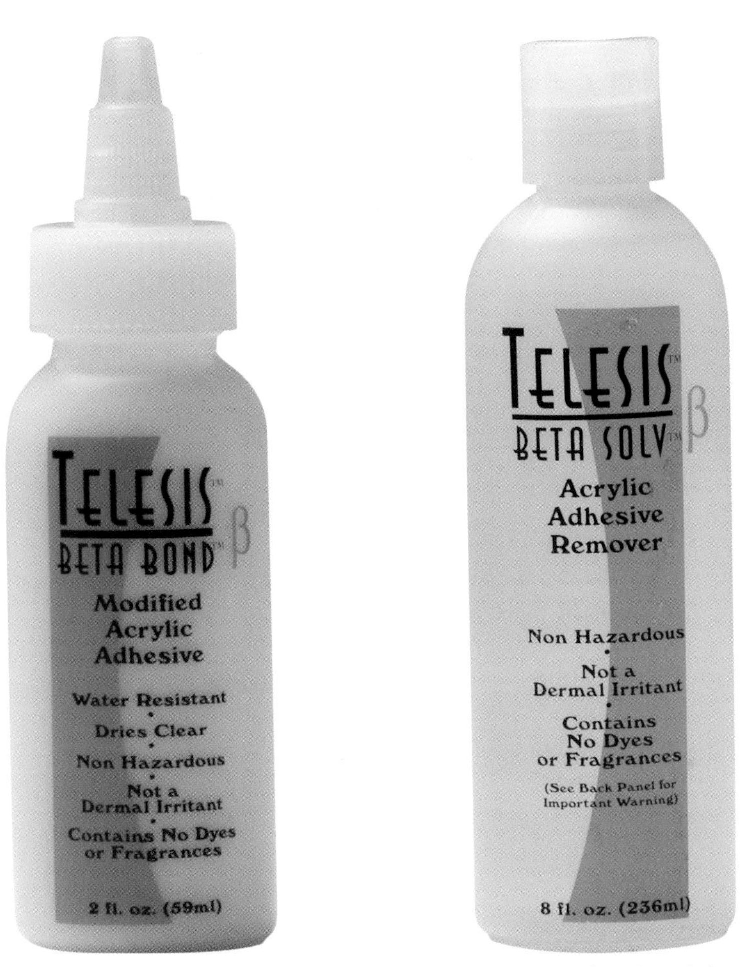

Figure 5.136 Telesis Beta Bond

Figure 5.137 Telesis Beta Solv

All spirit gum adhesives can be removed with isopropyl myristate, Super Solv, and Bond Off. The following are some specialist removers:

Ardell LashFree Eyelash Adhesive Remover

This aids the removal of eyelash adhesives, and is gentle on the eyes.

Ben Nye Bond Off

This is a remover for spirit gums and Pros-Aide products.

RJS Adhesive Remover

An alcohol-based cream remover that removes adhesives from skin and hair.

Bloods

Bloods most often will come in different formulas to mimic real-life traumas: fresh wounds and old wounds, internal or external. There are bloods that will need to work in tubings, on top of appliances, and Lars Carlsson has come up with a blood effect using flock. Whatever the effect, blood, along with adhesives, lace, and prosthetics, will need to be removed painlessly at the end of the day. The following are blood products that can be used alone or with other products like Illustrate palettes, bald caps, hair gels, hair creams, or prosthetics.

Fleet Street Bloodworks Dry

This blood stays looking wet when dry, and can be used in hair. It comes in liquid blood dark, and liquid blood fresh.

Blood Pastes

Blood paste can be used alone or with other products, and dries in place after application. Use a product like K-Y to maintain a wet look.

Street Plasma Soap

This soap removes most residues left by blood products.

Figure 5.138 Fleet St. Drying Blood Dark

Figure 5.139 Fleet St. Drying Blood Fresh

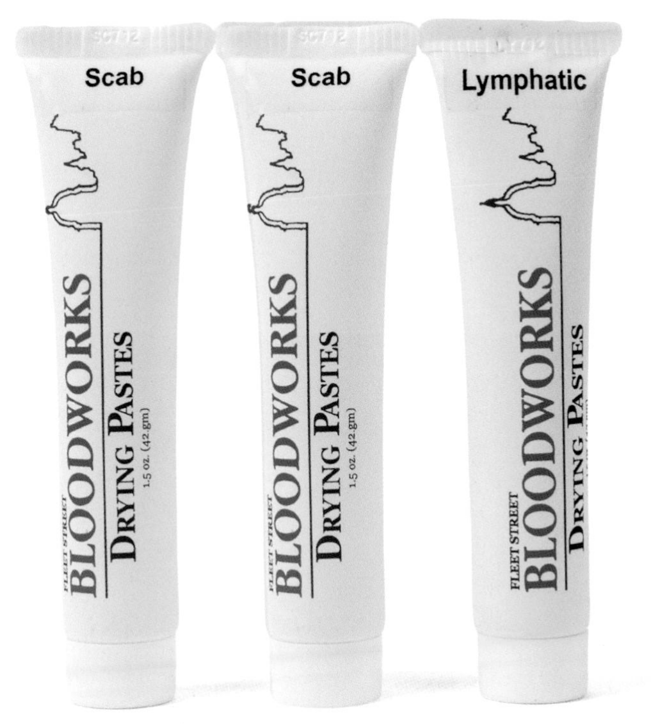

Figure 5.140 Bloodworks Drying Pastes

Figure 5.141 Telesis refresher

Figure 5.142 Fleet St. Plasma Soap

K.D. 151 Flowing Blood

This comes in in bright, dark, and extra dark. Flowing blood will not bead up, and works well on top of appliances, bald caps, and so on.

K.D. 151 Pumping Blood

Available in bright, dark, and extra dark. Pumping blood is used in tubing that simulates blood expelled at a fast rate.

Flocking Blood

Lars Carlsson explains:

"Anyone who has ever worked with fake blood knows how difficult it can be. There is a possibility of staining clothes, skin, equipment, the set, and your actors. Especially in theatre, which can have incredible blood scenes. I sat down with staff and the wardrobe department to figure out a non-staining blood. After testing all types of pigment and colours, the answer was obvious. Flocking! It is made of fibers, which can't stain anything, and you can get them in more or less any color. Mix flocking with sorbitol for a semi-liquid blood, and with a soft hair wax for a blood paste. The recipe is simply to keep adding flocking until you have a color you like and the thickness that you want."

Working with Silicon

Lars Carlsson's Silicon Head with Lace Front Wig

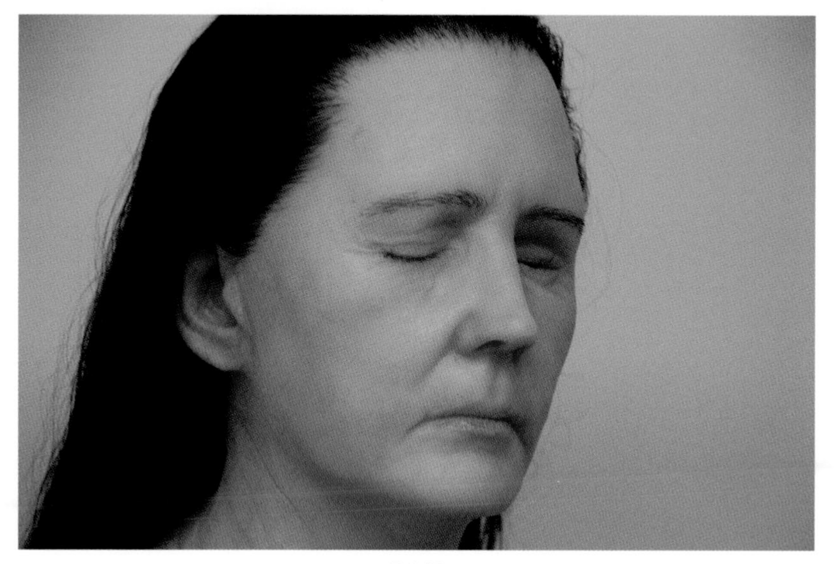

5.143

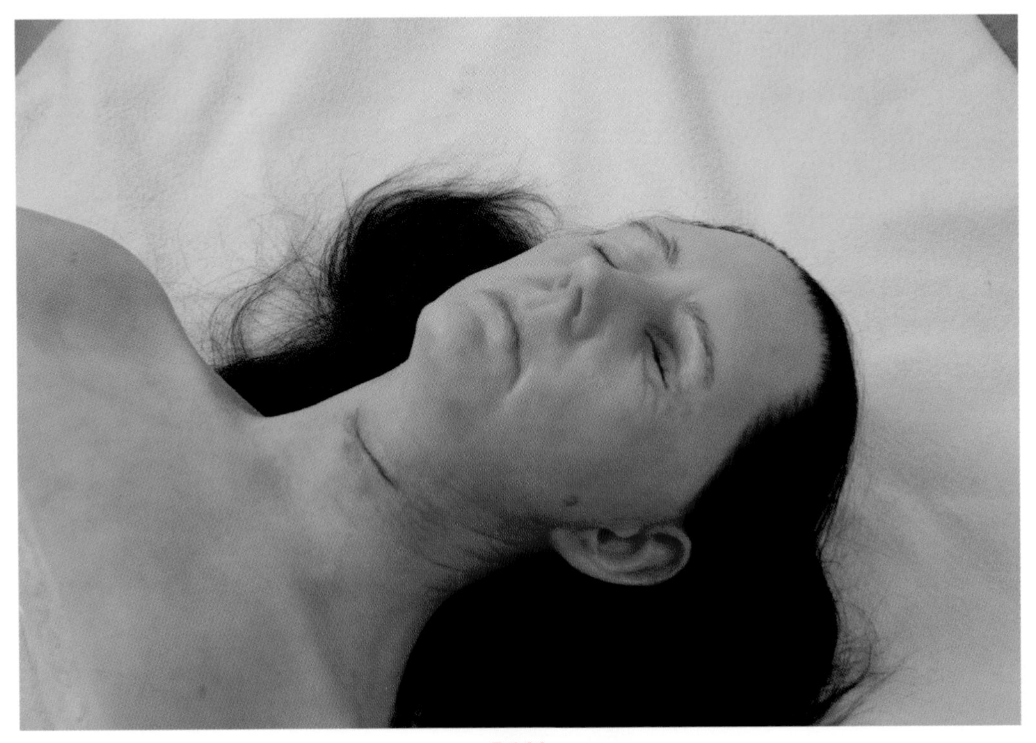

5.144

5.145

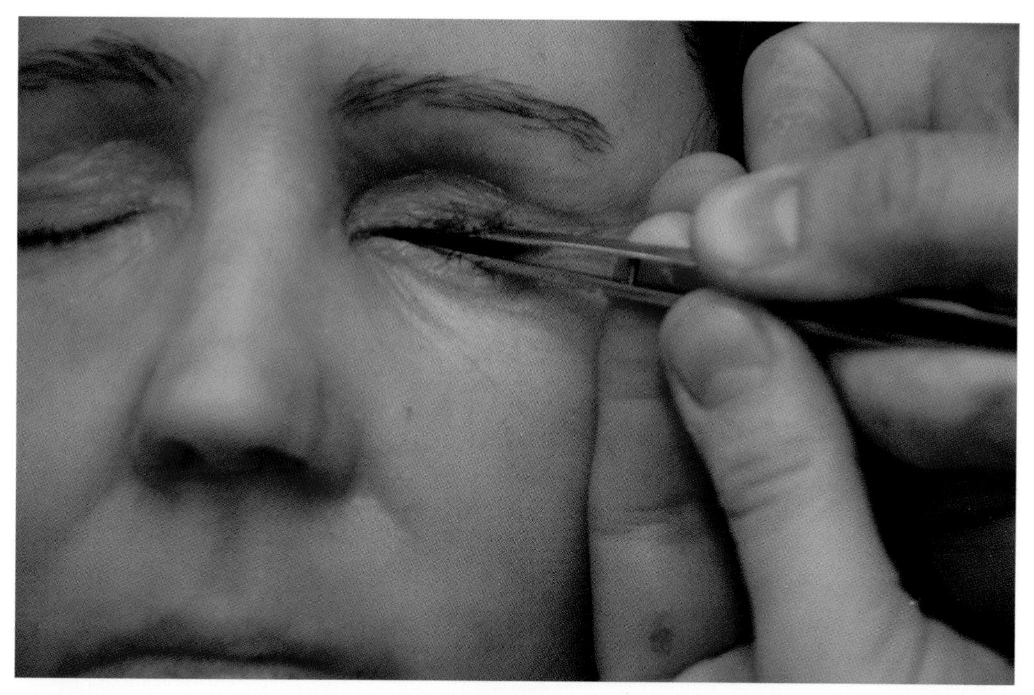

5.146

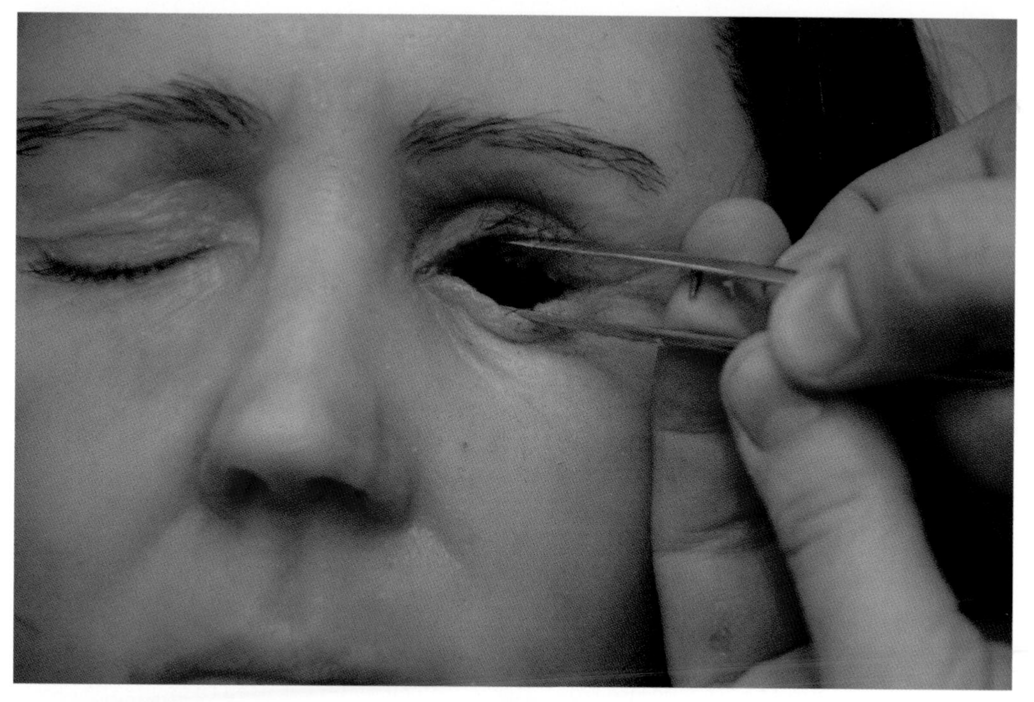

5.147

5.147

Figures 5.143, 5.144, 5.145, 5.146, 5.147, 5.148 Lars Carlsson silicon head

Lars Carlsson's work is incredibly realistic. He knows how important it is that skills in makeup and hair blend together seamlessly, and in theater or film, one person will often be hired to design the whole look of the show, both hair and makeup.

"It is crucial to wear proper gloves and to work under forced and proper ventilation with gas masks with correct filters when working around products like heptane," says Lars, a professional with a working lab. "Do not breathe in. For other safer alternative products to Heptane, we recommend d-Limonene, and Dow 0S-10 solution. Follow all manufacturer instructions, with proper ventilation.

"D-Limonene is a solvent, derived from citrus peels. You can use this product in smaller spaces like a hair and makeup trailer. Dow Corning 0S-10 is nontoxic, colorless, odorless, and can be used in small spaces."

The products you end up using on the actor and on the silicon piece will be two different things. Inks like Skin Illustrator are a safe and effective way to paint on the actor. Adhesives, silicon, or gelatin prosthetics plus lace front wigs will all be materials used to create the lookalike on the silicon head.

For his work in the film *Irene Huss: The One Who Waits in the Dark*, Lars used a silicon piece with hand-punched hair plus ventilated lace wig. There had to be a perfect match between the actress and the silicon head:

"When making a head like this, working with silicon gives me the translucency that's needed. Your cast must not be too transparent or the piece will not look real. Too opaque, an opposite problem occurs and you will be forced to over paint. Painting silicon starts with a base from Smooth On called Psycho Paint."

Lars takes us through the process as follows:

Painting a Silicon Cast

1. Mix a small batch of Psycho Paint then dilute it with heptanes. This will stop the setting process of the silicon.
2. Add pigment, such as Kryolan Supracolor grease paints, that has been previously dissolved in heptanes (see above for a nontoxic alternative) and stored in a solvent-proof bottle.
3. Never paint a silicon cast more than a week old. Any older, the paints will not stick well.
4. Before painting, wash the whole surface first with acetone or IPA to remove all dirt and grease.
5. Take a quick swab of heptane (see above for a nontoxic alternative) all over the cast. This seems to open up the surface a bit. Paint will then stick better.

Suggestion: Kryolan 091 Light Blue works well for veins, as does Ben Nye Death Purple for some shading.

"The hair," continues Lars, "is a partly ventilated lace wig with an inch in the front punched in. The work has been entirely done with my crown punch needles using human hair. Punch needles are used to punch the hair into the silicon piece. There are different sized needles for the various materials you would use, like heavy, normal, or fine. Punch needles work by grabbing small strands of hair and inserting them into the piece. After the hair has been inserted, an adhesive of choice can be added to glue the hairs down. In general, hair that is punched, left longer on the inside of the piece, will have a better hold. I purchase hair from Blond and Braun in Austria and Fischbach Miller in Germany, both reliable companies selling top-of-the-line hair."

Bald Caps

Bald caps are used in the hair department for a number of reasons, such as to protect the hair from prosthetics applications, for life casting, and to place under wigs, for example, where there is forgiveness if most of the edges are hidden.

Bald caps used for furthering a continued design can be made fast in the hair and makeup trailer. Mannequin heads, life casts of the actor's head, and Kryolan's Red Head all are good choices for making homemade bald caps, a simple process using materials such as PS Composites. The head is measured, then those measurements are transferred to the head form. Spray Pam on the measured head first, then apply the bald cap material in thin layers, allowing it to dry between each layer. Follow with talcum powder, then start this step again four times. Each layer will pull back slightly from the original edge, which will keep your edges thin. When done, peel the cap off the head, powdering liberally to prevent edges from sticking. Painting can be stippled in with your desired tones before the cap is removed from the head.

Flock or a loose powder can also be added directly into the cap material. I highly recommend professionally made caps for situations where edges will be under scrutiny. To apply a bald cap, see *The Makeup Artist Handbook*, 2nd edition by Gretchen Davis and Mindy Hall (Focal Press).

Bald Capping Material

1. PS Composites Pro Plastic Baldcap Encapsulator
2. Kryolan Glatzan Cap Material
3. BCM-16 Bald Cap Material

Paints

Products recommended for coloring hair and hair pieces are I recommend for coloring hair and hairpieces are Pax Paint, RMG, Illustrators Grunge Palette, Illustrators Scalp, Illustrators Blond, Temptu Dura Liquid Pro set Hair, Temptu Dura Pro Palette Earth, Temptu Dura Pro Palette Hair, Temptu Dura Pro Palette Inked .

Figure 5.149 Illustrator Grunge Palette 1

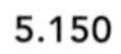

5.150

Figures 5.150 and 5.151 Hair Illustrator Scalp palette

5.152

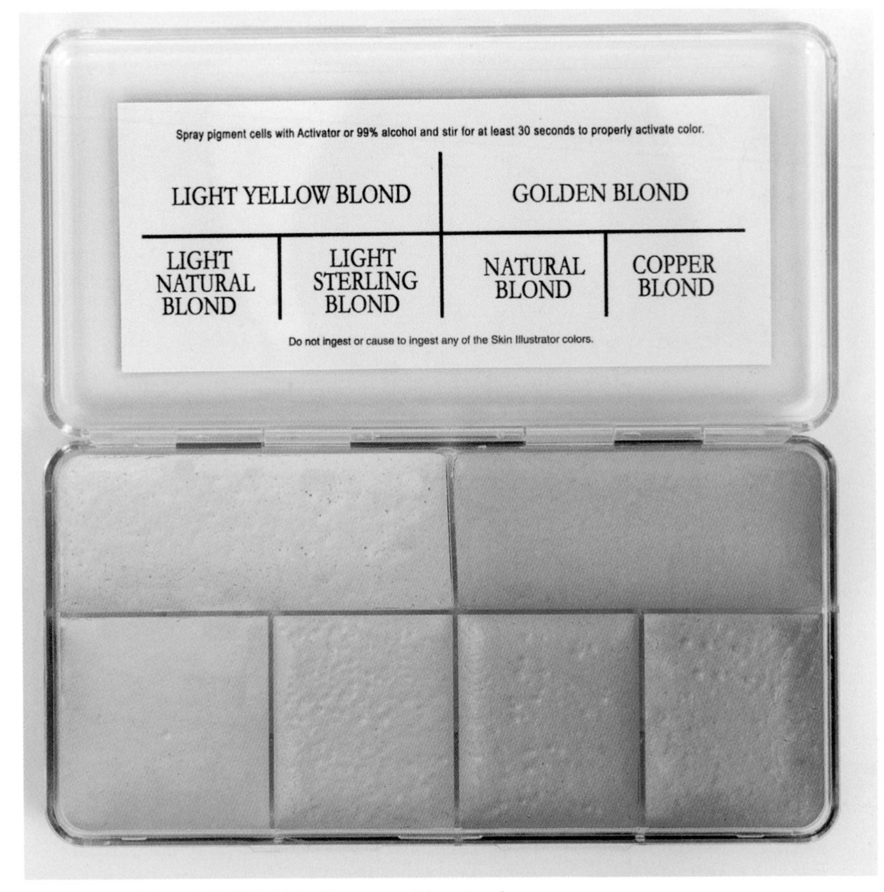

Figures 5.152 and 5.153 Hair Illustrator Blond palette

Figure 5.154 Temptu Dura liquid Pro set Hair

Figure 5.155 Temptu Pro Dura Earth palette

Figure 5.156 Temptu Pro hair palette

Figure 5.157 Temptu Pro Inked palette

Credits

www.bennye.com

Dave Bova: www.davebovadesign.com

Lars Carlsson: www.makeup-fx.com

www.davines.com

Jill Glaser, Makeup First School: www.makeupfirst.com

www.jennyboot.nl

www.kd151.com

www.kentaroyano.com

Keratin extensions: www.patrickevansalon.com
www.kryolan.com

www.lordandcliff.com

Lord & Cliff fusion: www.lordandcliff.com

PC Composites: www.pccomposites.com

www.ppipremiereproducts.com

Psycho Paint: www.smooth-on.com

www.skinIllustrator.com

Yvette Rivas: www.imdb.com/name/nm1006360

Jennifer Stanfield: www.imdb.com/name/nm0822145/

www.temptu.com

TAKE
2
9D
Day Night Int Ext
Mos
Sync
Filter

CHAPTER SIX
Education

Film Productions

After you have been hired, at some point you will be asked to fill out a slew of important forms at the production office. There will also be production meetings, show and tells, testing for hair and makeup, plus fittings. If you are department head, you'll also be responsible for all paperwork and information about the film for the crew that works under you. First step is to fill out start papers and all relevant paperwork, then pick up the shooting schedules, production schedules, and the days in/days out, which will keep you informed about when meetings are scheduled. There is a good chance production has already been emailing you these schedules. Most forms are kept in or right outside of the offices, hanging on the wall in folders. This is to keep crew from asking payroll unnecessary questions about commonly used paperwork. What a difference it makes when you know who and where to go for various answers within a production office. Only ever address a question to the correct department, and try and do a little research first if unsure who to talk to. Always enter an office, and especially a payroll office, quietly. When speaking with someone, use a soft voice. Someone at another desk could be crunching numbers, in a meeting, or on the phone.

The following positions within the production office are important to all crew members (see page 213). These are who you go to to obtain start papers, apply for petty cash, and request PO (Purchase Order) forms just before filming begins.

Suggestion: Before inquiring about filling out forms for petty cash, or start papers in the accounting office, have a conversation with the UPM (Unit Production Manager) about wages for you and your crew, your department's budget, petty cash amounts, kit fees, or anything that has to do with money.

PreShoot Shoot Dates tells you of any upcoming shooting that will happen before principle shooting begins. This form tells you scene numbers, how many pages in the scene, what day we shoot, what is the action, location, and actors in the shot.

Scheduled

Preshoot Shoot Dates Test Day, Mon Date				
Scene Numbers	1/8 pgs	Day	Scene Location Scene Action	Actors in scene

End Test Day Tues				
Scenes: Numbers	1/8 pgs	Day	Scene Location Waking up at dawn	1, 2 Actors in scene
Scenes: Numbers	1/8 pgs	Day	Scene Location Scene Action	1, 2 Actors in scene
Scenes: Numbers	pgs	Day	Scene Location Scene Action	1, 2 Actors in scene
Scenes: Numbers	pgs	Day	Scene Location Scene Action	1, 2 Actors in scene
Scenes:	**pgs**	**Int Day**	**Scene Location Scene Action**	**1, 2**
Scenes: Numbers	2/8 pgs	Day	Taxi Riding around town	2, 4, 5
Scenes: Numbers	1/8 pgs	Day	Taxi Argument In Taxi	2, 4, 5
Scenes: Numbers	2/8 pgs	Day	Taxi Taxi stopped at apartment	2, 4, 5
Scenes: Numbers	3/8 pgs	Day	Scene Location Scene Action	2, 4, 5
Scenes: Numbers	pgs	Day	Scene Location Scene Action	2, 4, 5
Scenes: Numbers	pgs	Day	Scene Location Scene Action	2, 4, 5
Scenes: Numbers	1/8 pgs	Day		BG 10
Scenes: Numbers	1/8 pgs	Day		BG 5
End of Tuesday				

Figure 6.1 Shooting Schedule

Your schedule to follow in preproduction.

Schedules tell you when you have meetings, and Makeup and Hair testing that you need to prepare for.

- Pre-Production Schedule –

Pre-Production

Schedule Dates

Thursday, Dates

---

* * * NO SHOOTING ON THURSDAY

9:00am – Camera Assistants Prep

9:30am – Wardrobe Show and Tell

11:00am – Actor Arrives Airport

12:00pm – 12:30pm Meeting, Makeup and Hair

12:30pm – Location Scout:

12:30pm – 1:00pm –Production Meeting

3:00pm – 6:00pm – Meeting In Screening Room (All Dept. Heads)

TBD – Actor Arrives

Friday, Dates

---

* * * NO SHOOTING ON FRIDAY, Date

10:00 am – Rehearsal with Cast and Director

10:00 am – Fitting Session

10:00 am – Hair and Makeup load in

11:00am – 1:00pm – Rehearsal with Cast

12:30pm – 3:00pm – Tech Scout, (All Dept. Heads)

Sunday, Dates

TBD – Actor arrives

Monday, Dates

Make-Up / Hair / Costume Camera Test

Tuesday, Dates

9:00am – Shooting Begins on Main Stage

Monday, Dates

Rehearsals

Tues. Dates

Rehearsals

Wednesday, Dates

10:00am – Cast Reading

Thursday, Dates

Rehearsals

Friday, Dates

Rehearsals

Saturday –

BEGIN PRINCIPAL PHOTOGRAPHY !!!

Future Meetings:

TBD – Makeup Hair Testing

TBD - Additional Choreographer Meetings

Figure 6.2 Pre-production schedule

Dates

Name of Show

Day Out of Days Report for Cast Members

Pages

Month/Day											
Day of Week	Mon	Tue	Wed	Thu	Fri	Sat	Sun	Mon	Tue	Wed	Thu
Shooting Day	1	2	3	4	5			6	7	8	9
1. Name of Actor	SW	W	W	W	W			W	W	W	W
2. Name of Actor		SW	W	W	W			H	W	W	W

One of the documents for your files is how many days each actor is working. This is helpful to know for continuity and budget reasons when the actor comes in and out of shooting days.

Dates

Day Out of Days Report for Cast Members

Dates

Title of Show

Day Out of Days Report for Cast Members

Pages

Days out of Days Report is an important form. For example if there is an actor with tattoos or an effect that the department head needs to create, design or order you'll know the number of days the actor is expected for the show. Your budget and supplies on hand will reflect that.

Dates | Title of Show | **Pages**

Day Out of Days Report for Cast Members

Month/Day	04/13	04/14	04/15	04/16	04/17	04/18	04/19	04/20	04/21	04/22	04/23
Day of Week	Wed	Thu	Fri	Sat	Sun	Mon	Tue	Wed	Thu	Fri	Sat
Shooting Day	33	34	35			36	37	38	39		
55. SOLDIER										/	
56. HOTEL CLEANING LADY										/	
57. INTERVIEWER										/	

These schedules can change over and over throughout the shoot. Actors are added or dropped. It is your responsibility to stay on top of any changes and adjust accordingly.

Dates | Title of Show | **Pages**

Day Out of Days Report for Cast Members

Month/Day	04/24	04/25	04/26	04/27	04/28	04/29	04/30	05/01	05/02	05/03	05/04
Day of Week	Sun	Mon	Tue	Wed	Thu	Fri	Sat	Sun	Mon	Tue	Wed
Shooting Day		40	41	42	43	44			45	46	47
55. SOLDIER				SWF							
56. HOTEL CLEANING LADY									SWF		
57. INTERVIEWER											SWF

Whenever there is an actor coming on board for the first time, department heads will have a meet and greet to discuss their looks and any wants or needs before their shoot date. The director can also be involved in these discussions.

Figure 6.3 Days in and Days Out Report

Unit Production Manager

Kathleen Courtney, UPM (United Production Manager), explains, "When a crew member is new to the workings of a production office, they often learn the hard way who does what and how they interact with the different positions. A UPM, is a DGA (Directors Guild of America) position in the USA, and is the person responsible for facilitating the physical production of a film on a daily basis, during preparation, shoot, and wrap of the production. The UPM's main duty is to spend money effectively, while staying true to the director's vision and keeping within the financier's budget. Depending on when the UPM joins the film, he or she usually helps to finalize the budget, hires most of the crew, approves all expenditures, monitors costs of all departments, approves call sheets, production reports, cost reports and budgets (along with the line producer), deal memos, start paperwork, and time cards, and often sign checks as well. Budgets are worked out with a line producer, who is usually in charge of that area, but on a small film it's often one and the same person. Department heads should come to me with concerns regarding unforeseen costs, crew on their team, schedules, or incidents on set. Department heads should not bother a UPM with questions concerning lists, schedules, accommodations, and all things that are specific to the POC (Production Office Coordiator) and/or found in the AD's world. If you're not sure, the POC can usually direct you to the proper person to address concerns.

"A UPM is part of the hiring process. He or she will not necessarily choose the crew members, though this does happen, but the Director looks to the UPM to vet candidates, only bringing him or her the appropriate choices for a particular film. I will research rates and various sensibilities, as well as knowledge on how someone works on set, in order to find the best people for a film. Deals are also negotiated by myself, except for anyone who is listed in main titles, for example the costume designer, production designer, DP (Director of Photography), and editor. When everyone is on the same page, it makes for a well-oiled machine. A good team, specifically in hair and makeup, is talented, quick, pleasant, professional, and tireless!

"One question that is often asked is, should you send in a resume to production? The answer is yes! The UPM can often look high and low for the right people. I've even asked my agent to get my name out there. Production receives the bulk of makeup and hair resumes, compared to the other departments. Even if department head positions are already filled, there are often jobs going in other areas in makeup and hair, like keys, second units, day players, seconds and thirds. I will send quality resumes to department heads so they can crew up. Department heads are always looking for talented people.

"What should you do, running a department? Don't forget to regularly NDB your team up to crew call! This can be a constant battle. Also, match your time cards to the production report (times that are given the AD team at wrap). If these are not done properly, or the times don't match, I'll have to hunt people down, addressing the differences in times. Filling out time cards and start papers correctly is a win for everybody.

"Watch your department's budget. Not caring that you are spending excessively is just wrong. Be sure to fill out POs and check requests.

"One of the most important things: Watch what you say. Bad mouthing crew to an actor or other crew members is so damaging. Makeup and hair have such incredible power. Your department can start the day for everyone with joy or conflict. Joy is good.

"Finally, always wrap up loose ends with the POC and UPM. Tell the UPM when you have completed your wrap. Continuity books should go to the POC."

Accounting

Judith Blinick, payroll accountant, says, "Like many people, I fell into the entertainment industry. My high school friend's father worked in WB publicity. I was entranced by the lots we'd go visit. It looked like old Hollywood and everyone seemed so nice. My friend got into the mailroom, but no such luck for me! Years later she knew someone who worked in accounting. I got the job! So what that math was my worst subject! Just like makeup artists and hair stylists, accountants freelance. Local 871 (script supervisors and production coordinators) took us in, but we are not part of the bargaining unit, so we don't have to be in 871. We can get our 'nonaffiliate' IA benefits without being in the local. However, we don't have representation or wage control: It's as negotiated. Sometimes studios will keep the accounting staff working so they can have peace of mind, knowing their staff is up to speed on their particular studio requirements, but in the end we are usually out there looking for work, just like you.

"Payroll accountants, like myself, process all the start paperwork, which has become a monstrous job with all the forms that have to get signed. Obtaining all the necessary signatures can be a job in itself, and crew can be careless when they fill out start papers. When a show starts, there are huge amounts of start packs. Even under the best of circumstances it takes hours to get through them. Information obtained through start packs is entered into an Excel spreadsheet. The spreadsheets are then used for quick reference when starting the payroll process. From there, a crew member's time card is brought out and compared to the production reports for discrepancies. They are approved by the accountant and UPM or production supervisor then sent to the payroll service. A couple of days later, edits are sent from the payroll service and I check them against my breakdown, make corrections, then release them so checks can be printed.

"All accountants run their departments differently. Some accountants have their first assistants run the department, as this helps accountants focus on budgeting and estimating. The first assistants generally manage the team, handle petty cash, reconcile, review the input of the second assistants, interface with the studios, and make sure the studio requirements are met. They will also code purchase orders and generally step in as needed. Since every office is different and the people in them change often, you have to be flexible enough to adapt to different accounting practices on different projects. Accounting offices shift with their own hires' strengths and weaknesses. Here is a rough breakdown of the positions within an accounting department. The bigger the show, the more multiples there are of the same position. Responsibilities may be distributed differently, but this provides a good overview."

First Assistant Accountant

The first assistant accountant manages the team.

Second Assistant Accountant

Second assistant accountants match purchase orders to invoices. They will enter purchase orders, invoices, and petty cash into the accounting software, auditing their input. They are also responsible for reconciling P-cards and Amex bills, and help in auditing the petty cash.

Clerk

Clerks file, hand out the purchase orders, and keep a log, making sure departments are returning what they take out. They will redistribute correct purchase orders, open the mail, answer phones, and help out as requested.

Suggestion: A safe bet would be to inquire about your petty cash to the clerk and not disturb a first accountant unless needed. That would also include calling the payroll office by phone.

Cast & Crew, Entertainment Partners, and Media Services are payroll services that also supply the accounting software used by production. These companies are employers of records. It is their responsibility, as well as the production company's, to see that the crew is paid correctly. Also, when you are applying for unemployment, it is the payroll service that is your employer, not the production company. You slow up your claims by sending them to the show. Payroll services also keep us up on the government requirements, like I-9 changes, the Wage Theft Prevention Act, which now requires yet one more form that nonunion people must complete in order to get paid.

Judith says, "If a crew member thinks they have been paid incorrectly, they should contact me, not the payroll service. For address changes, W-4 changes—anything payroll related—they should contact me. The time not to contact the payroll accountant is on the day the payroll is being processed: Sunday and sometimes Monday, depending on the day the payroll accountant has decided to work."

Judith warns about some common mistakes crew people make, including "not signing all the paperwork. I can't tell you how many emails I send out with unsigned forms or requesting missing information. This takes a lot of any accountant's time, which could be spent processing the payroll. We all know it's a lot of pages, and that people have done it over and over again, but we are required get it all back *signed*. Another common oversight is not filling out all the information on the paperwork: All of it needs to be done. If a crew member doesn't fill out the show's title, production company, addresses, etc., who does? The accountant! Frequently employees also forget to write in the proper boxes for their position, including starts, deal memos, and time cards. No one is a mind reader. Unfinished paperwork will go into a pile until I have time to research who that individual is. This is frustrating and time consuming for me and can cause a delay in payment for you."

Judith goes on to explain some of the terms common to the accounting department, which you should know, as well as how they pertain to you.

Start Papers

The start form and I-9 (and Wage Theft Prevention Act Form if you are non union) are what the payroll service needs in order to pay you. Everything else is from the studio: confidentiality memo, safety memo, conflict of interest form, sexual harassment memo, code of conduct, accounting procedures memo—it seems there is a memo for everything, and the staff in payroll hate it as much as, and I can almost guarantee probably more than, you do. Don't shoot the messenger! Read your contracts carefully. Crews have lost pay by not understanding individual companies policy. Especially kit fee forms.

Petty Cash

This is cash that is given to a crew member to make small purchases (there is usually a cut, for example $300) at places where we don't have accounts. The receipts are then taped on paper and put in a petty cash envelope with the breakdown on the front. Once completed, it is submitted to accounting for reimbursement. Accounting always demands the petty cash requirement for the crew in writing. Please follow the rules so you can be reimbursed. The receipt will need a company stamp, if it's not already printed on it. Please give detailed information on the purchase, so we know where to code it: For example, perhaps you buy makeup or hair supplies for a particular star. There might be a specific account for that star's product, rather than it being charged to general makeup purchases. Without that info, it will be charged to your account.

Prepaid gas receipts are unacceptable—anywhere—but over and over again we see them turned in. There needs to be a final receipt showing what was actually paid, not just the amount you initially gave the cashier. Personal credit card purchases are another problem, as generally these are not accepted by the studios. Try to have us open accounts so you can use purchase orders, not petty cash. If you are at a vendor where we do have an account, use it. Don't give us cash back unless you are reducing or closing your float. We reimburse you for what you spent, and that combined with your cash on hand should total your float amount.

Time Cards

Time cards record what hours you worked, when you took a meal, if you had a nondeductible meal, if you get a box rental, computer rental or car allowance. Your hours should match the production report, or you'll likely get a call or email from me or the UPM.

NDB, (nondeductible breakfast) is to break meal penalties. If you don't eat in six hours, meal penalties compound and can cost the company a lot of money. Because makeup, hair, costume and some other crew are often called in before the general crew call, they kick in to meal penalties before lunch. An NDB gets them in sync with the rest of the crew and the time is not deducted from their day.

BOX RENTAL WEEKLY INVOICE

Production Company: E

Crewmember's Name: Position: Hair

Employer: ______________ Incorporated:

Loanout Company: Yes: ______ No: ______

Federal I.D. #: Put Here______________

Check one:

Rental Rate: $__________ Per Week: ______ *(see footnote below)*

Date Rental Starts: Per Day: ______

Week Ending Date: ______________

Inventory: *(check one):* On File: ____ Attached: ____

Additional Inventory: *(attach pages if necessary)*

ITEM:	VALUE:

I attest that the described equipment represents a valid rental for this production.

______________ ______________

Crewmember's Signature Date

______________ ______________

Approval Signature Date

* If weekly rental exceeds $300.00 per week, a bid form must be submitted to and be approved by Sourcing.

Figure 6.4 Box rental invoice

Every department head runs their crew differently. Personally I like to fill out all time cards and keep them in the makeup hair trailer. This keeps the time cards looking uniform and correct. This includes box rentals and start papers. Box rentals are turned in weekly, and we attach these to the time card.

Itemized Make-up Kit:
Name of Crew Member
Address

Eye pencils 275.00	Sunscreens 55.00
Eye shadows 340.00	Cleansers 500.00
Brushes 675.00	Lash curlers 175.00
Lipsticks 250.00	Tweezers 75.00
Blushes 325.00	Concealers 220.00
Foundations 450.00	Baby wipes 50.00
Powders 260.00	Hair products 530.00
Lip pencils 300.00	Set chair 172.00
Brow pencils 154.00	4 make-up bags 100.00
Press powders 175.00	Adhesives 850.00
Sponges 300.00	Eye blower 45.00
Puffs 180.00	Camera 375.00
Tissues 100.00	

Totals:

Figure 6.5 Kit list

An itemized kit list is turned in with your start papers. You must have this before the papers can be processed. This is just an example. A kit that is brought into a feature film is extensive. The totals would be high.

Below is an example of a memo: memos remind crew of the importance of privacy. You are at work. Family and friends should not visit. Your websites should not have selfies, bragging, or actor's information.

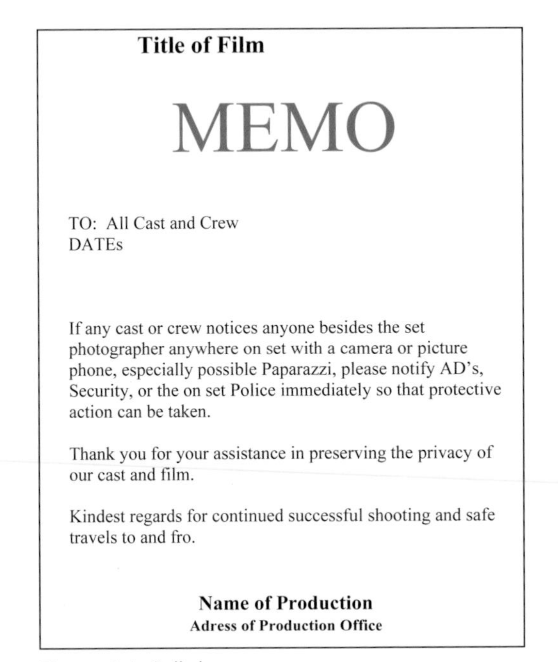

Title of Film

MEMO

TO: All Cast and Crew
DATEs

If any cast or crew notices anyone besides the set photographer anywhere on set with a camera or picture phone, especially possible Paparazzi, please notify AD's, Security, or the on set Police immediately so that protective action can be taken.

Thank you for your assistance in preserving the privacy of our cast and film.

Kindest regards for continued successful shooting and safe travels to and fro.

Name of Production
Adress of Production Office

Figure 6.6 Call sheet

Be sure the production office has a list of everyone working on a regular basis as day players or BG artists. Your people will need to be emailed call sheets at the end of each shooting day. It will be your responsibility to read a prelim (advance call sheet) each day and give to the AD department the correct names of who will be working the next day. The crew count can change daily.

Photography Shoots

The Photographer

Figure 6.7 "Garden of Memories" (Jenny Boot Photography)

Jenny Boot, photographer, explains how a shoot comes together: "Designing a photography shoot starts with images that pop into my mind. Sometimes the images are formed like a daydream. Lovely pictures start to form. This is the motivation to create. It's not until after a shoot that I'll recognize the images I imagined. Drawings can also be helpful in the design process, although my drawings are something only I would be able to understand. Mood boards are created for crew to have a better understanding on what is about to be shot.

"Fashion is often an intimate connection between myself and the model, although working with crew such as hair stylists gives me another point of view. At one time I used to work as a hair stylist, therefore my eye can automatically see where hair should be moved or styled on my models. This inside knowledge is valuable when hiring someone else to work with me. Stylists I hire must have such a talent that I can trust their skills without question. When we forget each other is there, that's when the photographer and stylist become one mind. The best photographs are formed that way.

"For 'Garden of Memories' the summer weather had an influence on me. I was inspired to create an image of lightness. Fond memories of childhood and freedom followed through these series of photographs.

"In the image the model was laying in water. As she rose up out of the water I knew what image I needed to take. Her hair was laid purposely in composition along with the natural elements the water brought with it.

"There is something to be said for stylists who can also convey naturalness even when using styling products."

Photography is a different beast than film and television. For one thing the pay structure can be different. Extremely creative individuals work in print and expectations for your skill set will run high.

Public Relations

Janice McCafferty, CEO and founder of Janice McCafferty Communications, Inc., knows all about what makes a successful stylist. As a licensed hair stylist and esthetician, Janice served on the board of Cosmetologists Chicago. Until she finished her presidency, the public relations committee was her responsibility. It was here that Janice gained her passion for garnering awareness of the industry. During her tenure Janice worked for well-known educator Xenon. Believing in him, Janice propelled Xenon into countless publications. Her addiction to nurturing artists through PR has been gratifying. Today there are very few people who do not know the companies she has made into household names, like CHI or BioSilk.

"When looking for makeup and hair stylists to represent something unique, a story is what draws me in," says Janice. "Their talent and connections also have a big influence. I would never take on a stylist that I could not promote.

"Fortunately over the years I have developed countless relationships with makeup and hair stylists. Not only in salons, but film, television, and editorial. My career, which involves many hats in the area of beauty, helps me to connect the right stylists to the right promotions. For a stylist to be represented properly by me, they would need a resume, biography, samples of work, client list, website, and a social media presence. Today, beauty writers or editors need everything ASAP. If you do not have the time to devote to PR, I won't be able to do my job properly.

"Professionalism is so important. Successful hair stylists have deep passion for what they do. Knowledge is key. Professionals are up on all the trends, and respect themselves and their reputation. You are your own calling card. Just imagine that how you act is a reflection on who you really are. I won't bring on stylists who don't respect themselves or others. Xenon would always say it's not brain surgery.

"As a PR representative, I show the public that makeup and hair stylists are not all these crazy personalities, but hardworking professionals doing their jobs. One of the most egregious acts stylists can perform is to not be on time, along with gossiping and not taking their career seriously. Thank goodness no one I represent has these problems.

"PR means creating unique story ideas to attract the attention of the media, releasing press releases, or on collections that stylists might represent. Also, our agency helps makeup and hair stylists on their media kits. We keep abreast of trends and news, and offer their styling tips to media on a daily basis. It is basically our job to get someone's name we represent out to the public. There they gain the recognition both parties are looking for. A PR agent looks for what you have that we can work with. That translates to celebrity clients, red carpet events, editorial work, or photo shoots that create collections. What do you have to offer in the form of special services and promoting your salon?"

Useful Resources

State Boards of Cosmetology

Different media have different rules. You will know what fits best for your personality and skills. As a hair stylist, going to a cosmetology school is that first step. As of now, for example, to work as a hairdresser in film in the US, you must have a cosmetology license. Not only will going to school get you a license, but you will learn valuable skills in both styling and dealing with the public. Every state has its own regulations for obtaining licenses. The following list will help weed through the system.

Alabama: www.aboc.state.al.us

Alaska: www.commerce.state.ak.us

Arizona: www.azboc.gov

Arkansas: www.arkansas.gov/cos

California: www.barbercosmo.ca.gov/

Colorado: www.dora.state.co.us/barbers_cosmetologists

Connecticut: www.ct-clic.com

Delaware: www.dpr.delaware.gov

Florida: www.myflorida.com

Georgia: http://sos.georgia.gov/plb/cosmetology/default.htm

Hawaii: www.hawaii.gov

Idaho: www.adm.idaho.gov

Illinois: www.idfpr.com

Indiana: http://www.in.gov

Iowa: www.idph.state.ia.us

Kansas: http://www.kansas.gov

Kentucky: www.kansas.gov

Louisiana: www.legis.state.la.us

Maine: www.maine.gov

Maryland: www.dllr.state.md.us

Massachusetts: www.mass.gov

Michigan: www.michigan.gov/cosmetology

Minnesota: www.bceboard.state.mn.us

Mississippi: www.msbc.state.ms.us

Missouri: http://pr.mo.gov/cosbar.asp

Montana: http://bsd.dli.mt.gov

Nebraska: www.hhs.state.ne.us

Nevada: www.cosmetology.nv.gov

New Hampshire: http://www.nh.gov

New Jersey: www.state.nj.us

New Mexico: http://www.rid.state.nm.us

New York: http://www.dos.state.ny.us

North Carolina: http://www.nccosmeticarts.com

North Dakota: www.governor.state.nd.us

Ohio: www.cos.ohio.gov

Oklahoma: www.cosmo.state.ok.us

Oregon: http://www.oregon.gov

Pennsylvania: www.dos.state.pa.us

Rhode Island: www.health.ri.gov

South Carolina: www.llr.state.sc.us

South Dakota: www.state.sd.us

Tennessee: www.state.tn.us

Texas: www.license.state.tx.us
Utah: http://www.dopl.utah.gov
Vermont: http://vtprofessionals.org
Virginia: http://www.dpor.virginia.gov
Washington: http://www.dol.wa.gov
West Virginia: http://www.wvbbc.com
Wisconsin: http://drl.wi.gov
Wyoming: http://cosmetology.wy.gov

Websites

www.aliexpress.com (shears)
www.alternahaircare.com
www.andis.com
www.americancrew.com (hair products and supplies)
www.badgerandblade.com
www.beauty.com
www.braun.com
www.bumbleandbumble.com
www.caboki.com
www.carolsdaughter.com
www.cinemasecrets.com
www.cobella.co.uk (wigs)
www.colormevanessa@yahoo.com
www.concoction.com
www.cricketco.com (Centrix shears)
www.concoction.com
www.daggettandramsdell.com (treatment products, razor bump products, makeup products)
www.davines.com (high-end hair product line, color line, and treatment products)
www.devacurl.com
www.domecaresolutions.com
www.donnabellahair.com (Donna Bella hair extensions, hair products)
www.dyers.org
www.eclipsehair.com
www.evelom.com
www.fda.gov
www.fekkai.com

www.fellowbarber.com
www.fhiheat.com
www.folica.com
www.frendsbeauty.com
www.fxwarehouse.info
www.goldwell.com
www.grainger.com (Eclipse shears)
www.hottools.com (Marcel irons)
www.instyler.com
www.janicemccaffertypr.com
www.jennyboot.nl
www.jeromerussell.com (spray)
www.joewell.com
www.kamisori.com (shears)
https://www.linkedin.com/kathleen/courtney
www.kd151.com (blood, adhesives)
www.kenra.beautycarechoices.com (hair products)
www.kentbrushes.com
www.kerafiber.com
www.kerastase.com
www.kiehls.com
www.kryolan.com (makeup and hair products)
www.loreal.com
www.maekup.com
www.makeupforever.com
www.manicpanic.com
www.mariobadescu.com
www.masonpearson.com (brushes)
www.matrix.com
www.mcmcfragrances.com
www.miragehairfibers.com (Mirage Hair Building Fiber)
www.monroebrush.com
www.murad.com
www.mymatrixfamily.com (Logics Color)
www.naimies.com
www.nigelbeauty.com

www.ojon.com
www.oribe.com
www.oscarblandi.com
www.oster.com
www.osterstyle.com
www.panasonic.com
www.patrickevansalon.com
www.philipkingsley.com
www.pomades.com (Fiber Grease)
www.ppi.com (adhesives, Illustrate palettes, makeup effects, and much more)
www.proproductsandmore.com (cutting capes, clippers, trimmers, shears, scissors)
www.realcolorwheel.com
www.redken.com
www.ritahazan.com
www.rouxbeauty.com (Roux 'Tween-Time)
www.royalshave.com
www.sallybeauty.com (Eclipse shears, streaks, and tips, Claudia Stevens hair highlighter, professional hair and beauty supply store)
www.scissormall.com (Eclipse shears, Shisato)
www.senspa.com
www.sephora.com
www.shearprecisionstore.com (Shisato)
www.shoptoniguy.com (Color Smash Hair Shadow)
www.skinillustrator.com
www.sleekhair.tumblr.com (also http://instagram.com/sleekhair)
www.smoothies.com (Blax hair ties)
www.soniakashuk.com
www.stilazzi.com
www.sultra.com
www.target.com
www.temptu.com (Temptu Dura palettes, Air Pod Airbrush System)
www.theartofshaving.com
www.tinsleytransfers.com
www.topnotchbarber.com
www.toppik.com
www.topshop.com

www.touchback.com

www.trendskin.com

www.tressa.com

www.tricut.com (shears)

www.wahl.com

www.wella.com (Wella Koleston)

www.westcoastshaving.com

www.wigwarehouse.com

www.wolfefx.com (Wolfe Glitter)

www.xfusionhair.info (Hair fibers)

Makeup and Hair Unions

Union representatives can fall under many umbrellas. For instance, makeup and hair can sometimes be represented locally under stage hands or under regionals. To understand your rights and how to join unions, contact www.iatse.net or the list below.

Local 706
828 N. Hollywood Way
Burbank CA 91505
www.local706.org
info@ialocal706.org
Jurisdiction: Hollywood

Local 798
152 West 24th Street
New York, NY 10011
www.798makeupandhair.com
Iatse798@local798.net
Jurisdiction: New York

Local 830
28 Mabel Drive
Seekonk, MA 02771
Ribeef11@aol.com
Jurisdiction: State of Rhode Island

Books

Art Deco Hair, by Daniela Turudich (Streamline Press)

As Seen in Blitz, by Iain R Webb (ACC Editions)

Audrey Style, by Pamela Clarke Keogh (Aurum Press Ltd)

Chocolate Hair Vanilla Care, by Rory Mullen (CreateSpace Independent Publishing Platform)

Encyclopedia of Hair: A Cultural History, by Victoria Sherrow (Greenwood Press)

Fashioning Japanese Subcultures, by Yuniya Kawamura (Berg Publishers)

Fashions and Costumes from "Godey's Lady's Book", by Stella Blum (Dover Publications Inc.)

Hair: Fashion and Fantasy, by Laurent Philippon (Thames and Hudson Ltd)

Hair: Guido, by Guido Palau and Andrew Bolton (Rizzoli International Publications)

Harry's Cosmeticology, 8th Edition, by Ralph Gordon Harry (Chemical Publishing Company)

In Vogue, by Alberto Oliva and Norberto Angeletti (Rizzoli International Publications)

J.D. Okhai Ojeikere, Photographs, by Andre Magnin (Scalo)

One Thousand Beards, by Allan Peterkin (Arsenal Pulp Press)

Pure Beauty, by Sydney Summers (Lucrative Life Publishing)

Sephora: The Ultimate Guide to Makeup, Skin, and Hair from the Beauty Authority, by Melissa Schweiger (William Morrow)

Soul Style, by Duane Thomas (Rizzoli International Publications)

Style Book II, by Elizabeth Walker (Flammarion)

The Allure of Men, by François Baudot (Assouline)

The Allure of Women, by François Baudot (Assouline)

The Look Book: 50 Iconic Beauties and How to Achieve Their Signature Styles, by Erika Stalder (Houghton Mifflin Harcourt)

The Science of Black Hair, by Audrey Davis-Sivasothy (Saja Publishing)

GLOSSARY

Acetone
An organic compound, a colorless, flammable liquid used often as a solvent or cleanser.

Adhesive
A substance that binds two surfaces together.

Adhesive Removers
A variety of substances that remove adhesives. It's recommended to use the corresponding remover to the adhesive you are using.

Air Brush
Air Brushes are used with compressors to spray materials onto a surface.

Aloe Vera
Succulent plant that is found in a variety of treatment products. Has healing properties.

Alopecia Areata
Autoimmune disease that causes hair loss.

Aluminum Beads
Beads made of aluminum, used for attaching extensions.

Amino Acids
Building blocks of proteins.

Andis
Leader in hair products, including clippers and trimmers.

Anlagen
Growth stage of hair follicles.

Anorexia Nervosa
Eating disorder caused with obsession about weight.
Art of Finger Waving by Paul Campari (Bramcast Publications).

Atomizer
Container for a product that can be sprayed or misted onto a surface.

Badger Brushes
Brushes of all kind using badger hair. For example hair, makeup, and shave brushes.

Bald
All hair shaved from the head.

Bald Cap
A latex or a natural material cap that is used by hair or makeup stylists under wigs or prosthetics, or to create a bald look.

Bald Cap Material
Polyurethane material with plasticizers.

Bleach
Chemicals mixed together that remove color or disinfect.

Blocked Nape
Cutting a straight line across the neck.

Blond and Braun
Shop with online facility, that carries hair, wigs, hair products, and makeup accessories.

Boar Bristle
Brushes made from boar hair.

Bowl Cut
A straightforward haircut that resembles an upside-down bowl.

Broadway
Theater district in New York City.

Burn
When skin has been wounded by sun, electricity, fire, or chemicals.

Burr Cut
Same as a military cut but using blade size 1.

Business Cut
A haircut that is on the safe side. Not too long or short. Conservative.

Butch
All-around clipped haircut.

Cabo Transfers
Transfers made with Pros-Aide , Cab-O-Sil, and plasticizer.

Caesar Cut
A short but fringed haircut.

Canvas Block
Canvas block used to style wigs.

Chin Beard
A beard or facial hair on chin and no moustache.

Circle Beard
A round goatee and connected moustache.

Clarifying Shampoo
Removes built-up products and restores shine.

Clairol
Personal-care product line.

Clippers
An implement used to cut hair.

Closed Curl
When the middle of a pin curl is closed.

Colored Foam
Temporary color in hair foams used to alter hair color.

Combs
Grooming, teasing, heat resistant, spring, folding, detangle, styling, lifting.

Conditioner
Product used to treat damaged hair.

Crew Cut
Hair on top of head is tapered from longer to shorter at the crown. Sides are tapered short.

Curling Irons
Different-sized barrels that hold heat used to curl or texturize hair.

Dandruff
Dead skin cells shed from the scalp.

Dermis
Layer of skin between epidermis and subcutaneous tissue.

Diffuser
Helps to muffle sound on a hair blower, plus it channels the air flow in a controlled manner.

D-Limonene
Made with oils extracted from citrus rinds and used as a cleanser.

Dow Corning OS-10
Fluid used as a thinner, or cleanser, in special effects work.

Dreads
Matted coils of hair.

Epidermis
The outermost layer of cells.

Facial Hair
Beards, moustaches, sideburns, and scruff.

Fade
Shorter tapered sides to a longer top.

Faux
To mimic hair styles, like faux Mo Hawks.

FHI
High-end heat products, like curling irons and blow dryers.

Finger Wave
Pinching the hair to create a wave in the hair.

Fischbach Miller
Shop that specializes in hair, wigs, and all related products.

Flat Irons
An implement that heats up, used to straighten hair.

Flat Top
A crew cut with a gradual long-to-short taper from the crown, then cut flat straight across the top.

Flock Material
Tiny bits of flock material used in a flocking machine or mixed into transparent effects products, to color.

Full Beard
A large full moustache and beard.

Fu Manchu
Moustaches that start at the corners of the mouth.

Garibaldi
Full beard with a rounded shape at the bottom.

Gel Product
A product, usually made with polymers, that works to style or hold shape.

Goatee
Facial hair that is located on the chin.

Goldwell
Product line that carries temporary colors for hair, like foam mousse.

Groomers
Personal implements used to trim facial hair, nose hair, eyebrows, or body hair. Often portable in nature, running on batteries. Most groomers have exchangeable heads for different grooming purposes.

Grosgrain Ribbon
A strong flexible ribbon with grooves, often used to block a wig.

Guards
Used on clippers to adjust the hair length being cut.

Hair Blower
An electrical device used to blow air for purposes of drying and styling.

Hair Chalk
Used wet or dry for a temporary color in hair.

Hair Extensions
Real or synthetic hair wefts that are applied

to someone's hair by several different systems.

Hair Fibers
Fibers often made of keratin that are applied by atomizer to give the appearance of fuller hair.

Hair Follicle
A opening, bulb or oil gland from which hair grows.

Hair Lace
Lace that is used to ventilate wigs or facial hair. Film lace is considered the best.

Handlebar
A moustache that curves upward at the ends.

Heat Spray
Product that protects the hair from heating implements such as flat irons and curling irons.

Henna
A dye that is extracted from a plant and used in henna tattoos or body art.

Heptane
Colorless and flammable, a toxic liquid that is often used as a solvent. There are now safer and non-toxic solvent alternatives.

High and Tight
A military alternative to the crew cut. Sides are cut short with a fade into the longer hair on top.

Hood Dryer
A stand-up dryer with adjustable heights. The hair and makeup trailer uses portable hood dryers with a soft hood that is applied directly onto the head.

Horizontal Curl
When pin curls are lined up horizontally.

Hydrogen Peroxide
An agent that contains water and oxygen. Used throughout the hair and cosmetic industry.

Illustrator
Product developed by award-winning makeup artist Kenny Myers. Long-lasting, alcohol-activated product. Comes in a wide variety of colors. Usage is endless.

Inflammation
Inflammation is a way the body tries to protect itself from harm. For example, by removing irritation or damaged cells.

Interchangeable Blades
Blades on a razor that can be removed and exchanged for another.

Interlocking Curl
When pin curls are formed and interlock with each other.

Ivy League
A hair cut similar to the crew cut or high and tight, but left longer for versatility.

Jojoba Oil
A natural plant extract from the seed of the jojoba plant.

Jon Dyers
Expert beard guy! www.dyers.org

Junco
A goatee that extends to the corner of the mouth but does not connect to a moustache.

Kanekalon Hair
An often-used synthetic hair product

that is soft and pliable for wigs and hair extensions. Can also be cut in small bits for laying facial hair.

Kerastase
A professional hair and hair treatment product line.

Keratinization
A process where cells under the skin convert to hair and nails.

Keratin Links
A small tube made of keratin, which is used to attach hair extensions.

Kirby Grip
Another name for bobby pin.

Life Casts
Casting a body to acquire exact measurements from the actor.

Makeup First School of Makeup Artistry
Makeup and hair school out of Chicago.

Mullet
Short hair cut on the sides and top, but longer in the back.

Mutton Chops
Large sideburns that stop at the corners of the mouth.

Myristate
Used as a thickening agent or appliance remover in cosmetics.

Open Curl
Pin curl whose middle is left wrapped open.

Pantone Color Wheel
Pantone is an organization that predicts what colors the industry should use for their products, and in this case cosmetics and hair colors.

Pax Paint
Pros-Aide that is bought pre-colored to paint appliances.

Pompadour
A hair style that is brushed up from the forehead.

Pros-Aide
Water-based medical adhesive used by special effects artists for prosthetics, and in the hair industry. Has multiple usages.

Protein
A protein functions in a variety of ways and contains at least one polypeptide.

Psoriasis
Cells that build up in one place, leaving patchy skin itchy and dry.

Punch Needles
Needles used to punch individual hair into silicon prosthetics or other manmade objects to give the look of hair.

RCW Color Wheel
Don Jusko's color wheel that shows us how to mix colors without using black.

Seborrheic Dermatitis
Patches of scaly red skin. Most often found on the scalp.

Single Blade
Long single blade housed in a case, often used in barber shops for shaves. The blade is sharpened on a strop.

Skeletal System
The bones of the skull, which hold and shape the head.

Soul Patch
A patch of hair found right below the bottom lip.

Taper Fade
Also in the taper cut, temple fade family, this cut is very popular.

Tattoo Transfers
Temporary tattoo applications. Leaders in transfer tattoos are Christine Tinsley, Rick Stratton, and Kentaro Yano.

Thinning
Losing areas of the hair or thinning out hair on the head that is full.

Tint
A temporary color that covers the existing shade of the hair without lifting it.

Toupee Clips
Clips used to attach toupees to the hair.

Van Dyke
Goatee that connects to the moustache.

Ventilating
Weaving strands of hair with a ventilating needle one at a time into a lace to create wigs and facial hairpieces. Also used to refront an existing wig.

Verdi
Rounded beard with the cheeks shaved clean and a moustache that borders handlebars.

Vertical Curl
Pin curls that are lined up vertically.

Wig Cap
The protection between the wig and natural hair. Wig caps are also used to help anchor the wig securely to the head.

INDEX

Page numbers in italics refer to figures.

accountants in film production 214–16
adhesives and removers for wigs 179, 188–91, *190–1*
airbrushes/airbrushing 61, *62*, 94, *94*
alopecia areata 22
aluminum curling irons 79
amino acids 4
anagen phase of hair growth 4
Andis Cool Care 100, *100*
Andis Masters clippers 102–5, *102–5*
Andis T-Outliner clipper blades *79*
anorexia nervosa 23
Aqua Bond 188
Ardell LashFree Eyelash Adhesive Remover 191
atomizers 93, *93–4*

badger bristle brushes 65–6
bald caps 176, 179, 199–200
ballhead pins 183
ball-tipped brushes 68
barber comb 70
barbering shears 75, *75*
beard brushes 68
beard/mustache trimmers 78–9, *79*
Ben Nye Bond Off 191
best badger bristle brushes 66
Beta Bond/Solv 189, *191*
bleaching hair 37, *46*, 46–9, *48–9*
Blinick, Judith 214, 215
blocking a wig *182*, 182–4, *184–6*
blonde hair: with cool skin tones 32–3, *32–3*; maintenance 49–50, *49–50*
blood paste 192, *193*
bloods/blood products 21, 192, *192–5*, 195
blow dryers 86–8, *87–8*
boar bristle brushes 65
bobby pins 91, *91–2*
Boot, Jenny *219*, 219–20
Bova, Dave 119
braids *123*, *127*
brow and lash tinting *51–2*, 51–3, *53*
Bumble and Bumble products *13–14*, *18*, *18–20*, 19

canvas wig blocks 183
Carlsson, Lars: blood products 192, 195; silicone work *195–8*, 198–9
catagen phase of hair growth 4
Centrix Q Zone blow dryer 86, *87*
ceramic brushes 67
ceramic curling irons 80
chalks for hair 56–7
chemical damage 20
clerks, role of 215
clipless curling irons 80
clippers *100–1*, 100–9, *102–7*
cold, dry weather 20
colored hair extensions *54*
coloring hair: application of *39*, 40, *40–5*, 46; bleaching hair 37, *46*, 46–9, *48–9*; blonde hair maintenance 49–50, *49–50*; brow and lash tinting *51–2*, 51–3, *53*; correcting of 50–1; dyes, tints, and bleaches *35–6*, 35–46, *39*, *40–5*; hair lightening *46*, 46–9, *48–9*; male hair 115–16, *116*; overview *27*, 27–34, *28*, *29–34*; paints for 200, *200–3*; *see also* temporary hair color products
color wheels *27*, *27–9*, *28*, *34*
Comare Mark II *72*
comb/brush attachment 86, *88*
combs 70–1, *71–3*
common damages on set 20–1
concentrate airflow attachment 86, *88*
copper coated bristle brushes 66
course hair 16
Courtney, Kathleen 213–14
crane shears 75
cranium overview 3
crayon/stick hair colors 61

creams hair color products 59
Cricket angle comb *73*
curling irons: burns 20; types of 79–80, *81–4*; working with 119–20
curly hair 12
cutting comb 70

dandruff 22
dark/black hair 33–4, *33–4*
dark hair, warm skin tones 29–30, *29–30*
Davines Bleach Powder/Paste *48–9*
Davines Oil Non Oil 188
Davines Tinted Shampoo/Conditioner *40–5*
Davines Toner *35–6*
detangling comb 71
DGA (Directors Guild of America) 213
diamond head shapes 9, *9*
diffuser attachment 86, *88*
diseases and disorders affecting hair 21–3
Dome Care products *114*
Don Jusko color wheel *27, 34, 55*
double process bleach 47
down and dirty method of hair extensions 155, *155–9*
DP (Director of Photography) 213
dreads: overview 17, *128*; sponges for textures 69; synthetic 172–4, *172–5*
dry, hot weather 17–18
dry hair 18
Dura Pro Temptu Hair *58*
dyes, tints, and bleaches *35–6,* 35–46, *39, 40–5*

early Egyptian style *127*
Eaton, Teri 24
Eclipse *60*
EJ lined razor *110*
electric razor shaves *112,* 112–13
epidermis overview 3
Evan, Patrick 37–9
Evian water spray 12, 14
exogen phase of hair growth 4
extensions *see* hair extensions

facial hair types 98, *98*
facial/shave brushes 68

FHI black combs *71*
FHI blow dryer attachments *88*
FHI Heat Platform blow dryer *87*
FHI Heat Platform curling irons *81–2*
fiber hair color products 59, *59–60*
film production: accountants in 214–16; overview 207; petty cash 216; photography shoots *219,* 219–20; production schedule *209–12*; public relations 220–1; shooting schedule *207–8*; start papers 216; time cards 216–17, *217*; United Production Manager 213–14
fine curls 14
fine hair 17
finger waves 122, *122*
first assistant accountant 215
flapper style *125*
flat irons: burns 20; overview 11; types of 84–5, *84–5*; working with 119–20
Fleet Street Bloodworks Dry 192, *192*
Fleet Street Bloodworks Fresh *193*
flocking blood 195
folding comb 71
Frends bobby pins 91, *91–2*
fusion hair systems 169, *169–72*

Galbraith, John Kenneth 6
Garbarino, Mark 21
"Garden of Memories" (Jenny Boot Photography) *219,* 220
Gator clips 92, *93–4*
gel hair color products 59
Gibson style *129*
Glamour curling iron *82*
Glaser, Jill 119–22
grooming comb 71, *73*
guard sizes for clippers 106, *106–7*

hair: color of 6; common damages on set 20–1; diseases and disorders affecting 21–3; overview 3–4; spa treatments *23,* 23–4; textures *11,* 11–17, *12–17*; *see also* coloring hair; textures of hair
hair brushes 65–8, *66, 67*
hair chalks 56–7
hair curlers/rollers: basics of using 120; hot curlers 88, *89*; hot rollers *120*; overview 90, *90*

haircutting shears 76
hair design: bald caps 176, 179, 199–200; bloods/blood products 21, 192, *192–5,* 195; dreads 172–4, *172–5*; finger waves 122, *122*; flat irons 119–20; inspiration for 123, *123–30*; measuring the head 176, *176*; overview 119; paints for coloring 200, *200–3*; period hair design 130–1; pin curls 120–1, *120–1*; silicone, working with *195–8,* 198–9; tattooing the scalp 186–7, *187*; ventilating 176–7, *177–9*; wet hair 188, *188*; *see also* wigs
hair extensions: colored *54*; down and dirty method 155, *155–9*; fusion hair systems 169, *169–72*; keratin links 140–1, *140–5,* 145; overview 11, *132,* 132–3; removal *138–40*; sewn-in 151, *151–5,* 155; tape-on 145–7, *145–50,* 150; toupee clips 160, *160–8,* 163
hair growth overview 4–6, *5*
hair-protecting product 16
hair stylists 1, *2*; *see also* tools of the trade
hair ties 90, *91*
half-radial brushes 68
Hall, Mindy 200
head shapes: diamond 9, *9*; heart 10, *10*; measuring the head 176, *176*; oblong 8, *8*; oval 7, *7*; overview *6,* 6–7; pear 10, *10*; round 9, *9*; square 8, *8*; triangular 11, *11*
heart head shapes 10, *10*
heat resistant comb 71
henna 37
heptane 199
Hi Lift colors 47
hot curlers 88, *89*
Hot Tools Marcel Irons *83–4*
hot weather 19
humid weather 19
hypothyroidism 22

image grooming brushes 67–8
inspiration for hair design 123, *123–30*
ionic blow dryer 86

Janice McCafferty Communications, Inc. 220
Joewell shears 74, *74*

K.D. 151 Extra Strength Ultra Matte Lace Adhesive 189
K.D. 151 Flowing Blood 195
K.D. 151 Pumping Blood 195
Kemp, Sandra 3
Kenra Hot Spray 16
keratin hair extensions 140–1, *140–5,* 145
keratinization 4
keratinocytes 6
kit list 218, *218*
Kryolan Supracolor grease paints 199

lash tinting *see* brow and lash tinting
leave-in conditioner 14
left-handed shears 77, *77*
level shears 75, *75*
lipocils 53

McCafferty, Janice 220
McNeill, Daniel 21
The Makeup Artist Handbook (Davis, Hall) 200
Marcel curling irons 80, *83–4*
mascara irritation 51
Mason Pearson brushes 66, *66*
Maughan, William L. 7
measuring the head 176, *176*
melanin pigment 6
memos 218, *218*
men's grooming: clippers *100–1,* 100–9, *102–7*; coloring and filling 115–16, *116*; intimate utensils 115; maintenance 116; overview *96, 97,* 97–9, *98, 99*; scissor over comb 109, *109*; shaving *109,* 109–15, *110, 112*; shaving a bald head 113–14, *114*
military brushes 68
Mills, Vanessa *46,* 47
Mohawk style *128*
moisture creams 15
Monroe brushes 66, *67*
mousse products 14
moustache brushes 68
Murad Acne Treatment 114, *115*

nano titanium curling irons 80
NDB (nondeductible breakfast) 216
negative ion energy curling irons 80
neurocranium 3
nylon bristle brushes 65

oblong head shapes 8, *8*
occipital bones 3
offset shears 75
Oster barber clippers *79*
oval head shapes 7, *7*
overbrushing hair 20

paddle brushes 67
paints for coloring hair/hair pieces 200, *200–3*
palm brushes 68
Pantone charts 27
parietal bones 3
Patchett, Tiffani 18–19
patch test for coloring 38
Patrick Evan Salon 37–9, 47
payroll accountants 214
pear head shapes 10, *10*
period hair design 130–1
permanent hair colors 37
petty cash 216
photography shoots *219*, 219–20
pin curls 120–1, *120–1*
POC (Production Office Coordinator) 213
pocket-sized brushes 67
polypeptides 4
pomade gel mix 69
portable hair dryers 88
powder tints 61, *61*
Prime Bond Plus 189
Prime On 189
prosthetic glues 21
proteins in hair 3–4
psoriasis 22
Psycho Paint 199
public relations 220–1
punch needles 199
pure badger bristle brushes 66

rainy weather 19–20
rake comb 70
rattail comb 70, *72*, 183
RCW Color Wheel *28*, *55*
redressing wigs 184
renting wigs 179
rewetting hair 12, 15
ripple pins 91, *92*
RJS Adhesive Remover 191
rollers *see* hair curlers/rollers
round brushes 67
round head shapes 9, *9*

scissor over comb 109, *109*
seborrheic dermatitis 22
second assistant accountant 215
semi-permanent hair colors 36
sewn-in hair extensions 151, *151–5*, 155
shaving: bald heads 113–14, *114*; men's grooming *109*, 109–13, *110*, *112*; skin problems from 114–15, *114–15*
shaving cream for adhesive removal 189
shears *74*, 74–8, *75–8*
Sigma Bond 189
silicone, working with *195–8*, 198–9
silicone-based adhesive 189, *190*
Silkomb *72*
silk pins 183
single-blade razor shaves *110*, 110–12
sivertip badger bristle brushes 66
skeletal system 3–6, *4*, *5*
skin problems from shaving 114–15, *114–15*
skin tones 29
slide cutting shears *78*
Sonia Kashuk makeup palette *30–1*, *33–4*
spa treatments *23*, 23–4
spiral curling irons 80
sponges 69, *69*
spray color products 58
spring comb 71
spring curling irons 80
square head shapes 8, *8*
Stanfield, Jennifer 7, 17, 130–1
Sta-Rite bobby pins 91, *91*
start papers 216
Stone, Susan 183
stove irons 85, *85*
straight-razor shaves 110, *110*
streaking products 37
Street Plasma Soap 192
styling/lifting comb 70

super badger bristle brushes 66
Super Million Hair *59*
Super Solv/Plus 188
swivel shears 77, *77*

Talika Lash Conditioning Cleanser *53*
Talika Lipocils *53*
tape-on hair extensions 145–7, *145–50*, 150
Taplet, Lennotch *97*, 97–8, 101, *101*
tattooing the scalp 186–7, *187*
tattoo palettes 57, *57–8*
teasing brushes 67
teasing comb 71
teflon curling irons 79
telegen phase of hair growth 4
Telesis Makeup Remover 189
Telesis 5 Silicone Matte Lace Adhesive 189
temporary hair color products: airbrushes 61, *62*; crayon/stick hair colors 61; creams and gels 59; fiber products 59, *59–60*; hair chalks 56–7; overview 54, *54, 55*; powder tints 61, *61*; sprays 58; tattoo palettes 57, *57–8*
temporary hair colors 36
Temptu Air Brush System *62*
Temptu Hair Dura palette *116*
textures of hair: coloring of 38–9; overview 11–12, *12–17*
texturizing shears 76, *76*
thinning shears 76, *76*
time cards 216–17, *217*
tints 37
titanium curling irons 80
tools of the trade: airbrushes 94, *94*; atomizers 93, *93–4*; beard/mustache trimmers 78–9, *79*; blow dryers 86–8, *87–8*; bobby pins 91, *91–2*; brushes 65–8, *66, 67*; cleaning of equipment 95; combs 70–1, *71–3*; curling irons 79–80, *81–4*; flat irons 84–5, *84–5*; Gator clips 92, *93–4*; hair curlers 90, *90*; hair ties 90, *91*; hot curlers 88, *89*; overview *64*, 65; shears *74*, 74–8, *75–8*; sponges 69, *69*; stove irons 85, *85*
Top Guard Skin Barrier 188
Toppik *60*
toupee clip hair extensions 160, *160–8*, 163
tourmaline blow dryers 86
tourmaline curling irons 80
triangular head shapes 11, *11*
trichotillomania 22
twill tape 183

Unlace-Wig Adhesive 189
up-do *124–5*
UPM (United Production Manager) 213–14

vegetable-based products 37
vent brushes 67
ventilating 176–7, *177–9*
viscerocranium 3

warm red-based skin tones 32, *32*
warm yellow-based skin tones 30–1, *30–1*
weather conditions 17–20
weaves 11
wet hair 188, *188*
wide-toothed comb 70
wig master 176
wigs: adhesives and removers for 179, 188–91, *190–1*; application of 179, 180–2; blocking a wig *182*, 182–4, *184–6*; redressing wigs 184
W.M. Creations, Inc. Xtra Hold Spirit Gum 189

XFusion *59*
Xtra Hold Spirit Gum 189

Yano, Kentaro 186, *187*

791.43027 DAVIS

Davis, Gretchen.
The hair stylist
handbook

SOF

R4002780020

SOUTH FULTON BRANCH
Atlanta-Fulton Public Library